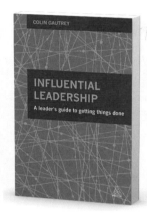

Influential Leadership

A leader's guide to getting things done

Colin Gautrey

First published in Great Britain and the United States in 2014 by Kogan Page Limited

2nd Floor, 45 Gee Street
London EC1V 3RS
United Kingdom
www.koganpage.com

1518 Walnut Street, Suite 1100
Philadelphia PA 19102
USA

4737/23 Ansari Road
Daryaganj
New Delhi 110002
India

© Colin Gautrey, 2014

ISBN   978 0 7494 7051 7
E-ISBN 978 0 7494 7052 4

British Library Cataloguing-in-Publication Data

A CIP record for this book is available from the British Library.

Library of Congress Cataloging-in-Publication Data

CIP data is available.

Library of Congress Control Number: 2014016507

Typeset by Graphicraft Limited, Hong Kong
Print production managed by Jellyfish
Printed and bound by CPI Group (UK) Ltd, Croydon, CR0 4YY

To my sisters,
Heather, Sandra and Carol.
With their love and support, these last few sad years
have had a silver lining.

CONTENTS

14   Influential leadership and persistence of purpose   259

An introduction to influential leadership

Leadership is about driving progress towards a vision or goal with the help and support of others. The quality of leadership varies greatly as do the behaviours, skills and characteristics of good leaders. It seems that no two leaders are the same.

One thing common to all leaders is the need to influence others. Leaders have to get people thinking, feeling and acting differently than they would otherwise have done. They have to create change in others. The more effective leaders are at influencing those around them, the more progress they will make. They will also gain recognition for their leadership ability.

When leaders are effective influencers they are able to win over opposition, motivate people to go that extra mile and get others to innovate and collaborate towards a goal or vision. Leaders all face challenges, but if they lead through influence then objections, problems and road blocks are easily overcome.

To achieve influence, leaders need to do a wide variety of different things such as visioning, inspiring, listening and coaching. Sometimes they also have to exert discipline, reprimand and veto. The means of influence are diverse, and effective leaders develop a keen sense of what is right, what will work and what to do in order to achieve the influence they need and get the result.

Leaders also have to be many things. It helps if they are charming, charismatic, demanding and tenacious. Yet the long list of leader attributes does not contain a definitive answer. This is because different environments require different attributes in their leaders: different leaders for different situations.

Leaders also need to develop a deep understanding of their environment and the individuals involved. This enables them to adapt their behaviour with precision and focus their attention where it will get the best return. This helps them to build trust, loyalty and long-term relationships while getting results fast.

Some leaders have big, bold ideas that they are working towards. They have glimpsed the future, seen how the world will be and are able to communicate this to others with eloquence. These I call visionaries. Others have a strong orientation to short-term imperatives. They are great at delivering what their organization needs right now in order to meet its targets and satisfy its stakeholders. These I call managers.

Managers struggle to find the time to look further ahead than their short-term imperatives and so continue to keep doing what is asked of them. Visionaries, on the other hand, struggle to get things moving because they are disconnected from the problems of today. *Influential leadership* is intended to help you, as a leader, to bridge the gap between managers and visionaries. Rooted in the practical world while also striving towards a bigger, better future, this book will help you to get things done for today, and for tomorrow. *Influential leaders* know where they are, where they are going, and pursue practical ways of leading the way.

The influential leadership framework

Influential leadership is a simple framework for applying practical influence in leadership situations. It aims to help leaders to achieve greater results today and to stretch them into a bigger and better future. It is predicated on three key beliefs:

- The primary work of a leader is to influence people towards a clear and ambitious vision of the future.
- Influence means getting people to do, think or feel differently, and preferably all three.
- Relentless focus is required on what needs to be influenced and the most effective means of achieving it.

The framework consists of three core elements that support each other:

- *Progress:* these are the results, both short-term and long-term, that accumulate over time. Influential leaders make significant progress, and fast.

- *Purpose:* from the long-term vision down to the short-term imperative, this is what the leader is aiming for. Influential leaders do not sacrifice the short term for the long term or vice versa.

- *Passion:* the emotion and energy that is poured into the purpose by the influential leader. This creates the resilience and inspiration to continue making progress.

The order that these core elements have been placed in is important. You might think that *progress* should come last. It is placed first because most leaders today are not making enough progress in their short-term objectives to create the time and the space to discover their longer-term purpose. What I have found is that as people get faster at influencing progress on their immediate priorities, it isn't long before they are looking around for new challenges. And this is just the time to begin stretching their vision and ambition.

Setting *progress, purpose* and *passion* in this order, they become a virtuous circle, with each cycle increasing the stretch and the achievement as competence and confidence rises (see Figure 0.1).

FIGURE 0.1   Influential leadership as a cyclical process

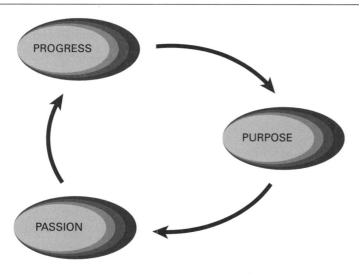

This book does not ignore the subject of *purpose* and *passion*, but it places greater emphasis on *progress*. This keeps it highly practical and of immediate value while also offering leaders the future potential to 'up the ante' while keeping their feet firmly on the ground.

In order to begin to make rapid and significant progress, leaders need to develop their knowledge, understanding and capability in five key areas. These areas have been derived from the work I have done over the last 10 years learning about influence and helping people to become influential. In reality, it merely segments the main topics into logical categories:

- *Power:* the bottom line is that if you want to be successful as a leader you have to be strong and powerful. Building greater power requires exercise and practice. It is something that everyone has to some degree, and is also something that everyone can improve on. Power helps to make it much easier to get things done and, frankly, forms the basis on which others do things for you.

- *Arena:* influential leaders also need to be acutely aware of the way things work in the arena in which they are leading – what is actually happening within their organization and in the wider world. External influences give shape to the way things work within an organization. The strategy adopted by the organization to succeed in its environment is the formal way in which things are shaped, but also belies the informal reality of the political complexity where individuals and agendas compete for prominence.

- *Strategy:* once a leader has developed a keen awareness of their environment, and is beginning to feel their power and strength growing, they need to put it into action and make decisions about exactly how they will move towards their goal. The goal will vary: from their grand purpose down to creating more time to think about their grand purpose – and everything in between. Coming up with a clear strategy is vital for economy of effort and ease of execution. This is the route-planning part of influential leadership.

- *Skills:* when the strategy has been decided, influential leaders need to deploy their skills in order to make it happen. In this area of the leadership framework you will learn the skills that are most critical to being great at influencing, which a leader has to be. These skills are not difficult to understand, and most of them are also not too difficult to develop and use. Leaders who focus on these skills will quickly see their influential leadership rise.

- *Style:* aside from the actual skills, there is a variety of ways in which they can be used. The skill remains the same but the style of execution can change. Choosing the right style for the individual and situation that the leader is working with makes a vital difference to the result. Get it wrong and people are easily distracted. Get it right and they will much more easily buy into what the leader is saying and wanting.

Proficiency in all of these areas provides the means of getting things done and these will be covered in considerable depth as you move through the book. And you do need proficiency in all five key areas, because they are inextricably linked and mutually supportive. The *influential leader* has to master all five areas to fully realize their potential.

Influential leadership capabilities

In order to develop your influential leadership, as you move through these areas I will address a range of specific capabilities, as set out in Table 0.1. These form my vision of a role-model leader. This will help to provide structure and also help you to focus on the actions that you will be taking as you develop your competence. Table 0.1 indicates the main chapters of the book that deal with each listed capability, yet most chapters in the book will contribute in some way to all of these capabilities.

Maximizing your development

People vary in their learning styles and what works for one person may not be good for another. Writing a book on this topic is challenging since it seeks to cater for as many preferences and levels of experience as possible and I have done my best to enable all readers to gain significant value from it. However, I do have some recommendations for you in terms of making the most of this book and developing your capability as an influential leader as quickly as possible.

This book is intended to be read from cover to cover. Until you are familiar with the whole it is not suitable for jumping around within the content. This is because of the interconnected nature of the different topics and also the logical building of understanding necessary before the action starts. At the very least, I suggest a rapid read through the entire contents (not a skim) so

TABLE 0.1 Influential leadership – specific capabilities

The capabilities that best describe an *influential leader* is someone who:	Covered in:
• knows that they are a leader and has decided where they will apply their leadership; • develops a clear sense of purpose and is able to communicate a compelling vision; • injects passion into their purpose and is able to maintain momentum; • is able to create space for their long-term purpose while delivering short-term results;	*Chapter 1: Building your purpose and passion*
• has a clear understanding of what influences people; • is able to recognize why different people are able to influence successfully;	*Chapter 2: Power – what makes people influential*
• can analyse what will work and what will not work for different people in different situations; • knows what makes them powerful and how to grow and utilize their power;	*Chapter 3: Why power works in the real world*
• has an intimate understanding of the individuals they are engaged with; • is able to appreciate the pressures and influences affecting their stakeholders;	*Chapter 4: Deeper understanding of people*
• continually develops their understanding of the political aspects of their domain; • can quickly assess the dynamics operating within any group of individuals; • develops a clear picture of the complete arena or organization where they are active; • is able to predict future scenarios and how they will affect their purpose;	*Chapter 5: Understanding your leadership arena*
• operates with high levels of personal integrity; • understands and makes clear decisions about ethical positioning;	*Chapter 6: The ethics of influence*

TABLE 0.1   *continued*

The capabilities that best describe an *influential leader* is someone who:	Covered in:
• develops coherent and robust strategies and plans to achieve their purpose and goals; • economizes their activities to focus on the most important stakeholders;	*Chapter 7: Creating your leadership strategy and plan*
• focuses on enhancing skills that are critical to more successful influence; • builds skills through practice, reflection and regular review;	*Chapter 8: Increasing your skills as an influential leader*
• develops strong networks, alliances and collaborations around their domain;	*Chapter 9: Developing powerful and influential networks*
• is able to create and build robust high-trust relationships; • understands and mitigates the threats to trust;	*Chapter 10: Establishing and building greater trust*
• has learnt how personality affects engagement and is tolerant of diversity;	*Chapter 11: Understanding influencing styles*
• can instantly adapt their behaviour to suit the individual they are seeking to influence;	*Chapter 12: Understanding and adapting your style*
• thinks carefully about the influence they want to create in any situation and responds appropriately to meet the needs of any individual;	*Chapter 13: Tailoring your approach for maximum influence*
• is meticulous in preparation, swift to action and tenacious in the pursuit of their purpose.	*Chapter 14: Persistence of purpose*

that you can gauge your familiarity with the concepts and make decisions about what you personally need to focus your time on.

Most of the chapters have exercises to help build understanding and also help you to make immediate progress on your goals and purpose. If you are doing a quick read you will probably skip over these until you have decided where you need to focus. Once you do get into the exercises, don't skimp on the time you spend on them. Many of them require additional research and collation of information, which can take days to weeks to assemble. All of the exercises require careful thought and lead towards refining or changing the action you take as a leader.

This may seem at odds with my earlier sentiment that as an influential leader you need to move quickly to the action. Quick but not so quick that you are exposed to the risk of being unprepared, ill-considered and naive. It is the careful analysis of the situation you are facing as a leader that will mark you out as being adept, and different from most of the leaders languishing at middle management levels. Doing these exercises carefully is a good illustration of 'pausing to go faster'. I promise you, as you become more familiar with the approaches it will get much faster as you swing up the learning curve. You will also be accumulating a much deeper level of knowledge about your environment and stakeholders, which can bring value and speed for years to come. So make sure to invest the time to do this properly.

Another strong recommendation is that you apply the thinking this book provokes directly to something that is very important to you. In Chapter 1, I help you to develop your thinking about your longer-term vision; however, that can take quite a while to refine and finalize. Because the framework of *Influential Leadership* can work on short- as well as long-term goals, don't allow any lack of clarity with respect to your purpose to stop you applying these ideas in the short term.

The whole idea of the *progress*, *purpose* and *passion* approach is that you need to focus on making some progress initially in order to free up time to do further work on your purpose. Lack of purpose offers no excuse for not ratcheting up the amount of progress you are making in your work. The more progress you are capable of delivering, the more time you will be able to allocate to the longer-term development. Just make sure you capture some of that time, otherwise you will fail to become an influential leader. Instead you will become a very accomplished completer finisher.

At times you may find the text easy or tough to follow. One of the major challenges I have had in writing this book is matching the explanation of the concepts to wide variations in reader experience. The way I have handled that is to keep the text as succinct as possible. That way, those with more experience have few pages to skim over while less experienced people have the opportunity to stretch their thinking and get glimpses of deeper ideas. In order to meet these varied needs, I have included at the end of each chapter an online resources section of further reading on the topic, which will also continue to build and provide case studies, examples and more depth.

As a final point, I wholeheartedly recommend that you do not make your study of this subject a private affair. As you develop your capability by studying the ideas, analysing your environment and engaging with your stakeholders, involve others in your learning. Friends, colleagues, team members and even line managers can all benefit your learning and, in turn, learn more themselves. They will thank you and your learning will be dramatically enriched. Many of the exercises lend themselves very well to team-based activities that you can organize.

The role of integrity

The field of influence is peppered with approaches that seek to coerce, manipulate or trick people into doing things that they either don't want to do or shouldn't do. The overriding purpose of all of my work is to help people with high levels of integrity to lead and succeed without the need to resort to dubious practices. Although the challenges to integrity are high, with a fair degree of caution and careful handling it is possible to find ways of leading with fairness and honest dealing. At times you may have to work a little harder, bring forward more competition than you need and some-times offer your opposition an advantage. But in the fullness of time, with diligent hard work the relationship benefits that you gain will far outweigh any disadvantages you may encounter along the way.

So, fuelled with good intent and honest endeavour, let's begin.

Building your purpose and passion

01

" *You can only be an influential leader if you have an ambitious purpose, and get moving.*

To become an influential leader you need to develop a clear long-term vision and also be realistic about how you are going to free up time to begin making progress. That means you have to also focus on your short-term objectives and make sure you don't miss anything critical. The grander your purpose, the more influential you will become – provided you are also making progress at the same time.

This chapter contributes to the following influential leader capabilities:

- Knows that they are a leader and has decided where they will apply their leadership.

- Develops a clear sense of purpose and is able to communicate a compelling vision.

- Injects passion into their purpose and is able to maintain momentum.

- Is able to create space for their long-term purpose while delivering short-term results.

Exploring your leadership purpose

You need to define your purpose in a manner that is appropriate for you. What is right for you will depend on many factors including your experience, age, values, position, responsibilities, capability and ambition. To make the most of the contents of this book, your purpose needs to be sufficiently stretching to mean that you will be stepping out of your comfort zone. It needs to be something that will force you to think differently, either about your current role or to take you into uncharted waters.

You need to take a sensible view on what to focus on right now while also adding a little stretch to challenge yourself.

Leadership arenas

Because leadership is all about getting things done, you first have to decide where you want to get things done, or rather, where you feel motivated to create some sizeable change from the way things are at the moment. This will be your *leadership arena* where you want to exercise your potential as a leader. Here are some of the potential arenas you could choose from:

- *Your job:* this is the most obvious. Assuming you are in a leadership position, have a team and result to achieve, you can immediately start to define your vision around the mission you have been tasked with. This could include changing the way the rest of your organization utilizes your services; or it may be launching your products into a brand new market. Provided you have the opportunity to be visionary, change hearts and minds and get others involved, this could be the ideal place to start.

- *Your organization:* you don't have to be leading the whole organization, leaders exist in many places and the most influential among them will be able to drive things forward across the whole organization. Creating substantive change in your organization could be a great place to focus, particularly if you are career-orientated right now and there is a distinct lack of leadership being displayed. There are many different types of organization and a good place to begin exercising greater influence is where you work. It doesn't have to be across the whole organization: you might choose to focus on your division. Alternatively, if you wish to focus on other types of organizations such as charities, clubs, political parties or religious groups, everything in this book will apply just as well.

- *Your society:* beyond formal organizations there are a wide variety of societal groups that you may be involved with. Often with these there is no formal leadership; no one is given the job of being the leader. They are much more open to ambitious and caring people to take on the leadership role and help the group move in a different direction. Potential groups vary greatly in terms of size and complexity, from local communities to the largest of all – the world. Provided that the group you wish to apply leadership in contains a reasonable level of complexity, you will gain a great deal from this book.

- *Your industry:* surpassing your company, perhaps you want to become a leading figure in your sector or industry. Becoming a thought-leader, spokesperson and shaper of a whole industry can be very rewarding, and also beneficial to the whole community. The semi-informal nature of this type of structure will make the ideas in this book not only fascinating, but also extremely useful as you work out how to make progress towards your purpose.

- *Your profession:* the only difference between this arena and the previous one is the source of the group members – they will come from many different industries. If your profession is mature there will be several formal organizations already established to serve different functions, but there will also be a range of much more fluid groupings to which you can apply your focus.

There are many other possible arenas and what is important is that you make a decision about which one you want to make some leadership progress in. At this point, it would be worth pausing and making a list of all the possible arenas that you are (or could be) connected with and that might be candidates for you to become an influential leader within.

Selecting your leadership arena

Now you have a list, apply a little more thought to it and see if you can select just one arena to focus on as you move through the book. Here are some questions to consider as you review your list of potential arenas.

Which arena:

- Contains the greatest need for change?
- Has a desperate lack of leadership?
- Is facing the greatest challenges?

- Presents the greatest potential rewards, not only for you, but also for the people in the arena?
- Do you care most about?
- Has the greatest degree of turmoil?

Try to decide which arena you would most like to become an influential leader in. You don't have to make a final decision right now, but at least decide which to focus on for the time being. Usually ideas and interest change as people become more skilled at capabilities presented in this book. When this happens to you, just come back here and repeat the process.

Analysing your arena

Once you've decided which arena to work with you need to go into a great deal more detail about what is actually going on there. While it would be tempting to rely on your own knowledge and assumptions, I strongly advise you to involve others in building your understanding, especially if the arena you have selected is large and/or complex.

Here are some questions to help you do your analysis:

- Where is your arena (organization/society/group) going wrong?
- What significant problems and challenges is it facing?
- How do external factors influence what is happening within the arena?
- What are the trends or changes taking place there?
- How do views about the challenges vary between key players?
- How are the politics affecting the current situation?
- What are the key beliefs and values that shape the way things work?

Make sure you answer these questions as thoroughly as you can. You don't have to do this immediately: take your time – this is important work. As well as talking to others connected with your chosen arena, make sure to also find written evidence such as articles, reports and newspaper comments. If you are to be an influential leader in this arena, you will have to become an expert in it, so don't skimp on your work. Generally, the bigger and more complex the arena, the more research you need to do. In Chapter 5, I will show you how to deepen the analysis of your arena in order for you to determine specific plans of action to influence those within it more effectively.

Deciding on your purpose

Having explored the nature of the arena you wish to exercise your leadership in, now you need to consider the different options that you could pursue, and settle on one that will become your *leadership purpose*. It will become the purpose to which you apply all of the ideas in this book, and one that will help you to learn more about being an influential leader.

It doesn't really matter how bold you are being, provided you have made a clear decision what to be bold *about*. Leadership is measured by substantial achievement, but it is also preceded by much trial and error. So start where you feel comfortable and stretch further as your confidence grows.

Considering the options

Returning to the arena you have been thinking about, assemble a range of options that could be your *leadership purpose*. Again, some questions to help you think this through:

- How should the arena change in order to succeed in the current climate?
- What does it need to stop doing, start doing or completely transform?
- What significant cultural or mindset shifts need to take place?
- List three things you think should change – significant things.
- Are these ideas radical enough, and different from what other prominent people are saying?
- What would create a seismic shift in this arena?

Okay, now it's time to begin making the decision – what is your *leadership purpose* going to be? Try to formulate two or three visions of the future that you could focus on. Deciding which one to go for may take a little while to finalize; the following questions will help you think this through:

- Which option is most attractive/fun/exciting to you?
- Which is of critical importance to you?
- How do the risks and rewards compare? For you and for others?
- What are the different timescales involved?
- How much effort might each take?

- How will each option affect other people in your private life?
- Which will be the most stretching?
- How do the options compare in terms of feasibility?

Feasibility is a tricky word and needs to be handled with care. Apart from technical probabilities, feasibility is an emotional judgement. What is feasible to one person may be ludicrous to another. Much depends on your experience, competence and personal disposition. Aiming low will make things easier, more assured, but less exciting. Aiming too high introduces the risk of being labelled a dreamer, a heretic and arousing resistance. However, the higher you aim the more you deliver, provided you have the tenacity to keep going. Feasibility is actually very personal.

You also need to take care when involving others at this early stage. Well-meaning friends are often quite good at knocking down your dreams and helping you to be realistic. All substantial change in the world began with a single person making a stand against everyone else, daring to be different, and having the courage to stick their neck out and be bold.

If you are just starting out as an influential leader, start aiming a little ahead of reality and make it a short-term purpose. As you progress in your practice, gradually increase your ambition and stretch further. Once you've made a decision about what you want to focus on – what you want your leadership purpose to be – write it down in a sentence or two.

Creating a compelling vision

You will achieve a great deal more progress if you can articulate your purpose in a compelling way. Because of the challenge of criticism, the stronger this is, the better. You will be striking out against the tide of public opinion and will need to prepare your approach as well as possible. This will help you to motivate people to first take notice, and then make a decision to support you before finally committing wholeheartedly to helping you to turn your vision into a reality.

To maximize attention, support and commitment, your vision needs to be:

- *Exciting:* with so many ideas competing for attention around your organization, where's the buzz that will make stakeholders sit up and take notice of yours? If you are struggling to get excited about your goal, why would anyone else?

- *Touchable:* stakeholders need to believe it is within reach. This is a difficult one, but unless people can believe your vision is capable of being realized, they will be reluctant to put effort into helping making it a reality.

- *Logical:* not normally a word you might associate with vision, but whatever vision you are putting out there needs to be credible and people need to believe it's a good thing to aim for. It either has to fit with everything else, or be an appropriate way of disrupting the status quo.

- *Beneficial:* along with stakeholders being able to almost touch your vision, they also need to feel they will fit into the new world and will be a beneficiary. While some altruistic individuals may accept their own demise, they are rather few and far between. And when I say benefit, I mean that they will need to benefit more from the realization of your vision than from any competing visions vying for their attention and buy-in.

Based on the description of the purpose you created earlier, rewrite it taking account of the ideas above and try to create a single-page flyer that could be used to get people excited about your purpose and vision.

If you are finding it difficult to develop a compelling vision, consult more widely about how others imagine what the world would be like with your purpose achieved. You can also start to imagine it from other people's perspectives. How might a customer describe the world with your goal achieved? What about other teams within the organization – how might they describe it to their friends?

If you cannot make a big goal compelling to the people you need to influence, you are likely to be faced with an ongoing struggle to get them on your side, and keep them on your side. The bigger the purpose, the more sensible it is to enlist the help of PR, marketing or communications professionals.

Right now, don't worry too much about creating a polished, finished product: run with a decent working draft and improve in the most appropriate way as you progress.

Protecting the short term

Before you get too carried away by your purpose, remember that influential leadership needs to balance longer-term progress with short-term results. The chief risk that you face is not being able to devote enough time to working on your purpose because of the demands you face right now. Losing your position because of poor performance is unlikely to help you progress towards your purpose – unless you are heading into a completely different arena.

Assuming that you are already working in the arena you want to develop your influential leadership within, pause for a moment and do an audit of where you are right now. Consider all of the important things that are going on in your life and work at the moment. Think about:

- What targets do you need to achieve at work this year?
- What missed objective could get you fired?
- What challenges and problems are you facing at the moment?
- What feedback have you had lately from your team, peers, family, friends and line manager?
- What goals do you have in your personal life for this year? Next year?
- Are you facing particular difficulties or issues at work (or at home) at present that you need to resolve?
- What are others expecting of you right now?

This thinking is really important as a backdrop to deciding on your purpose and will help you to keep your feet on the ground.

Boosting your motivation

To be an influential leader you need to be highly motivated in the pursuit of your purpose. This helps to generate the tenacity to overcome the inevitable challenges you will face. Problems, obstacles, delays and frustrations will need to be overcome as you strive for progress. The bigger your purpose, the higher your motivation and passion will need to be. Since you have now established your purpose, or at least the one you intend to start with, now is an appropriate time to boost your motivation.

The main principle here is that you need to find a way to keep going – or perhaps many ways to keep going. Starting this book and developing your initial purpose demonstrates the beginnings of motivation, but that is unlikely to be enough to see you through to the end. When the going gets tough, you need to be ready – you need to be at your peak in motivation terms so that you have the tenacity to stick with it.

One way to increase your motivation is to develop a list of personal benefits that success will bring to you. To this you can add a list of the negative consequences or losses you will incur if you fail. Some people tend to be more motivated by the gains they could make, others by the losses. In psychology, this is often referred to as 'moving towards' or 'moving away' motivation. Whichever you tend towards, that's okay – recognizing it will help you to focus your thinking.

In your notebook, start with your list of potential benefits. Use these questions to help:

- How will realizing your purpose/vision contribute to your bonus, pay review?
- How will it improve your career?
- How will realizing your vision raise your profile?
- Will it make life easier for you?
- How will others in your life benefit from your success?
- What problems will it solve for you?
- How will it improve the way your colleagues think about you?
- What new connections/friends will you make?
- Will it improve your personal life?

Try to make your list as long as you can, this will help later.

Now make a list of all the things you may lose, or the negative consequences of failing to achieve your purpose:

- What will you lose if you fail?
- How will your reputation be damaged?
- Will others think you have let them down?
- Could you get fired or rejected for promotion?

- What will more senior colleagues think about your failure?
- Will you have enough excuses to get away with it?
- Will anyone buy these excuses?
- What will your partner or friends think?

Make this list as long as possible too.

Which was the hardest list to create? Which is the shortest list? Which list makes you feel most motivated to achieve your purpose? Which list stirs your emotions the most?

Whichever list creates the greatest motivation in your mind is the one to keep near at hand. Make sure you review it regularly to maintain and increase your motivation as you progress. Keep it close enough that you can quickly refer to it when you start to hit problems. I have noticed that these lists are almost impossible to create when you are in crisis – referring to a pre-prepared list is much easier.

Protecting your motivation

Without wishing to pour cold water on your motivation immediately, no matter how strong your motivation is there will come a time, probably very soon, when it will drop. And when it does, you will be seeing the world in a different way. Once you've hit a few obstacles or had some criticism you will start to wonder whatever made you think your purpose was possible in the first place. When you do this, your focus will shift back to more pressing priorities and your purpose will be left until another day.

To lessen the impact this can have on your motivation and progress, recognize the inevitability of your motivation sliding and plan *now* the action that you will take when this happens. There are probably things you can do now to lessen the likelihood of falling motivation and/or the impact this could have. For example, actions you can take straight away might include:

- make a list of all the reasons why you must achieve your purpose;
- share your goal with friends who are good at supporting and encouraging you;
- don't share your goal with people who tend to have a negative slant on life (unless you absolutely have to);

- find case studies where you (or others) have succeeded with similar goals;
- raise your motivation to fever pitch by writing vision statements and benefit lists;
- make a public commitment to your purpose – right now;
- inspire and motivate others to believe in your purpose.

Similarly, an action plan to deploy if doubts hit you may be:

- reread your notes on reasons and benefits for achieving your goal;
- go for a walk with a friend who you can rely on to help you recover your positive frame of mind;
- brainstorm ideas with your team to find ways to make your goal happen even faster;
- distract yourself with other work for a few hours so you don't have time to dwell on your doubts;
- do something fun that will put you in a positive mood.

An important point to make about this contingency plan is to write it down before you need it. If you don't, the actual writing of the plan will be almost impossible when the doubts hit you – because you will be in a negative state of mind. You may be able to find it within you to take the actions you have already laid out, but it is unlikely that you'll be able to dream up a clever plan at that point.

What this is all about is doing everything you can to maintain your motivation and commitment until you have achieved your goal, or at least until goal realization is inevitable. Your positive expectation and frame of mind will make a significant contribution to your success and it is worth doing everything you can to protect it.

Assessing risks and opportunities

Besides building and protecting your motivation, it is also important to be aware of the diverse range of events that might happen that could seriously affect the pursuit of your purpose. Consideration of these now can enable you to be more proactive and reactive in the face of these events.

The severity can range from mildly frustrating to 'showstopper' level. At the opposite end of the spectrum, other things can happen that can dramatically improve your prospects. Often, at first sight, they have only a minor connection with what you are engaged in. Being prepared for these, spotting them when they occur and responding to them well is an important part of maximizing progress.

Ironically, those who get caught out here are often the people with the best execution skills. Their drive to get the result narrows their focus and they can easily lose awareness of what's going on around their project, goal or purpose. They easily develop blind spots and miss warning signs because they are so committed to (or sold on) the value of their result. So, it is prudent to stop from time to time in order to look at the risks you may be facing and the opportunities you could make more use of.

The level of detail you need to go into with this is dependent upon the size, scope, complexity and context of your chosen leadership purpose. The more complicated it is, or the bigger its potential impact, the more time and effort need to be invested in considering the risks and opportunities. Even in the simplest of scenarios, I believe that it is worth taking 10 minutes to quickly attend to this topic.

Strategic risks

Take a few moments to brainstorm all of the key things that could go wrong around your purpose:

- What might happen in the wider organization that could cause you problems?
- What crises could the organization face in the foreseeable future?
- What critical resources could be withdrawn?
- Is there something that may change in relevant legislation that could affect your purpose?
- Are there any significant technology considerations that may impede your progress?
- If your project wasn't to proceed, what would quickly take its place?
- If you were the CEO, for what reasons might you kill your project?
- What could happen that would really damage your progress?

Strategic opportunities

Now spend some time considering the opposite: what are all the things that could happen that would really help your progress?

- What are all the big exciting projects going on or being contemplated in the organization at the moment?
- Where is all the executive attention at the moment?
- If one thing were to happen to immediately make your purpose easier, what would it be?
- If I gave you one wish (related to your goal), what would it be?
- What event could happen that would really accelerate your progress?

Having thought about these risks and opportunities, ask yourself a hard question – are you still aiming for the right thing? The purpose of this question is not to try to dissuade you, but instead to pressure-test your resolve and ambition. This also helps to clarify the challenges ahead that you will need to manage in order to make progress.

Cultivating passion

Since influential leaders need to be passionate about their purpose in order to make swift progress, you need to do everything you can to cultivate the passion you feel about what you are aiming to achieve. When you have developed your passion, it will show and it will help you to become more influential.

In a work context, passion is an intensive emotion compelling unusual levels of excitement for a particular subject, cause or purpose. It goes beyond simple motivation and enthusiasm for a subject. It stands out because of the exceptional activity it creates. Passionate leaders tend to have an almost obsessional interest in their purpose. It seems to be the only thing that matters.

The root cause of the passion usually defies rational explanation, yet the effects are profound. If you have an extremely high level of passion for your purpose, what could possibly stand in your way? Objections and reason are swept aside and people get pulled along in the wake of the passionate leader. Certainty begins to set in and people believe your vision will be realized. This can then become a self-fulfilling prophecy.

Passion can be cultivated to deliver this level of success by making sure that you:

- *Attain high levels of passion:* if you accept that passion is a higher level of enthusiasm, and that enthusiasm is a higher level of interest, you can devise a route plan for progressively increasing the level of emotion for a given subject. Beginning with the ideas above on motivation, you can proceed to make it more and more prominent in your working life. The more often you are thinking about what your purpose is, and noticing the benefits that will accrue, the higher your levels of emotion will become.

- *Don't fake it:* people will be able to tell if you are not really feeling passionate. Building it gradually and robustly for your own benefit first is a good way of making sure that you only display what you are really feeling. If your passion for your purpose grows and develops naturally, it is far more convincing to people.

- *Maintain high levels of passion:* in the cut and thrust of organizational life there are many enemies to passion, especially in large cumbersome organizations where the weight of bureaucracy, processes and governance is a real passion killer. Maintaining passion requires daily if not hourly reinforcement, ideally through activity to deliver your purpose. This persistent attention will automatically increase your positive feelings towards your purpose and will ultimately lead you to the conviction that your purpose absolutely must be achieved.

- *Keep your passion focused:* some people are naturally passionate and get excited easily. One of the challenges these people need to overcome is dissipating their passion in lots of different directions. For passion to yield maximum results it has to be consistently applied to a specific purpose in a single-minded manner.

- *Remain alert for risks:* as your passion begins to take effect, you will be destabilizing the powers that be. This could bring forward political moves and you should not let your passion override careful consideration of the political effects of your influence.

- *Be sensitive to the culture:* before you unleash your passion, make sure you know how it will be received. The skill of demonstrating passion involves injecting enough to get noticed and pull people forward. Too much, too soon, and you could alienate rather than influence. As the right people begin to respond you can raise the levels again.

- *Keep control of your passion:* for the reason mentioned above, it is not always wise to show the full extent or strength of your feelings. Learning to manage your displays of passion will reduce the risk that you will overshoot or undershoot.

The last point in the above list is really important. Some would argue that unbridled enthusiasm and passion for a purpose is the only way to keep going when the going gets really tough. I agree. However, displaying uncontrolled passion is likely to unsettle stakeholders and make you look unprofessional and flawed in your approach.

Getting things done

Important points to remember as you begin to make more progress:

- Develop a purpose that is appropriate for you. The more experienced you are, the bolder your purpose should be.

- Focus on your short-term imperatives and your long-term purpose.

- Work hard to build your motivation and passion, because this gives you the energy to keep going.

- Keep your feet on the ground and remain alert to what is happening in the real world.

- As you make more progress, your boldness will grow.

- Influential leaders get things done.

Further reading

When you get a chance, make sure to check the further reading and resources for this chapter online at: **www.learntoinfluence.com/leadership**

Now, exactly what are you going to do as a result of reading this chapter?

As you move through the book I will help you to get much deeper into your leadership purpose and accelerate your progress. The next few chapters will help you to look beneath the surface of how and why people are influenced. These insights will be vital because they lie at the heart of how an influential leader gets things done with the help and support of others. By the time you arrive at Chapter 7 (Creating your leadership strategy and plan) you may have a very different view of how the world works, and thus will evolve and develop new ways to make greater progress.

Power – what makes people influential?

02

> *To gain the help and support of others, you need to know what influences people.*

Understanding why an individual will do something for one person, while ignoring another, is a fascinating voyage of discovery. And it is one that any ambitious influential leader needs to make rapid progress on, otherwise they will quickly find themselves in the doldrums and will fail to deliver.

To influence others you need to be powerful. The more powerful you are the more progress you will be able to make, and the quicker you will be able to make it happen. Studying the ways and means of developing greater power is critically important. By doing this you will be able to learn to make the right moves and develop in the optimum way to be able to fulfil your purpose.

This chapter contributes to the following influential leader capabilities:

Has a clear understanding of what influences people.

Is able to recognize why different people are able to influence successfully.

▶

As you read, what you will quickly notice is that there is no special magic going on here. Instead, very simple things are happening that create the influence, and the greatest progress goes to those who can consciously work these with skill. In the next chapter, I'll get into the underlying principles at play with power and show you how to leverage greater influence.

A quick introduction to influence

The need to influence is a fundamental human trait; it is instinctive. From your first few minutes of life you begin to learn how to influence: initially for nourishment, then to survive. The need to influence remains with us for life. As an adult, you need to influence people in your personal life and your work life: influencing them to accept you, buy into your ideas and remain loyal.

Without influence, people struggle. If you are unable to influence others to a reasonable degree, you will not be able to move forward. Sure, you will probably be able to influence sufficiently well to get food on the table and a safe place to live, but beyond that you'll be struggling. Becoming more powerful makes influence so much easier because it enables you to magnify your influence.

Not everyone needs to be concerned about power. If you can answer a resounding 'yes' to all of the statements below, you don't need to read this chapter and I'd be wondering why you bought this book:

- You have everything you want at work and in life.
- You are completely confident that you will be able to keep what you've got for as long as you want it.
- You are totally content with things the way they are.
- You strongly believe that if your desires or circumstances change, you can easily get what you then need.

I'm fairly sure that few readers will be able to give an enthusiastic 'yes' to all of these statements, and that there will be a wide variation on the scale of reader agreement. In many ways, the degree to which you are in agreement with these statements is a good indication of the amount of power you believe you have in your life as a whole right now.

These statements have been chosen carefully because they demonstrate what power can do, or rather, what it can help you move towards. You are human and are thus prone to moving the goalposts – and life has a habit of springing surprises. Over time, increasing your power will help you to take control and satisfy your needs and desires. It will also help you to respond faster and with greater confidence to the challenges thrown at you. As you take more control of what goes on in your life, you will then be able to provide greater service, help and benefit to others.

For example, powerful people tend to:

- enjoy greater autonomy and independence;
- possess the ability to have a greater say in their future;
- be able to overcome life's little (and big) problems quickly;
- be contented and happy;
- have more success in work and in life;
- yes, have more money too.

Besides, who wants to be a powerless leader? Unless you can be powerful you cannot lead – it is as simple as that. You don't have to be oppressive or dictatorial, but you do have to be powerful.

Before I start to explore what makes people powerful, I'd like to clarify a few concepts to ensure you gain the most from this chapter.

What is power?

If you want to be more powerful in your life and career it really helps if you know what power is and how it works. This knowledge can help you to make rapid progress and focus only on the things that will help you most. It will make you efficient in your acquisition of power.

During workshops I rarely get a clear answer to this question: what is power? This lack of clarity suggests that those attending the training are not moving as quickly as they could do and are probably missing opportunities to be more influential. How would you answer it?

What generally happens is people think about their experience of power and how it has affected them. Then they proceed to give lots of examples of things that are powerful, such as passion, energy, money, charm, fear, rapport, communication, teams, knowledge. The list is a long one and shortly I will go into these in much more detail with the *seven sources of power*.

The simplest answer to this question that I have seen comes from Jeffrey Pfeffer who wrote *Managing with Power* (1992). He defines power as: 'The capacity to influence'. In my work over the last 10 years, I like to add that: 'Influence is someone thinking, feeling or doing something different'.

One of my recent workshops arrived at the definition 'power is the capacity to get what you want'. At first sight this may appear a little selfish. Yet, sometimes, getting what you want means that you influence people not to change. Often the status quo is just the thing you need to keep.

The clever part of these definitions comes from the word 'capacity', because it means that power is available to an owner – they can use it as and when they wish, for whatever purpose they wish to apply it to. If you have power, you have a resource available and ready to use. A balance of £10 million in your bank account could be a very powerful resource that you can use when you like. That level of spending power can exert great influence over sales people, investment advisers and retailers.

This leads to another important point: merely having the 'capacity' can create the influence you want. Provided people know you have the capacity, they may be influenced by it without you taking any action at all. Salespeople drooling over your budget and thinking about their commission potential is one example. Another might be a relationship you have with the CEO. One of your colleagues may be far more compliant and nice to you if they fear you might whisper something detrimental about them to the boss. The next chapter will cover these ideas in much more detail. In the meantime, to help you understand clearly what influences people (rather than *why*), let me share with you a simple structure of power that encompasses all of the examples that I have heard in my workshops over the last 10 years.

Seven sources of power

In the pages that follow I will cover, without going into lots of theory, the wide variety of things that can influence people. In the process you will begin to discover what makes you influential at the moment, while also finding out what makes other people influential – perhaps you can be more like them. Often it is easier than you might imagine.

What follows is an outline of the broad categories based on the responses from thousands of individuals in my workshops, and a large amount of personal research too:

1 *Credibility:* the power derived from your professional standing and expertise.
2 *Character:* the underlying traits, values and beliefs that shape your behaviour.
3 *Presence:* the impact you create and the feelings you stimulate when people meet you.
4 *Position:* the roles you play and how you manoeuvre yourself into the limelight.
5 *Connections:* the network of relationships you have around you and your work.
6 *Skills:* those exceptional abilities you have that enable you to get things done.
7 *Agenda:* the issues and priorities you focus your leadership attention on.

As you read, pause every now and again to reflect on your own examples in each source of power. What have you seen influence others really well? Why does it work? This will help you to link it to your own experiences and make more use of the new ideas presented.

Source one: credibility

The power derived from your professional standing and expertise.

Credibility is the reliance awarded to someone based on trust and perceived expertise on the topic being considered. When making decisions, most people get input from others and they have to decide how much reliance to place on that input. Information from highly credible sources are more likely to be accepted at face value and not challenged, questioned or verified with another source. If someone doesn't think you are credible they probably won't believe what you have to say.

Credibility has capability and expertise at its heart. How people judge others' expertise varies, especially if they have a fair amount of knowledge on the same subject. While some may think a formal qualification in a subject is sufficient, more experienced people will be looking for a solid track record as well.

Sadly, credibility is also rather susceptible to assumptions and miscalculations. It is impossible to get all the facts and, by necessity, people take shortcuts in deciding on the credibility of an adviser. On the one hand, those seeking to establish their credibility are likely to conveniently cloud the communication in order to make their credentials appear stronger than they are. On the other hand, those receiving the messages may only hear what they want to hear.

Suppose I want to establish a partnership agreement in a new territory. I will get advice from a credible source otherwise I might get it wrong – and that could be both costly and embarrassing. To judge credibility I will certainly put a lot of weight on their qualifications and track record in this type of agreement. I will also be interested to notice how they communicate on their topic. Do they explain things with confidence? Do they respond clearly and assertively when questioned or challenged? Going deeper, I will want to know who else they have worked with, what endorsements they have and perhaps obtain some references. Maybe this is just me, but I'd also like to work with people who have been published in their specialist area and speak at conferences. These implied endorsements can make all the difference.

What has this got to do with becoming powerful? Remember that the definition of power I am using here is the 'capacity to influence'. The person who has high credibility is much more likely to be able to influence me to buy their services, and pay a premium rate. They may also be influential in their profession and be able to sway opinion for their own purposes. The power of credibility comes from the ability to demonstrate expertise in areas where lots of people need help – and if you can do that much better than anyone else, you will become influential – at least in your arena.

Most people do not think deliberately about how to establish their credibility in the minds of their stakeholders. Those operating in the external marketplace may do this quite naturally as it is part of their stock in trade. Some of them get into trouble with exaggerated claims (I will come to this in Chapter 6 on ethics), while other professionals are far less likely to think in terms of establishing their credibility and building trust, and this is a shame because it means they are missing out on major opportunities to become more influential.

Reflection questions:

- Think of a topic that is important to you right now. How would you judge the credibility of someone who could advise you on that topic?
- Who has leadership credibility in your organization and why?
- Why are you credible in your business/subject/service?
- How do you communicate your credentials?

Here is a list of things that people often cite as evidence of credibility:

- track record;
- qualifications;
- awards;
- memberships (trade bodies, committees etc);
- publications (books and articles);
- client lists;
- demonstrable command of topic;
- conference speaking;
- newspaper mentions;
- endorsements and testimonials;
- achievements;
- judging awards;
- promotions;
- social media statistics.

As beauty is in the eye of the beholder, the credence given to each of the above also depends on who is doing the judging. For instance, credibility as to the volume of Twitter followers and Facebook friends that one has is falling fast as more people realize how easy these are to manipulate.

Developing stronger credentials:

- Make a clear decision about what you want to be recognized as credible in (or for).

- Research credible people in your occupation, profession or specialism. What makes you think they are credible?
- Compare your credentials with theirs. What is the difference?
- How can you close the gap and boost your credibility?
- What have they missed? Could you capitalize on their gaps?
- What must you stop doing that might be damaging your credibility?
- Beware false claims and exaggerations: these have a habit of backfiring.

Demonstrating stronger credibility:

- When you engage with people, share your thinking and rationale. Tell them what you are doing, how you are doing it and why you are not choosing to take other courses of action.
- Don't take shortcuts without explaining why it is safe and sensible to do so.
- Imagine you are in an internal marketplace and you are the product. Decide how to establish and build your credibility.

To establish your credibility you do not need to become a show-off or a blagger. What you need to do is be clear about what you are about and then communicate clearly, assertively and consistently.

Source two: character

The underlying traits, values and beliefs that shape your behaviour.

It is difficult to estimate how influential it is to have strength of character, but it is big. It complements credibility – and if you have generous amounts of both then you're well on your way to becoming very powerful and influential.

In effect, this is concerned with your internal world and how it manifests in observable behaviour. The old phrase 'character building' seems to have been forgotten in leadership development, but many years ago it was top of the agenda for all those concerned with developing leaders.

This source can be split into the following: the effect created by character, the behaviours that create these effects and the underlying core values that drive those behaviours.

Consistency: the effect

People with strong and robust characters are generally a pretty stable bunch of individuals. They are known for their clear sense of integrity (however you wish to define it). The fact that people can rely upon them creates a high level of trust – people know what to expect and what is driving them.

For instance, if you are known for being tough but fair, those presenting proposals to you will know that they will get a strong challenge combined with support and help. This will raise their confidence and encourage them to stretch the boundaries of their competence – which is just what you want as an influential leader. However, if you are a soft touch, or fail to support them, their confidence will take a knock and they will be more cautious with their ideas and proposals.

Personality: the behaviours

Personality is usually regarded as the observable aspects of character. I will cover personality in much more detail in Chapter 11 (Understanding influencing styles). The main point I want to make clear now is that you need to have a strong personality if you want to become highly influential. This makes you more noticeable and more likely to be listened to. Weak personalities seldom influence to any great extent.

And don't think for a minute that I am only talking about the positive here. Negative personalities can be equally influential, albeit the aftertaste is unpleasant. That they are sources of influence cannot be disputed, nor should it be ignored. I am not suggesting that you should develop and display nasty behaviours in order to gain your influence – that flies in the face of leadership and does not create the long-term potential that a truly influential leader needs in order to reach their full purpose. However, you do need to understand and contend with these strong negative characters so that you can win through.

Personality traits that often get mentioned in workshops as being powerful and influential include:

- warm, engaging and charismatic (even charming);
- inspirational and naturally enthusiastic communicators;
- energetic and passionate drivers;
- demanding, challenging, tough and formidable.

The reason why these traits are influential is because of their effect on others. Some excite and motivate while others evoke fear and apprehension. Some do both at the same time. Others are sexy and attractive, and people love to be around interesting people – so much that they will move heaven and earth to get in their good books and be invited on to their projects. In effect, interesting people easily get people to go that extra mile.

Values and beliefs: the hidden drivers

Values are the deeply held beliefs and attitudes that govern the decisions people make and which in turn give rise to their behaviours or personality. The extent to which they are consistently applied generates their level of consistency.

From a power and influence perspective, the important thing to note is that if a leader does not have well-developed values, their behaviour will vary depending on how they feel on a given day. Put another way, if there are two conflicting values then the one that wins on any given day may produce a radically different behaviour.

Let me give you a simple example, taken from the health sector: *patients come first* versus *costs need to be tightly controlled*. Both are important and individuals will vary in terms of how strong each of these is within their overall value set. To achieve consistency in behaviour there needs to be a marked difference in the importance of each in the mind of the individual. If these two values are too close then they will conflict at times. Both of these values can drive through different behaviours and personalities. In this example, you would expect to see a more caring individual on the one hand, or a more insensitive and demanding personality on the other. Holding both of these contrary values at a high level will confuse followers and put them on edge.

Overall, strength of character requires a robust and strong set of personal values that are consistently applied. Then people will take notice, particularly if you can sparkle with it too.

Pause for a moment to consider the following questions:

- Who do you know with a strong personality?
- What is it about their personality that makes you say that?
- To what extent are they consistent?
- Can you list their top five values?

Strengthening and demonstrating your character:

- Know what your values are and how they interact with each other.
- Monitor your behaviour to ensure that it aligns with your values.
- Don't be shy; trumpet your values and let others know what to expect.
- When making decisions, explicitly connect them to your values.
- Ask others to challenge you if they think you have stepped out of line with your core values.
- Be bold, be strong, and act with conviction and certainty.

Powerful people know what they stand for and are prepared to demonstrate the courage of their convictions. This helps influential leaders as they generate clarity about what their vision and purpose is. This is real leadership!

Source three: presence

The impact you create and the feelings you stimulate when people meet you.

Much is made these days of *executive presence*, and with good cause – because it is a source of considerable power and influence. It is usually described vaguely as a collection of characteristics that combine to create an aura around the executive, making them immediately noticeable. When they glide into the room, everyone immediately feels and responds to their presence.

When it comes to becoming powerful as a leader, it matters little what you are or how you present yourself if you do not first consider what others are expecting of someone in your role. For me, true presence is displaying all of the qualities and characteristics that will convince others that you are ideally suited to your role, and that you believe you are too. You have to look the part, sound the part and believe the part all at the same time – super-confidence that never tips over to the dark side of arrogance. If you can do that, your influence will soar within your arena.

When I say all of the characteristics, I mean all of them, or as many as you possibly can. This is no easy task – and is made more difficult because of the diversity of roles and expectations. You may be the Director of Operations but that is just one of many roles you have to fulfil concurrently. Some will view your role as predominantly management while others may see you more in terms of a leader. Others may see you as a mentor and coach while your boss may view your role as being their number two. Expectations are very different for each of these roles and each of the observers.

In practical terms, you have to figure out the most important characteristics you need to display that will demonstrate your confidence to the greatest number of constituents. And herein lurks a twofold danger: you may focus on the wrong constituents or, worse, you may please the minority at the expense of the overwhelming majority.

The other danger is that by focusing on the audience you miss the point. If you spend time focusing on making people believe you are confident and in the right position then you will spend less time on actually becoming super-confident. If you are super-confident, the fact that some may think otherwise probably won't matter because your performance will win through.

If you want to create a more powerful presence, here's what you need to do:

- Determine your primary role definition.
- Quickly summarize what your main audience might be expecting of someone who is totally competent in that role.
- Spend a good deal of time working out what it will take for you to feel totally confident.
- Develop an action plan to develop your role confidence.
- Attend to the hygiene factors – eliminate things that could detract from your confident presence. Make sure you look the part as well as sound it.

The real challenge is in the third point in the above list. What exactly is confidence? In this context it is a feeling that you are in total control of your role, situation and subject area. You know from experience that whatever happens, you can handle it. Nothing and no one can faze your confidence. The depth of your knowledge and skill is always sufficient to meet the demands of the role and, probably, by some margin.

Much of this comes from robust and well-honed processes of enquiry, problem solving and decision making. These allow you to respond well to the unexpected and the novel. Many people I've coached over the years base their confidence on their technical knowledge and experience in a given area. When they are promoted to lead in a new area that requires different technical knowledge, suddenly their confidence disappears because they don't know as much about what they are doing as they used to in their previous role. What they need to do is to quickly transfer the base of their confidence to the processes. These confidences are usually highly developed but can be hidden from their self-awareness.

People who are totally confident subconsciously give themselves permission to relax and be at ease. The effect of this easy confidence is almost magical. The super-confident no longer need to keep trying to prove themselves to others. They are good and they know it. They can handle with ease anything that comes their way. Nothing surprises them or disturbs their relaxed approach. That's real presence.

Visual impact

You also need to at least be aware of the effect your visual presence has on others. To many this is more of a hygiene factor in the professional world, but it is nevertheless an important one. Certainly the way you dress, the way you move, and the way you look can help to complete the picture or can make presence more difficult to achieve.

Unfortunately there are few hard and fast rules. This was illustrated when one coaching client asked me what he should wear to create the right impact. Without knowing his audience it was impossible for me to say. As I helped him to explore this aspect he began to cite differences between how men dress in London compared to Switzerland. As a director, in certain places people expect you to have your initials on your shirt cuffs. In other places, that goes unnoticed, unlike the watch you are wearing. To maximize your presence you need to tune in as much as you can to others' expectations without getting too consumed and distracted by it.

Another interesting example was a newly appointed director almost running down the corridor to meet me. We subsequently discussed the impact that his running to meet me could have on the perceptions of others. To many, it gives the impression that you are in a rush, not in control and that you are struggling to keep up. In contrast, if you are relaxed and confident, don't saunter, but do glide along the corridor!

Don't get too obsessed about visual impact, however – focus first on building your super-confidence that will command attention, respect and influence. Be the part, then look the part, naturally.

Source four: position

The roles you play and how you manoeuvre yourself into the limelight.

To become powerful it certainly helps to get yourself into a good position. Position means much more than simply being given a particular role or title by your organization, even though this type of position is the most understood and easy to recognize.

Beyond this, you have people who are given temporary positional power as project leaders, managers or sponsors. All of these have been given responsibilities by the organization and the power to do certain things. Other powerful positions sit to the side of organization control. Union conveners, spokespeople and staff representatives can all exert significant influence on organizational life.

Then there are the myriad positions within the social fabric of the organization. Party organizers, newsletter writers and 'go-to' people all have positional power. This can even go as far as the company joker – the life and soul of the Christmas party who has the position (attention) and can flatter or ridicule with equal mirth those he or she likes or dislikes.

Formal positions

Formal positional power is based on the control of:

- *people:* how they are recruited, rewarded, deployed and dismissed;
- *resources:* such as facilities, processes and raw materials;
- *markets:* authority to engage with the markets and customers of the organization;
- *money:* deciding on which project, programme or division to favour;
- *information:* the insight into what is going on, be that management information, market intelligence or communication mechanisms.

To a large extent, formal position works because of the responsibilities and permissions bestowed on the individual by the organization. It is also clear that the ability to influence is also found in the expectations placed on an individual in a given role.

For example, a role such as Operations Director usually comes with the authority to decide where to allocate resources (physical and financial) and control over large numbers of people. It is also generally viewed as mission critical for the organization. Alternatively, being the Compliance Officer means having the ability to veto plans on the grounds of legal requirements or to avoid reputational risks – at least in theory.

There are many other roles within organizations that are formally created and can provide the incumbent with significant power if positioned well. These include consultants, mentors, coaches, researchers – the list is long. The extent to which these can provide power will vary depending on the way they have been created and the powers that have been vested into the role. Just giving someone a title doesn't make them powerful.

For all of these roles, the influence comes from the degree to which they own decision-making authority in a realm that is considered to be important (more detail on this in the next chapter).

Informal positions

There is also a multitude of roles where the positions have not been formally created. Instead they have become initiated by the individual. Clever people are able to position themselves where they can become influential by virtue of the support they give, or the value they bring.

This includes mentoring, coaching and consulting, too. You don't have to be formally given these roles for friends to come to you seeking your help and support. And the more you do this, the more influential you will become, at least in their eyes.

Some informal roles are quite functional:

- organizer: such as the Christmas party, or planning the quarterly team-building event;
- facilitator: helping two people to resolve their differences, or leading another team through a creative brainstorming or problem-solving process;
- communicator: volunteering to write a department circular or a blog sharing news, or even offering to write up the minutes of a meeting;
- number two: although not formally recognized, most teams have an individual who is usually regarded as the second in command – the one everyone turns to when the boss is away.

Others roles are more social in nature:

- Confidant: the person who everyone turns to when they have a problem and need to talk something through.
- Joker: there is one in every team. Their role is to lighten the mood, release the tension and help everyone to have a good time at work.
- Gossip: speaks for itself.
- Friend: everyone needs friends, even people in high places.

What you may notice about the roles above is that they are voluntary and the success (or power) that can be gained from the relationships they build varies, depending on the abilities of the individual holding the role. They also demonstrate that you can gain positional power without necessarily gaining formal approval.

An extension of this comes from informal groups. There is a wide array of groups that emerge organically in large organizations. These are collections of individuals who recognize that they have something in common and they usually cross over the usual functional boundaries. As soon as they notice this and start to communicate, they become an informal group. They are informal because they have not been designed and created by the organization itself – instead they have self-organized. However, all of them can develop to the stage where they begin to look very formal. Chapter 5 (Understanding your leadership arena) will go into much more detail on this topic.

In order to strengthen your position:

- Clarify your formal terms of reference – your decision-making authorities.
- Extend the scope of what you currently do. What are others not doing that you could do?
- Write down and agree additional responsibilities as soon as it becomes clear you can fulfil those duties.
- Ensure your decisions are reinforced by proactively managing your superiors' expectations. If you think someone is going to appeal, get in their first.
- Forge alliances with other decision makers so you can support each other.

- Make sure to use the power that you have.
- Stay alert to change and competition.

Finding a position:

- Look for opportunities to create informal groups. Find the commonality between talented people and make a role for yourself.
- Keep close to HR and Talent Management people. You may be surprised how influential they can be when your boss is selecting his or her successor.
- Remain vigilant in respect to any changes to the challenges that your organization faces. How could you help? Spot a problem, volunteer to find the solution.
- Find additional ways that you can help senior people. What can you do to make their life easier, their work more successful?
- Keep your ear to the ground and dialogue with your network about what is really happening in the organization.

Source five: connections

The network of relationships you have around you and your work.

Without doubt, connections can make you more powerful. By connections I mean your network of friends, associates and contacts. These people can be useful for:

- helping you meet specific challenges;
- providing you with information and insights you would not otherwise have;
- introducing you to other people you need to connect with;
- supporting and advocating your work around the organization (and outside too);
- helping you to find new opportunities;
- alerting you to problems moving in your direction;
- counselling and supporting you in times of need.

All of these provide you with the capacity to influence people in order to support the achievement of your goals. In turn this enhances your credibility because of your strong track record and results. Thus a virtuous circle is created.

On top of this, having a strong network of connections can also help increase your influence in a number of other ways:

- *Association:* when people see you associating with other powerful and influential people, they will ascribe greater power and influence to you. If you are moving in those circles, you must be worth getting close to.

- *Visibility:* the more extensive your network, the more powerful people will notice you. Providing you have a positive profile and fit, they may wish to draw you into their circle, especially if you are supportive of their agendas and can add value.

- *Access:* if others have problems or difficulties and they know you have an extensive network, they are likely to approach you for help. When you do help, they usually reward you with goodwill, thanks and greater support for your goals. You don't have to wait for others to come to you, you can proactively connect people who need to talk to each other.

- *Advocating:* similarly, when you are recognized as having a good network, others may be more cooperative and helpful to you because they hope that you can put in a good word for them with other powerful people. The opposite might also be true: they may be more cooperative for fear of you giving negative feedback.

Whenever you connect two people you are losing an element of control. If others have to come through you to get what they need that provides you with a source of power and influence. Once you've connected them directly, they don't need you any more. Another way of looking at this is that that while you are giving up some control, in return you are building a stronger relationship with either or both of the other parties. People who are secure in their power don't need to become paranoid about controlling access to their networks. Influential leaders are secure and confident. They are much more concerned with the long-term benefit of strong relationships.

Another feature of the *connections* source of power is that of uncertainty. In many instances, those who are being influenced by the extent and quality of your network are making guesses about what you may or may not be able to do. Because they are rarely able to judge the exact nature of your relationships, it is only through experience that they can see what you are able to achieve with your network. Less confident leaders frequently exploit this by dropping names into their conversations, and attempt to exaggerate the nature of their relationships to create greater influence. This can work when directed at less experienced people, but long term it is not the best way to become more powerful.

'It's not what you know, but who you know' gets truer with each passing year. Being able to talk to the right people, in the right way about the right things can dramatically accelerate progress towards your purpose. Although less experienced people may criticize you for doing this, other successful people will recognize the good intent and strategic way that you, as an influential leader, are making things happen and getting things done.

Strengthening your connections

There are a lot of resources out there to help you to build a stronger network – networking is a large and important subject, so study it well. Chapter 9 (Developing powerful and influential networks) will explore this in much more detail. Meantime, here are a few important ideas to start you thinking:

- Remember that this source of power is about building high-quality relevant relationships.
- Analyse your current network in terms of: quantity (how many?), quality (how good?), reach (where?), relevance (to your purpose) and influence (can you influence them?).
- Look for development areas to strengthen the overall quality of your network following your analysis, perhaps by filling in some gaps or deepening core relationships.
- Make sure you add value first. Rewards will come later. No one likes being connected to someone who is only interested in taking.

Source six: skills

Those exceptional abilities you have that enable you to get things done.

People don't get ahead and become highly influential by being the same as everyone else. In this source, it points to the particular skills you have that really stand out. You are not just good at these, you are exceptionally good, and others know it. These skills need to be relevant to your *leadership arena* and the work you are engaged with.

For example, imagine you are well known for your ability to build rapport and connect at an emotional level. This can increase your influence as an influential leader because:

- Being more approachable you will hear more about what is really going on in the organization.

- People are more likely to come to you for help, and in return will help you too.

- Others will open up and be more honest with you.

- You will have deeper relationships and greater loyalty among your connections.

- New people will proactively come and introduce themselves. This gives you early opportunity to shape and influence.

- Others will proactively help you in case they need your help at a later date.

Other skills that are particularly useful in generating greater power and influence include:

- *Charm:* yes, this is a skill that can be learned. People tend to want to be in the company and good books of charming people because it makes them feel good about themselves.

- *Motivation:* the ability to get people to want to do what you want them to do is really useful. It avoids the need to force or manipulate and increases commitment.

- *Inspiration:* if you have the skill of being able to inspire others around you, the discretionary effort and energy they will put into your projects will exceed your expectations.

- *Rhetoric and persuasion:* the ability to structure your communication to get people on side in the most effective manner is one of the key skills you need as an influential leader. Arguably, without this skill you cannot be an influential leader.

- *Negotiation:* not only a handy skill when you need to use it, but also, awareness that you have it will affect others, making them think hard before they try to get more than their fair share from you.

Chapter 8 (Increasing your skills as an influential leader) is dedicated to this element of the framework: which skills contribute to your power. For now, it is worth simply pointing out that, in terms of power, skills can do much more than simply help you to do your job well. The recognition that you have certain skills will help you to be more influential.

Source seven: agenda

The issues and priorities you focus your leadership attention on.

What is noticeable about all powerful and influential people is that they have very clear opinions about a whole variety of things in the wider organization. They have also chosen to focus their agenda in a particular way. Their focus may be orientated towards fixing a certain problem or issue that the business faces. Or perhaps they have decided that the wider population needs to view things in a specific way. Whatever it is, they have clarity – and most people are able to recognize this.

If you have been working on your *leadership purpose* in the previous chapter, you will already have a clear notion of your own agenda. However, because this source is defined as what you focus your leadership attention on, it can also include other things beyond or outside of your defined purpose.

For instance, you may be focused on someone else's agenda. Without having a clear notion of what your purpose is you can still jump on other people's agenda and use it to focus your effort and influence. This quite often happens in large organizations when a new CEO arrives. They most certainly have an agenda, and the wise senior managers will be very tempted to pick up and run with elements of that agenda. For instance, if you get a new CEO appointed with a cost-cutting agenda, it would be sensible for you to begin focusing your attention on saving money before you are forced to. This could help you to become more visible, valued and influential with the new CEO.

Alternatively, due to your role responsibilities, you may have to focus on specific problems that might otherwise hold little interest for you, or relevance to your purpose. Examples of this include annual budgeting, planning, audits and governance. All of these are important aspects of organizational life, but usually fall well outside of notions of purpose, unless you happen to be the chief compliance officer.

Agenda gains its power and influence in three ways:

- Clarity: the easier it is for people to see where you are trying to go, the more likely they will cooperate and do what you need them to do. If they are left guessing about your direction, they may not know what to do for the best.

- Confidence: clarity exudes confidence. When people see confidence they are more likely to be influenced than when they see doubt and uncertainty. Confidence conveys credibility.

- Buy-in: if those exposed to your agenda like what they see, and realize they will benefit from getting there, they'll help you all the way.

The topic of agenda will be returned to time and again throughout this book. As an influential leader you have to have a clear agenda and be able to see and understand other agendas, at both an individual and group level.

The power of reputation

During workshops, reputation is often cited as being powerful, something that helps people to be influential. And it can be highly influential. But what does it mean?

Reputation refers to the widely held, consistent and distinctive expectations about an individual. These expectations relate to who you are, what you do, the way you behave and how you react and interact with others. Reputation goes way beyond where a personal brand may take you, because the impression created is repeated and strengthened over a long time and in a peculiar way. Your reputation is something that can make you truly stand out from the crowd, perhaps by becoming only one in 10,000 people to hold your particular reputational distinction. To give you power, reputations need to be more than noticeable and distinctive. To really stretch, you need to have a reputation for something that people truly admire and are moved by.

Reputation invariably contains a unique blend of the sources of power that have been considered in this chapter. It is the cumulative effect of all of your sources of power. Yet there is no ideal or perfect way of doing it. Reputations come in all shapes and sizes, from good to terrible. While I'd like to think that any reader of this book will be strongly favouring the positive, I need to recognize that many powerful people are influential because they have a fear-inducing reputation that puts people around them on their guard and scares them into capitulation, sometimes even before the monster has entered the boardroom.

What people with fearsome reputations need to realize is that they create a perilous position of vulnerability and perpetual stress. While others may be able to go and work elsewhere, people with fearsome reputations are stuck with their negative means of influence because they have created a reputation others don't want to employ. So, do yourself a favour and concentrate on building a strong and positive reputation that will have enduring influence throughout your career.

To understand how reputations are built into great power, the field of impression management suggests that it can be broken down into three key areas:

1 Substance: this comprises your technical knowledge, experience and skills – the tools of your trade. Mainly derived from *credibility* and *skills*.

2 Direction: this provides the energy and focus for your content. The sources in play here are *character* and *agenda*.

3 Communication style: this is the way you express yourself, in all its forms. This also draws on your *skills* and your *presence*.

These three elements of reputation are contextualized and given substance through your *connections* and from your *position*. Thus, you can see how all seven sources of power play their part in reputation building.

When it comes to building greater power, many people focus sporadically on building the individual sources but rarely sit back and ask two critical questions: 1) What reputation do you wish to create? And: 2) What is the best way to build this reputation?

Being able to answer these two questions takes an investment in time and energy. Any attempt to move towards clarity will yield benefits because of the way it focuses on particular outcomes. The next chapter will help you to answer these questions in detail.

Before that, I'd like to encourage you to do a little application of the ideas in this chapter. This will help you to see what is really going on around you.

Applying sources of power to your world

As you have been reading I am sure you have been thinking of your own examples related to people you know. Now I want to take that a stage further with an exercise that will probably take you about half an hour.

The purpose of this exercise is to get you thinking more deeply about the different sources of power that people have, by assessing individuals you know well. This will help you to notice what is working for others and increase your awareness of what is working, and could work, for you. In later chapters I will refer you back to this exercise to extend and deepen your analysis.

Exercise

The power analysis exercise

The guide below explains how to set up the exercise that will be used many times in this book. To get started you need to:

1 Find seven pieces of card, about half the size of a business card. Write the power sources on them, one per card: *credibility*, *character*, *presence*, *position*, *connections*, *skills* and *agenda*). The purpose of the exercise is to consider the order in which the sources create influence for the subject of your analysis (to begin with, the subject will be individuals).

2 Create a page in your notebook, with seven rows and ten columns. Enter the name of each power in the first column, one per row. This will create a place to record your analysis as you complete each exercise so that you can easily refer back to it (there is a completed example below if you need to refer to it).

3 Whenever you are completing a power analysis, keep the source descriptions nearby so that you can easily refer to them. At the beginning you may also need to refer back to this chapter and the more detailed descriptions of each power source.

Power source description reminder

- *Credibility:* the power derived from your professional standing and expertise.
- *Character:* the underlying traits, values and beliefs that shape your behaviour.

- *Presence:* the impact you create and the feelings you stimulate when people meet you.

- *Position:* the roles you play and how you manoeuvre yourself into the limelight.

- *Connections:* the network of relationships you have around you and your work.

- *Skills:* those exceptional abilities you have that enable you to get things done.

- *Agenda:* the issues and priorities you focus your leadership attention on.

Analysing others

To begin, I'd like you to identify three or four people you know quite well who are influential. If you are working for a large organization, try to select people who work there. Alternatively, think outside of your organization and even outside of your working life. To make this exercise useful, the important thing is to find people you are quite familiar with.

Taking each individual in turn:

- Sort the cards into priority order based on what it is about the individual that makes them influential with you. Think about examples of when they have easily influenced you to do something, or to feel a certain way. Which source of power is most prominent in your mind about the way they are able to influence you?

- Once you have finalized the order, write down the ranking in your notebook under a column headed up with the name of the individual and 'me'.

- Next, think about how the individual is able to influence other people. There may be variations because you have a special or different relationship with them. Consider their work and the people they engage with. What is it about them that sways opinion, mobilizes action and gets things moving in the direction they want? If you do notice differences, move your cards around and complete another column with rankings under the title of the name of the individual and 'others'.

- Before you move to the next individual, pause and reflect more deeply on how each source of power is used by them. For instance, when you think about their credibility, what aspect of their credentials is working for them? It may be their public profile, testimonials or their track record of results. Go deeper on each source of power.

Repeat this for three or four individuals if you can. What you will end up with is a page in your notebook that might look like the example shown in Figure 2.1.

FIGURE 2.1   Power analysis exercise

	Paul/Me	Paul/Others	Chris/Me
CREDIBILITY	1st	1	3
CHARACTER	5	6	1st
PRESENCE	3	4	2nd
POSITION	7	7	6
CONNECTIONS	2nd	2	7
SKILLS	4	5	4
AGENDA	6	3	5

In the example shown in Figure 2.1, Paul is a highly respected specialist who is influential because of what he knows (*credibility*), and also who he knows (*connections*). Although he is by no means a weak character, he doesn't really use his force of personality to influence (*character*). However, he does exude quiet confidence and always makes a strong impact (*presence*).

Chris, on the other hand, is a hard-hitting project manager who uses his assertive personality and physical presence to push things through. Although he has an incredible track record he lets that speak for itself, but everyone knows he is going to deliver. Perhaps as part of his personality, he doesn't really have time to bother with small talk and would far sooner just press on and deliver.

Analysing yourself

Now it is time to start applying this to you. What is it about you that helps you to influence other people? Why do people do what you want them to do? How are you able to land your project and get people collaborating effectively?

Using the cards again, sort them in your own personal order. Make sure to think of specific examples of when you have been influential. Think carefully enough about it that you can be ready to explain your rationale to a friend. In fact, why don't you do that now? As with all of these exercises, they are much better shared and explored with friends and colleagues.

Once you have finalized your order, enter them in your notebook in another column.

The results

Before you move on, you might find it useful to take a look at the overall table you have created in your notebook. What differences do you notice between the individuals you have considered? How does their power differ from your own? Are there any common themes about your selections? For instance, did *character* always come first? Just pause a moment and reflect on what you have done.

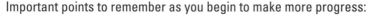

Getting things done

Important points to remember as you begin to make more progress:

- Power is the capacity to influence someone to think, feel or do something different.

- Power provides the means by which an influential leader is able to obtain the help and support of others as they pursue their purpose.

- Without power, leaders struggle to influence.

- Power has the potential to make substantial positive progress.

- There are many sources of power that combine to form a leader's reputation.

- Once you learn what influences people, you can more effectively increase your influence.

Further reading

When you get a chance, make sure to check the further reading and resources for this chapter online at: **www.learntoinfluence.com/leadership**

This concludes our initial consideration of what can make leaders strong, powerful and influential. You will work with these more deeply as the book unfolds and this is one reason why this section is placed at the beginning of the book. In particular, in the next chapter I will explore why these sources of power work, and why they sometimes don't work. Once you understand this you will be able to begin focusing your time and effort as an influential leader in ways that will be more effective.

Why power works in the real world

03

When you understand why different sources of power influence, you can begin to learn what will work for you.

Learning what can give people the power to influence is only the beginning of the journey towards becoming an influential leader. It is quite difficult to be all things to all people and therefore you need to be able to focus your time and effort on building the right sources of power for you.

The next step towards being able to determine where to focus your power building is to understand how and why power works. From this understanding you will be able to economize your time and effort without losing progress towards your goals.

This chapter contributes to the following influential leader capabilities:

Can analyse what will work and what will not work for different people in different situations.

Knows what makes them powerful and how to grow and utilize their power.

The five principles of power

Power is the capacity to influence.

This clear working definition of power leads nicely to the next question: how does it work? There seems to be a great deal of mystery surrounding power, and this is encouraged by the powerful. Why should they help others to learn how to become more powerful? Unfortunately for them, you are about to find out how deceptively simple it all is.

After a massive amount of study, coaching and thinking, I've simplified power down to just five key principles. The benefit of this simplification is that keeping these principles in mind you will be able to maximize your power without getting lost in the complexity.

Here's a quick summary of the principles of power that I explore in this chapter:

1 *Consequences:* power creates waves and needs to be handled with care.

2 *Calculation:* power is all about individuals making personal decisions in order to satisfy their needs and wants.

3 *Supply and demand:* you will be powerful if people want what you have, and especially powerful if they can't get it elsewhere.

4 *Perception and reality:* it is not so much about what power you have, but what power people think you have.

5 *Utilization:* your power and influence will grow if you use your power.

Principle one: consequences

Power creates waves and needs to be handled with care.

As soon as you acquire power, things will begin to change, often without you consciously attempting to make things happen. These consequences fall into four broad categories:

1 Results: the tangible achievements you are able to secure. This is what you are intending to get done.

2 Impact: how others behave and help you to achieve your goals.

3 Relationships: the way you engage and relate to others and, critically, how they relate to you, will change dramatically as you grow in power.

4 Yourself: power will have a big impact on your own attitudes and beliefs.

In each of these categories there are pros and cons that need to be borne in mind as you prepare to develop greater power as a leader.

Results

Providing you are keeping well focused, as your power grows you will find that you are able to achieve the results you set out to achieve more quickly and easily. The flow of achievements will steadily increase and become much more straightforward and efficient. The days of struggling to get what you want will fade and be replaced with a confidence that you can get the results – all you need to do is to set the goal.

Unfortunately, greater ease of accomplishment heightens the need to be crystal clear on what it is you do want. It is all too easy to go charging down the road to a goal only to realize when you get there that the world doesn't look quite as good as you expected – be careful what you wish for. This can become evident before you get to the end of the road too, so if you are not clear from the beginning, your followers could charge down many dead ends and have to keep doubling back to find an alternative route. This wastes time, energy and goodwill, and will damage your leadership credibility.

In practical terms this may mean that although you get a good result for you, it may not be the best thing for other stakeholders who have a marginal interest in what you are doing. When you were deciding on your goal they probably didn't feature too much in your consideration so were easy to overlook. After you have achieved your result, they may be spurred into action as they realize what you have done. This could create unwelcome consequences for you.

Another reason to be careful with your results is that the amount of challenge you get will diminish as your power grows. You need to be sensitive to this and make sure that you continue to get the challenge you need to ensure your results are safe. Ensuring that your team members and others around the organization feel safe to raise their voice and challenge you is vital to getting good results. And it is important that they do this at the right time. Many will hold back until the problems they can see become extreme – by which time the cost of correcting the problem will be greater.

As your power and results grow, so too will your reputation. If you have managed to avoid the results consequences, you will soon set up a virtuous circle that will lead to greater success.

Impact

Another consequence that power creates is that people will be more likely to do what you want them to do. This is great news for an influential leader as it is the magical ingredient in getting things done in an (apparently) effortless way. Limited power means you have to rely on persuasion, cajoling or even bribing people to do things. Huge amounts of power will make people flock to the door, willing to help.

This presents many challenges and unintended consequences because you are becoming less of an actor as your power increases. People will increasingly take it upon themselves to make the decisions about what they do for you. Either because they have less time with you, or because they are more motivated to figure it out for themselves. The reality is that you are less likely to know exactly what is going on.

Little surprise that one of the consequences is that you may yield to the temptation to micro-manage. You have less time and an increasingly clear view (vision) of what needs to happen. More on this point in a moment.

Another phenomenon you need to be careful of is that if you are getting more of what you want out of people, particularly those who do not report directly to you, it means that someone else is getting less from them. Watch out for peers responding to your growing influence.

Relationships

Many of you I am sure will have experienced the trouble caused when you were promoted within a team. Instead of being one of the team, you were placed in the leadership position. This immediately changed the relationship between you and them. It usually comes as a surprise the first time it happens in a career, filtered out by the fluttering ego delighted at gaining promotion. Only with experience do you learn to anticipate the consequences, and work proactively to minimize the negative impact.

It is more difficult to notice and handle changing relationships in the wider organization as you grow in power – and they will be changing faster than you can talk to them. Elevation to senior levels means you have less time for networking and may not realize that a relationship has turned negative until a problem occurs. One new director observed the immediate swing from struggling to get meetings with people to suddenly having to bolt his door as they all wanted his attention.

A main change that occurs in relationships as you grow in power is trust. Because you are becoming more powerful, can you still be relied on? With greater responsibilities people will expect you to act differently, but how different will that be? Now you are a member of the inner circle, or you sit at the top table, maybe you will not be their friend any more. People around you will be looking for the clues to give them the answer to the question: can they still trust you? Many will presume, until proven otherwise, that the power will go to your head. Until trust can be re-proven, you are likely to experience a great deal more caution in these relationships.

This works both ways: now you are more powerful will you still be able to trust them? Research has shown that managers are prone to be suspicious of subordinates offering help and assistance, especially when it is not expected. What are their real motives? That subordinates have noticed you have more power and are clamouring for your attention will only exacerbate your suspicions if you are not careful.

A final factor to consider is how your friendships will change. It is impossible to totally detach your personal life from your work. Who you are at the office inevitably spreads to who you are at home and with your friends. As your beliefs, attitudes and confidence change, people will notice. Friends may not like what you are becoming. Close friends may not like the new you. Partners will also see a different you. Because these relationships are important, it is vital that you are proactive at protecting them.

All of this means you just need to be sensible and alert. These things don't always go awry, and being a little more careful is the easiest way to re-establish the excellent working relationships.

Yourself

The final category of consequences, and perhaps one of the most important, is what greater power will do to you. As will be explained in Chapter 8 (Increasing your skills as an influential leader), self-awareness is a key skill that needs to be honed. Observing the changes within your attitudes, beliefs and behaviour is vitally important as an influential leader.

> 'Power tends to corrupt, and absolute power corrupts absolutely. Great men are almost always bad men.'
>
> John Dalberg-Acton

This quote is a great attention grabber, and certainly sounds a warning bell that power can exert a tremendous effect on those who acquire it. While I agree with why it was said all those years ago (1887), what it misses is the fact that corrupt power is far more noticeable than ethical power. History is littered with the notorious, but the virtuous leaders struggle for prominence, even if their actual achievements are far greater.

However, rather than getting into a moralistic debate about the uses and abuses of power, the important thing to note is that as you grow in power, you are going to be changing. This is something you need to watch carefully if you are to avoid power going to your head. These changes are difficult to anticipate and notice, often until someone gives you some rather tough feedback.

Here are some of the things to watch out for:

- Over-confidence: as power ascends it is the most natural thing in the world to relax and feel more at ease with the world, and your work. This is good, but you also need to watch out for complacency, tempting shortcuts and dismissing challenge because you can.

- Risk taking: linked to the above, your propensity to take risks will grow. The more successful you become, the more you will believe that you have the golden touch and that the risks are pretty minimal – you can handle just about any trouble that heads your way.

- Reduced analysis: why bother? You know what the answer should be so why spend so much time analysing it to death? Besides, even if there is a slight flaw in your thinking, no problem, you can handle that. Tread carefully.

- Increased visibility: once others in the organization start to realize you are becoming more powerful, they may see you as a political rival. You will start drawing attention and you need to be prepared for it.

- Vulnerability: as you begin to move in more powerful circles you automatically become a little less secure. Not only is your power growing, but so too are your responsibilities and others' expectations. These things can easily conspire to create greater personal strain and stress, which if ignored can damage your health and make performance even more difficult.

No doubt you will notice other consequences along the way, but it is important that you pause for a few moments to reflect a little more deeply on the ones outlined above. Consider others you know who have risen to power. How did they change? What traps did they fall into? What would you have done differently? Even better, why don't you go and ask them? Perhaps they may be a great mentor for you as you develop your ability to get things done!

Principle two: calculation

Power is all about individuals making personal decisions in order to satisfy their needs and wants.

Power works because of the way people view your power as being capable of either helping or hindering their own progress towards their goals. Since you are not the only person in the world attempting to gain their help and support, they may have to choose between you and someone else. They will calculate the relative merits of each competing course of action.

Disturbance factors

Wouldn't it be nice if all of these calculations were done based on clear logic? The real world is much more interesting than that. Decisions defy logic due to a range of factors going on inside the mind of the individual making their choice, including:

- Imperfect information: rarely is it possible for an individual to have all of the facts that they need to make an accurate decision. There may be a great deal of guesswork going on about other people's agendas, plans and promises.

- Incompatible choices: often the decision will offer alternative risks and rewards that are difficult to compare. For instance, on the one hand they may solve some of their problems today by offering their help to you but, on the other, their career prospects may be improved by helping someone else who offers them the opportunity to present to the board.

- Emotional interference: emotional reaction to the options are more influential than the facts – and they are very personal. What moves one person may completely fail to move another. The obvious example is that friends are more likely to help than enemies, even though you say and do exactly the same things. It is tough decoding emotional reactions and even those who are reacting will find it difficult to explain why they feel the way they do.

- Gut feel: as either an intuitive feeling of the right course of action, or an inexplicable and deep emotional hunch, the inescapable fact here is that people make decisions and cannot always explain their rationale.

- Social proof: the concept popularized by Robert Cialdini (author of *Influence: The psychology of persuasion*) is that people seem to be greatly affected in their decisions because of what other people are doing. Popular products sell in part because they are popular – people make the assumption that so many others cannot be wrong.

- Peer pressure: humans are very responsive to comparisons with others and are highly motivated to maintain or increase their position relative to others. They certainly don't want to lose their current standing.

All of these factors make it extremely difficult to predict with a high level of certainty how an individual will make a decision to be influenced by you, especially in a group setting. These will be explored in great detail in Chapter 5 (Understanding your leadership arena).

Decision stimulus

Aside from the actual task of making a decision, it is also important to consider how an individual became aware that they needed to make one:

- Extrinsic direct: the most common reason why the need for a decision becomes apparent is when someone makes a specific request, often an urgent demand at an inconvenient moment. The implication of calculations starting this way is that they immediately create a negative disturbance to work in progress – which means that to comply with the request, something else has to be sacrificed.

- Extrinsic indirect: here someone else is making the request on behalf of the beneficiary, or subtly suggesting what should be done. This is particularly potent when the requester has little or no apparent personal interest in the outcome. This level of independence adds a huge amount of credibility to the request.

- Intrinsic: people spend a great deal of time wrapped up in their own concerns, trying to figure out what to do for the best. Internal requests are highly potent because there is little need to question the credibility or reliability of the person making a request and the individual does not feel as if they are being forced into something. They are in total control.

The stimuli above are ordered from least to most effective. So if you can find a way for people to convince themselves that they should be doing what you want them to do, you are certainly an influential leader.

Individual disposition

The final factor to bear in mind when considering how people make their calculations about what to do is their own general psychological disposition and character. Perhaps the more obvious points to notice are:

- Optimism versus pessimism: some people quite naturally see the positive in everything while others obsess about all that is wrong. You need to be alive to this possibility because it makes such a difference to the way in which you might choose to articulate your requests and proposals.

- Personality clashes: there is a strong tendency in humans to prefer the company of those with similar personalities. Research is clear that influence is going to be much easier if the people you need to influence are similar in personality to you. Much more on this aspect in Chapter 11 (Understanding influencing styles).

- Pain versus pleasure: some people focus more of their attention on how to avoid problems while others immediately latch on to all they can gain from an opportunity. Again, there is a big difference in the way you might articulate your requests.

- Trust versus distrust: unless people trust what they are hearing and believe what is being presented, influence is unlikely. Sadly, because of past experiences, some people find it very difficult to trust what they are hearing and will need a huge amount of convincing. If you know how much someone trusts you, you can approach them more effectively.

As with all generalizations, there will be exceptions and it is your job as an influential leader to keep these in mind and make conscious decisions about the way people are assessing your requests.

Decision examples

The bottom line is that power only works if people make a decision to do what you want them to do, or what they think you want them to do. The best way of getting them to decide in your favour is to utilize the sources of power that will be effective with the people you want to influence.

Before moving on to the next principle, pause for a moment and consider the following case study of how calculations work.

CASE STUDY

Serena is an ambitious new graduate accountant. How do different sources of power affect her decisions, from the obvious to the more obscure influences?

- Position: those who have a higher grade than she does carry more decision-making authority and potential to help or hinder her career.

- Credibility – experience: people who have greater experiences within the company (either in accounting or not) are likely to be able to influence Serena easily because they could help her to figure out what she should do. She is also much more likely to take their advice at face value.

- Connections – network: colleagues who know people they could connect her with are likely to be able to easily get her attention provided she knows they have that network and they are able to give her hope that they will make an introduction.

- Credibility – reputation: some people in accounting have the sort of reputation that make Serena fearful of stepping out of line. These people are notorious for the way they can demolish ill-prepared juniors in meetings.

- Connections – associations: if someone happens to be dating a director, they have the potential to put in a good word for her, or a bad one, so she is likely to be rather helpful to them.

If you need to, now would be a good opportunity to return to the previous chapter to look again at the detail of these sources of power and see how they could be influencing your calculations right now. The more you can link these ideas to your own world, the more quickly you will grow in power and influence.

There is a risk here of becoming paralysed by all this talk about how people make decisions. So many things to think about. This is where experience and lots of practice comes to the fore. Learning what makes people tick, and how different people are making their calculations, can be fun too. It you approach this area as a puzzle to be solved rather than an insurmountable problem you are much more likely to make good progress. I'll return to this topic in Chapter 4 (Deeper understanding of people).

Principle three: supply and demand

You will be powerful if people want what you have, and especially powerful if they can't get it elsewhere.

Power functions according to the market laws of supply and demand. If you have a source of power that a lot of people value and want, and they can only get it from you, then you are in a very powerful position.

For instance, if one of your sources of power is the status or position that makes the final decision on which projects are given funding, people will be very keen to keep on the right side of you. They will do what you ask them to do. On the other hand, if there are many sources of funding then their choices are more varied and they are much less dependent on your favourable consideration. The scales have tipped in their favour.

What if you have a problem that needs the assistance of a specialist lawyer? If there are only a few people with that expertise they will be able to charge high rates, especially if lots of other people have the same problem as you. The more demand there is for their services, the more they can charge and the more selective they can be about who they favour with their expertise. Of course, their fees may get so high that you make the decision it is better to keep the problem rather than solve it, or you may look for alternative ways of removing the issue.

Demand-side considerations

For your sources of power to be powerful, people have to:

- want what you have, or at least feel they will benefit;
- know that you have it;
- believe you may be willing to supply it;
- think that they cannot get it elsewhere on more favourable terms.

Notice that I am using the word 'want' rather than 'need'. The difference is the individual's conscious awareness. Quite often people say to me that their stakeholders need their help and would really benefit from it. However, if the stakeholders are not aware of this, then influence is going to be difficult to achieve.

Interestingly, *need* doesn't even have to exist in order for people to *want* something. I'm sure that you have often wanted something that you don't really need. There is perhaps an ethical question about supplying to wants rather than needs, and I will get to that Chapter 6 (The ethics of influence).

In addition to thinking about the obvious economic and practical causes of demand, such as the need for funding, resources and solutions to problems, there are also a number of psychological causes of demand, particularly when it comes to how power and influence work. When all other things are equal in a calculation about what to do, these factors will weigh in heavily:

- Responsibility: a key finding of Frederick Herzberg (author of *Motivation to Work*) was that one of the strongest motivators in the workplace is the desire for responsibility. People are naturally looking out for ways to take on more responsibility, sometimes just for its own sake rather than the monetary rewards that it could bring.
- Respect: this draws directly from the power of credibility in that individuals want to work with people they respect and admire. They want to be led by people they look up to. They want to do things for these people and become part of their team.
- Fun and friendship: since people spend so much time at work, many will gravitate towards people they enjoy working with. Enjoyment is an oft forgotten element of the business of leadership. Happy people do more, and make greater progress.

- Belonging and security: these deep human drivers are highly influential in the way people make decisions. If what you have to offer plays to these lower-level motivations it may swing the calculation in your favour.

Motivation is such an important element of influence that I will develop this further in the next chapter.

Supply-side considerations

Returning to market economics, those who possess or control access to products and services that are in high demand are able to achieve greater profit margins. To gain maximum influence, work to gain control of the things that people want most. Here are a few examples:

- Sales people: access to the end users or customers is a very powerful position; because they 'know' the customer, they are able to block or promote organization-wide ideas. They will jealously guard that access (limiting supply) because the customer insight is one of their key sources of power with which they can influence the business. Other key power sources for them are revenue (perhaps profit and loss) and also the customer relationship.

- Personal assistants: because they stand on the door to the executive suite, to get in you have to go through them. Not only do they have the keys, they also have intimate knowledge of their boss's schedule, and can even whisper in their ear. In the past I have been tipped off by a PA as to when would be a good time to drop in on her boss, and also when definitely not to show my face. They are also really good at advocating people they like to their bosses.

- Old hands: these are the people who have been in the organization since it began, or often it seems that way. They know every nook and cranny. The odd thing is these people are often not seen as being powerful, yet they are able to use their knowledge to completely block an ambitious upstart who has annoyed them. In many cases they are the custodian of the corporate intellectual capital and, when push comes to shove, the senior people know this and will protect them.

- Information control: anything that people need to know can have value if the demand is high and supply is restricted. Management information is necessary to be able to make decisions about corporate strategy. Market and customer insights are vital to be able to design, develop and deliver successful products. The information you have or are able to deliver will make you powerful if it is in high demand and you are the only one who can provide it.

- Resources: in an organization driving down costs, financial expertise and process change people will be in demand. Being in a position to choose where to allocate these types of resources can place you in a great position. Who you choose to favour with the best people on your team will mean that those needing the resources will work hard to gain your cooperation.

Of course, good influential leaders will not abuse their domination of supply, but they will use it to slide smoothly through the problems they encounter along the path towards their goal.

Principle four: perception and reality

It is not so much about what power you have, but what power people think you have.

If you think about a recent time when you were influenced to do something – why did you do it? To what extent was it a decision (or calculation) based on fact? Most likely there was a great deal of guesswork involved, even if you do call it gut-feel or intuition. The subjective element of decision making is greater than you may realize. Basing decisions on emotions is not something that many people would be prepared to own up to. Indeed, many corporate decisions are made initially with emotion and then justified by teams of analysts.

When people are making decisions in response to your requests, remain alert to the gaps between their perceptions about your power and the reality. I have noticed that, in the main, people tend to underestimate their own power and overestimate the power of others. This widens the gap and introduces risks that you need to be careful of, as well as opportunities you can make use of.

Underestimating your own power

The obvious implication here is that you will not leverage the influence you could do, therefore you will miss opportunities to get things done quickly and easily. Your evident lack of confidence will actually begin to diminish your real power.

This goes deeper than humility, where you might present yourself as being less powerful than you actually are. What is happening here is that you believe it. Sometimes this can be as simple as assuming people will say no – so you don't ask and therefore avoid possible rejection. Sometimes people don't ask even when they have been given permission and encouragement – they still talk themselves out of making the request.

Overestimating your own power

This risks the appearance of overconfidence and arrogance. You will not take long in overstepping the mark and that could create significant political risks as others queue up to put you back in your place. On the other hand, your self-deluded state may be believed by others and help you to grow your power quite quickly. As time passes, this gap will need to be closed by increasing your actual power to match your perceived power.

If you are doing this consciously, presenting yourself as more powerful than you actually are, you risk appearing manipulative and political. You may not be able to see your lack of confidence, but others will, particularly more seasoned campaigners. The notion of 'fake it until you make it' has a somewhat dubious reputation.

Others overestimating your power

You might be forgiven for thinking this is a good thing. If people imagine you to be capable of things that you are not, then they will do far more for you because of their overestimation. Imagination can develop into fantasy, and people's internal dialogue will convince them that you have the power to make things happen far beyond the reality.

However, the inherent risk is that one day they will find out that you are not actually able to whisper in the ear of the CEO, or call in favours from your vast network. Then your reputation may be severely affected.

Others underestimating your power

Here you have done yourself an injustice by not presenting yourself well enough. The consequence of this is that you will not get as much done as you could do, or you end up surprising people when they do realize what you are capable of. Neither overestimating or underestimating your power is tolerable for an influential leader – especially the latter, due to the likelihood of appearing Machiavellian.

A simple illustration

Whenever you go to a conference, one of the attractions is likely to be the credibility of the speakers. You will be keen to hear from them, learn from them and are likely to take action. Before you take action, you will need to be satisfied that their advice is good and a large part of it will rest on their credentials.

Credentials are prone to misunderstanding. You might be impressed with their biography. The mention of having worked with numerous business schools may be a good indicator, but what does that actually mean? There is a world of difference between working with a business school on a long research programme and popping in to speak to the odd class. But there is only room on the brochure to mention that they have worked with business schools and the rest is left to your imagination.

Is this misrepresentation? I tend to think that is a value judgement. What is lying? Is missing out certain facts lying? To some it is, to others it is not. Chapter 6 (The ethics of influence) will challenge you on this topic.

The bottom line

The important point I want to make here is that whether you like it or not, people will make guesses about you based on what they see, hear and imagine. The greater the gap between perception and reality, the higher the risk becomes that your reputation will get damaged when they find out. The extent to which you encouraged this misinterpretation will determine the depth your reputation will sink to.

As an influential leader, you need to keep a close eye on how others are perceiving you and take steps to be prudent in managing the gap. Resist the temptation to let them get carried away, which they will, especially if you're pretty good anyway.

Principle five: utilization

Your power and influence will grow if you use your power.

To become strong and powerful you need to make use of the power that you have, otherwise you will quickly begin to lose it or, at least, its usefulness will diminish. This is not to say that you should throw your weight around and dominate others, but people do have to know that you have power and will use it when you need to.

For instance, if a primary source of power that you could have is a large amount of cash (or budget), provided others know that you have it, and they would like some of it, it will influence them to try to get into your good books so that you may be induced into sharing some of it with them. However, this will only work until they realize, if this is the case, that you are miserly and will never share your money with anyone. Once they realize this, they will wander off elsewhere to look for people to help who may be a little more generous than you. No, you don't have to give your money to just anyone, make them work hard and ensure that you share it sensibly with those whose help you the most. When you do this, make sure others know that you have shared, and why, so that they can learn what they need to do in order that they may also obtain some of your money.

Similarly, if you have a big stick but everyone knows you just like to wave it around and that you would never dream of using it, they will not be frightened by it and will begin to ignore it. No, I don't advocate hitting people with big sticks, but it is a nice illustration of how all sources of power need to be utilized to keep their impact in working order.

To many, power is regarded as an ugly concept. To be powerful is to dominate and abuse. Hopefully, having read so far, you will have a different idea as you will have seen the tremendous positive that can come from combining power with an ethical approach. Yet many don't see this and shy away from using the power that they have at their disposal. That is a choice, and one that damages their ability to get things done. Influential leaders need to build their base of power and exercise it ethically so that it grows and becomes even more useful in helping them realize their purpose (more on this in Chapter 6).

So, with power, if you don't use it, you'll lose it.

The complexity of power

These five principles of power are very simple on the surface, yet in practice operate at a very subtle level, exerting their influence and getting things done. Learning how power is working in a group or *leadership arena* where you want to be successful as a leader will take time and careful study. Real life is never as simple as the principles would have you believe.

One of the reasons for this is that people are usually unclear about exactly what they want – having instead perhaps just a vague notion of what they want to achieve. This immediately casts doubt on their ability to appreciate the consequences of the power around them. It also makes their calculation somewhat prone to error, and certainly difficult to predict. If they don't know what they want, how can they tell that you will be able to help them to get it, or stop them from getting it?

Another complication is that people respond to the different sources of power in different ways. Because individuals have had different experiences, hold different values and have different ambitions, it can be very tricky working out which sources of power will work, and which will not.

An easy example to illustrate this is qualifications. As part of credentials, you either have a qualification or you don't. People who value qualifications in general, and your qualification in particular, are likely to award you with greater credence. Others who have no qualifications may still be influenced, but it may be purely because they feel intimidated by your intellectual prowess. Or, they may simply dismiss you because unlike them, you haven't got a degree in the school of life. The responses to qualifications are usually quite obvious.

More difficult to notice is the way that presence or gravitas influences people. Presence works at a feeling and emotional level. While some emotions are easy to spot, most are not, especially with more senior people, or those who prefer to keep their emotional world to themselves. Quite often you only get to find out how people feel about what is happening when their behaviour has revealed it, which might be some time after the point at which they were exposed to the presence of the influencer. This is especially likely because they may fear revealing their true feelings to a powerful individual. This will delay disagreement and drive it underground (I'll talk more about how emotional preferences can interrupt relationships in Chapter 11).

The only way to overcome the challenge of this complexity is by regular practice. Observe power in action, analyse what is happening and draw conclusions. Then test those conclusions. This is mission critical for influential leaders.

To help you to do this, I explore below a number of roles that you will be familiar with. Then I'll challenge you to figure out how these sources and principles of power are working around your organization or in your leadership arena.

HR directors

Generally, HR directors seem to draw their power and influence from:

- *Connections*: their extensive network around the organization gives them a broad understanding of the politics, agendas and rivalries amongst the workforce. They also have a keen insight into the mood of the people and the culture.
- *Position/agenda*: as custodians of the people strategy they will have a significant influence on things such as pay awards, training, promotions and dismissals. This is used as a foundation for establishing a clear people agenda, which they are usually very good at focusing on.
- *Credibility*: their ability to do their job and instil confidence among stakeholders also adds power and influence, especially if the organization is suffering from poor industrial relations or frequent employee litigation.

In order to be powerful, they need to use their power by acting on the political insights they gain, and doing so for the good of the organization (*principle five: utilization*). If they are not seen by the other executives to be doing this, their credibility will fall rapidly.

Often, HR directors appear less powerful than they actually are. Much of the networking that they do goes unnoticed so that the majority of people in the organization are unaware of the full impact they are capable of having (*principle four: perception and reality*). Sometimes, this perception of low power is also held by the incumbent who fails to recognize the way they can leverage these relationships, or does not have the confidence to use their connections.

When it comes to *supply and demand* (*principle three*), the ability of HR directors to influence depends on who they are attempting to influence. Other powerful directors and executives may not feel they have the need for the services of HR directors. Worse, HR directors may be considered to be a hindrance, especially when HR is restricting the directors' activities on recruitment or reward. More junior people, perhaps those in the talent pool, usually need to build new connections, which HR people have a plentiful supply of. Add to this their ability to inform and advise senior directors on new appointments and they have a great deal to offer ambitious individuals.

The actual level of influence that HR directors exert, and where they do this will vary widely. If they present themselves well and demonstrate their effectiveness, people around the organization will start to take more notice of them (*principle two: calculations*) and find creative ways of getting closer to them. Others will be more likely to want something from them and thus will be more amenable to their influence in return.

Finally, the consequences of their power (*principle one*) will mean that if they are really good at their own PR they will not need to work hard to get people to approach them. On the other hand, if they don't, they hand the power to other powerful people.

Getting it right also means that HR directors generally develop the power of *presence*. Their deep inner knowledge of the workings of the organization, and the circles they move in, helps to add a highly confident demeanour. They know who the rising stars are, and they know what the executives are planning. In many organizations, I have seen HR directors become the closest confidant of the CEO, advising on just about every decision they make. Sadly, I've also seen them overreach themselves and lose badly in head-on political battles with other powerful executives.

Operations directors

It is extremely difficult to generalize on this role because of the diverse range of organizations that they work in. However, from what I have seen, they tend to focus their power and influence on:

- *Position*: their role usually gives them responsibility for large resources of people, money and assets. Since they are also responsible for service delivery or production, their position in the overall executive team carries significant clout.

- *Credibility:* due to the complexity of their work, the experience and track record is usually left unchallenged. Add to this their reputation for moving fast to manage crises and solve severe production problems and they become formidable.

- *Character:* usually people in these positions demonstrate extremely strong personalities with tremendous resilience. They tend to be direct, fast and don't suffer fools gladly. In so doing, they become dependable for the organization.

For operations directors, using their power is never a problem (*principle five: utilization*). Indeed, they often seem to enjoy making things happen so much that they do it far too often rather than empowering their people to do more for themselves. The 'just do it' mentality is never far from their lips. Potentially, using their force of character to influence people weakens their position due to the damaged relationships and reduced commitment (I'll talk more about this in Chapter 13).

When it comes to perceptions, operations directors and others may think that they are more powerful than they actually are (*principle four*). Although their influence within operations is likely to be absolute, when it comes to making some of the bigger financial decisions, deciding on promotions and bonuses, or purchasing new IT services, they may falter in the face of other executives who have a broader remit and need to cater for the whole organization.

There is little doubt that operations directors are masters of *supply and demand (principle three)* as this is their stock in trade. The organization needs them to deliver and cannot survive long without it. They also have huge freedom to adjust the allocation of resources (be they people or budgets) within their realm. Since these are often two of the most valuable assets in an organization, this places operations directors in a very powerful position.

At an individual level, the influence of the operations director will be keenly felt by thousands or tens of thousands whose livelihood (*principle two: calculations*) is to an extent dependent on their support (either as a member of their team or in other connected businesses in the supply chain). Additionally, anyone who wants to get something done that involves the cooperation of the operations division will feel their influence too. Gaining the favour of the operations director for a new system can build careers, deliver promotion and help others achieve bonuses. People will also be considering the disadvantages they will bring forward if they don't get their support.

The consequences of a powerful operations director (*principle one*) can be substantial. With high-volume manufacturers or high-value service the rewards to the organization of having a powerful individual in this position will be significant. Because of the large numbers of employees, their position of power will also mean that others will be working hard to find ways to influence them and they need to make sure these are focused efficiently.

Other examples

Space does not permit me to explore other roles here, however the online resources offers further insight into roles such as financial controllers, compliance managers and CEOs. See: **www.learntoinfluence.com/leadership**

Exercise

Target group analysis

The real question that needs to be asked now is, who do you need to influence? Only when you have an answer to this can you begin to figure out which sources of power you will need in order to maximize your progress. There is absolutely no point in developing an impressive list of qualifications if the senior people in your target group deride such qualifications. That approach might be more useful if you are seeking to develop your industry standing because that arena is more likely to be using qualifications as evidence of credibility.

First you need to list the groups that you are interested in. The prime candidate as an influential leader is your *leadership arena*, which is where you want to achieve your purpose. One of the challenges this presents is that if you are being big and bold with your vision, it is likely that this group will be too varied in their responses to different power sources. For instance, you may wish to dramatically change the way your industry functions in order to create a massive improvement in its carbon footprint. Within your arena you would have competitors, media organizations and public interest groups to name but a few. Each of these groups will respond to different power sources, or rather, will be influenced by different things.

Incidentally, there is an exercise in Chapter 9 (Developing powerful and influential networks) that will help you to explore the make-up of your leadership arena and you may find it helpful to pause a moment and see if that will help you right now to identify the groups you need to analyse.

Ultimately, you will need to be able to influence all of the groups within your arena but, to start with, focus on the most important ones to gain a clear understanding of what is involved in the analysis process. It will also move you more quickly into action. As time allows over the coming months, you can then extend your analysis into further groups.

To consider how power and influence is working in each important group, answer these questions:

- Which sources of power are most influential (refer back to the previous chapter for a reminder of the different sources if you need to)?
- Which sources are being used by the most successful people in the group?
- What needs and wants do people have within the group?
- Which sources are most effective at meeting these?
- Which sources are in short supply?

It is important to make generalizations. This is not about what will move an individual, but generally how people within the group will respond to different sources. In reality this is the beginning of analysing the culture.

A good way of consolidating your thinking and making it more useful is to add an extra column to your growing Power Analysis table for each group you are considering (see the end of the previous chapter). This time, what you need to do is to order the various sources as they appear to be effective in the group you are analysing. This will be particularly helpful in the next section where you will be asked to consider what you need to do next.

Once you have worked out how power and influence is working within your target group(s) you can then decide how best to proceed.

Boosting your power

The process of becoming more powerful is easy enough – getting there may take a little longer. First, you work out what sources would be useful in the pursuit of your *leadership purpose*. There is little point in developing a source that is not going to be useful – no matter how attractive you think it is. If you have applied yourself well in the exercise above you should now have a fairly clear idea of what the important sources are.

The next step is to compare this with what you already have by way of power. What you need to do is to boost the sources that will have the greatest impact in the group(s) you are targeting. This may vary between groups and it is difficult to try to cater for all of them, so you will have to prioritize the most important sources that will have the best impact across all of your target groups.

This leads to five possible options, which are presented in order of usefulness, ease and speed. To be honest, the final option – re-educate the groups – is by far the hardest to achieve and will take many years of effort. I've included it in order to really stretch your thinking.

Reposition and highlight current power

Quite often people are not making the most of what they already have. One common example is the boost that credibility can gain from people knowing more about your previous experience. When joining a new company, conventional wisdom suggests that you need to be careful to avoid repeatedly referring to your past employer, which risks alienating your new colleagues. However, many people swing too far the other way and never refer to their previous experience. That leaves others guessing, or not even thinking about it (remember the principle of *perception and reality*).

What you need to do is to dispassionately consider what you have that could be of value to your target, whether or not they are aware of it. If you think it can, or might, be of interest then consider alternative ways that you can bring it to their attention. You don't have to do a hard sell, just find simple discreet ways to let them know what you've got available.

One great way of doing this is to talk to people. Be open and meet up with people who you know well in the group and explain that you are looking for ways that you can provide better service, or be more helpful to them and what they are trying to achieve. Find out more about their agenda, what they are trying to achieve and then start introducing ideas on how your particular experience can support them. While you are doing this, look out for ways in which your other sources of power could work there too.

The great thing about this option is that it is relatively straightforward and involves better communication rather than any actual change in your capabilities.

Enhance current sources of power

It is generally regarded as being more effective to build on strength than weakness. If you can identify something that gives you power and then extend and develop it further, this is likely to be an easier route to follow than attempting to develop a source of power from scratch.

Part of the secret to doing this is to focus even harder and more rigorously on what makes you unique in your strongest sources of power. Bolstering your knowledge might be one example. Strive to become an industry expert. From this you could move on to becoming the expert's expert and a thought leader in your field. One of the great benefits of becoming a specialist in a particular field is that you are continually reading and thinking about your subject. Others will be thinking about a wide range of other subjects and they are unlikely to be able to match your depth of knowledge.

This applies to all sources of power, even presence. If you are well known for your grace and poise, how could you become exceptional?

Build new sources of power

If the power you need to influence a group is more or less absent from your portfolio, you need to be quite careful that it is realistic for you to aim to secure it. It may be that you are just not suited to that source of power.

Building connections is a good example. You may be able to get by with sufficient networking, but making it a real strength generally requires a personality that is curious and interested in meeting new people. If you don't happen to have such a personality then networking will be hard work. You can still be an influential leader without being an exceptional networker, however, so you may benefit more from directing your development effort into one of the other power sources.

Unfortunately, having a complete absence of a source of power that you need in order to be successful in your leadership arena may indicate that you have chosen an arena that is not suited to you. In which case, return to the first chapter and take a hard look at your thinking on your leadership purpose.

On a brighter note, some power sources are easier to acquire because their absence from your power profile is not because of any weakness in your skills – you simply don't have that power. *Position* and *agenda* are two good examples. Talking your way into a favourable position requires careful thinking, strategizing and engaging with stakeholders. Once you've got them on-side, hopefully the position you want will be on its way. This is not about overcoming weaknesses, it is about filling a gap and acquiring something new. Agenda is also easy to build from scratch. Just make some decisions, get really passionate about it and start communicating to the right people.

Beg, borrow or steal power

This is a very tempting option, and easier than trying to turn a weakness into a strength. There are two main ways of doing this. First, you can reflect on the power that you need to acquire to succeed in your chosen arena or group, then find people who have it and strike a deal. Find something you can do for them to win their support and loyalty. This takes time and requires huge amounts of trust in the relationship. This approach requires mutual benefits so that each party will honour the alliance.

However, there is a significant danger involved. As you will remember from *principle two: calculations*, there will always be a balance to be struck. If the other party is calculating their gain and is happy with this, then fine. Over time, this balance can change, perhaps because you are not fulfilling your side of the agreement, or their circumstances change and they no longer gain so much from the deal. If they switch their allegiance elsewhere they could leave you high, dry and powerless.

You also have to keep in mind *principle three: supply and demand*. If you have competition offering the same benefits then why should your powerful friends stay loyal to your cause? If you become too reliant on someone else's power to achieve your purpose you are making yourself vulnerable.

A slightly more robust approach is to 'empire build'. This only really works on the positional and credibility sources of power where you are able to gain responsibility for more resources: people, money, assets or knowledge. Convincing your line manager to give you more responsibility for more departments is one main way of attempting this. This only works if the new responsibilities come with power attached, such as people and budgets.

Even here there are traps for the unwary. For instance, don't imagine for a moment that others don't know what you are attempting to do. Political adversaries will be watching you closely and may counter your attempts to acquire more power. There is also a danger of acquiring unsuitable or harmful assets. I remember watching from the sidelines as one colleague fought hard to gain control of a team without realizing the problems the team were struggling with. Although he got what he wanted initially, six months down the line he was still beset with all the problems he acquired with the team. In actual fact, the previous owner put up a fight to keep control of the team, which turned out to be a ruse to make the other manager more vigorous in the takeover.

Tread carefully and don't become too dependent.

Re-educate the groups

Since this book has a wide readership, this option is included for completeness. What it involves is taking steps to change the culture and/or opinions of the members in a group so that they place a higher value on the power that you have.

One example might involve changing the way an organization regards professional qualifications. You might choose to attempt this because you are extremely well qualified, you have an extensive network of other well-qualified people and you believe that a high level of education would dramatically reduce the risks the organizations runs. Usually this is pitched against the embedded cultural value placed on experience and credence given to people who have been there and done it, rather than read about it in a book.

Achieving a change like this in any sizeable group requires meticulous planning, the power to make systemic changes in many different areas of the organization and, hence, the wholehearted support of the most powerful executives – and lots of time.

Getting things done

Important points to remember as you begin to make more progress:

- Power provides enormous potential for an influential leader, and for the people who benefit from their work.
- Power works primarily on an economic model of exchange.
- The process of becoming more powerful can be summarized by three questions:
  - What power have you got?
  - What power do you need?
  - How are you going to get it?
- Tuning in to the power sources that will be most effective in creating the influence you want to build is highly efficient.
- The effect of power is largely dependent on the perceptions of the people being influenced.
- Developing greater power is a strategic imperative for the influential leader.

Further reading

When you get a chance, make sure you check the further reading and resources for this chapter online at: **www.learntoinfluence.com/leadership**

It is important to note that, in the context of influential leadership, building your power is concerned with your baseline capacity to get things done rather than moving forward and influencing specific outcomes. As you utilize your power you will naturally apply them to these ends, but when it comes to boosting your power, this takes time.

Return every couple of months to this topic. As you learn more about power and start to accumulate successes, you will start to see the world in a different way. More importantly, your notion of what is possible will rise.

Now I'd like to turn your attention to a more detailed look at what makes people tick. How those on the receiving end will be making their calculations and responding to the power they see in you.

Deeper understanding of people

04

It is very difficult to influence people if you don't understand what is driving them.

You can influence people in many ways, but one of the most effective is by tailoring your approach in such a way that it connects directly with their world. Then they notice that you understand them, are taking their situation fully into account and will welcome your approach. This means you have to invest time and energy in finding out as much as you can about the important people around your purpose. If you don't you'll be attempting to influence mainly on guesswork.

This chapter contributes to the following influential leader capabilities:

Has an intimate understanding of the individuals they are engaged with.

Is able to appreciate the pressures and influences affecting their stakeholders.

As you read this chapter you will learn more if you focus on one or two stakeholders who you need to understand better. By doing this you will gain practical benefit and also highlight the gaps in your knowledge of them that you need to fill. You can also use this chapter as an opportunity to focus on yourself and improve your self-awareness – why you do what you do.

Current performance

As people spend the majority of their waking hours in the workplace, begin developing your understanding of an individual by asking the question – are they doing a good job? People who are performing well act and react in very different ways to those who are under pressure. People whose jobs are at risk will be making decisions driven by the need to remain solvent, whereas those who are flying high will be taking more risks and hoping for greater rewards.

When analysing an individual in this respect, there are a number of things you need to gather evidence about, or seek insight on:

- Job role, descriptions and instructions form the starting point. What is the formal role they have been asked to fulfil? Many people these days have several different roles, and some of these will be unofficial, so try to discover the full range of things that they are being asked to do and by whom.

- Targets, objectives and key result areas will help you to establish the performance expected of individuals. Although this may appear to be a difficult area to explore, most people are fairly open about what they are trying to achieve, especially if they think you may be able to help.

- Current performance levels will illuminate the degree of pressure an individual may be under. For each of their roles, explore the difference between expected and actual performance. This will be harder to find out and you may find people covering this up if they are struggling.

- Performance comparisons need to be understood so that you can determine the position of an individual relative to their peers and competitors. Even a bad performer can feel safe if everyone else is performing even worse than they are. This means you have to analyse other people at least at a cursory level. Only go deeper with them if you believe you'll get extra benefit.

- Wider organizational issues and pressures also need to be factored in. What is the context of their job and performance? Even a well-performing person could be on the verge of being exited due to a planned restructure.

Some of these things may be very difficult to discover, but very worthwhile if you can. Usually the clues are there once you decide to look for them. There are also many opportunities when you can ask an extra question or two during a meeting in order to learn more. Most people miss these, mainly because they have not decided that they need a deeper understanding.

Friends, associates and enemies

You are being influenced all the time by the people around you, just as everyone else is. Considering the people around the individual you are analysing begins with noticing who they are. Begin by making a list of who they are:

- Who do they spend most time with?
- Are there people who they try to avoid?
- Who do they refer to most often?
- What about disputes and arguments – who have they fallen out with recently?
- Where does the challenge come from?
- Do they have special people they turn to for advice and guidance?
- Where do they turn to for support, information and resources?
- Are there any special clubs or associations where they socialize with others?
- Who would they say are their friends and enemies?

Once you have a list, work through it thinking more deeply about the people who you believe have the greatest impact on the individual you are analysing. Try to answer all of these questions:

- How would you describe their relationship?
- Do they trust each other? What evidence do you have?
- Why is this person able to influence the individual you are analysing?
- Can you recall specific situations when their influence was successful?
- Are there times when they fail to influence?
- How does influence work the other way around?

There are many other parts of this book that explore the interactions of others in more detail, particularly Chapter 7 (Creating your leadership strategy and plan) and Chapter 9 (Developing powerful and influential networks).

In respect of the individual you are analysing, it is also important to build up your understanding of the groups they are a member of. Groups such as their team, profession, division and sports clubs will all exert a measure of influence over their behaviour and decisions. The degree to which they identify with each group will dictate the level of influence. If membership is important to them they are unlikely to go against any of the group norms of acceptable behaviour, and they will not risk alienating themselves from the group.

Therefore, it is advisable to learn all you can about the groups that they are involved with and the strength of their involvement. While the formal groups such as team and profession are obvious, the informal ones may take a little careful observation to notice – and it is these that are likely to exert the greatest influence over their behaviour, so it will be worth the effort (the next chapter will delve into groups in much more detail).

Power and influence

A critical component of your understanding of another individual is what makes them powerful and able to exert influence over others. This will help to identify what will be most likely to work when you attempt to influence them. It will also illuminate how they may respond to your attempt.

Exercise

In Chapter 2 I introduced an exercise that you can use to analyse the sources of power that make people influential. You can use this again to deepen your understanding of the individual you are analysing now. Use the same process with the cards to consider the order in which the different sources of power are being used.

On your Power Analysis chart, complete a column for each question so that you can refer back to your rankings later: 1) Why is this person influential with other people? 2) Why is this person influential with you?

Make sure you explore each source fully to determine exactly how they are gaining influence. For instance, what is it about their credibility that is really working for them? If you can deconstruct this you can begin to notice not only what they are using, but also what may work well with them.

Influencing others

How does the person you are analysing use their influence? What exactly are they doing as they attempt to get people to do what they want them to do? To do this, think of specific people you have noticed them influencing, then see if you can apply each of the principles of power to that situation (consequences; calculations; supply and demand; perception and reality; and utilization).

How do they vary their approach, depending on the target of their influence? Look for themes and trends in their activity. For example, depending on the group they are working in, they may choose to influence through consultation, collaboration or force. These different approaches, and more besides, will be covered in detail in Chapter 13 (Tailoring your approach for maximum influence). Here I am encouraging you to notice the things that they are doing to influence and, also, how well their approaches are working.

Considering this aspect will help you to learn how they operate, how aware they are and the level of sophistication they deploy as they do their influencing – extremely useful if you want to learn how to influence them.

Being influenced

How are other people around the organization influencing the person you are analysing? A good way to explore this is to draw up another column on your Power Analysis chart to capture your thoughts on how the different sources of power work to influence them. Take your cards and reflect on the way they are being influenced by others. Which source of power is most effective at influencing them? Why? What comes next?

As you do this, what will be fascinating to see is how your impression of the way they influence others compares to the way they get influenced in return. In my experience, there is often remarkable similarities in the two columns. This makes sense because people tend to value and respect the sources of power that they use, and are thus more likely to be influenced by those same sources of power. For instance, people with high levels of credibility will be looking more closely at the credentials of others before they accept their influence. Similarly, those with large networks may not respect people who are not well connected.

Once you know what they believe makes them powerful you can tailor your approaches to illustrate the benefits they will gain. If you subtly show them how it will strengthen their position of power and influence you are well on your way to successfully influencing them. I'll talk more about this in Chapter 13 (Tailoring your approach for maximum influence).

Values analysis

If you want to understand why people are doing what they are doing, you need to try to get into their system of values and beliefs. Decode these well and you will be able to explain why they do what they do and be able to learn how they may respond to new situations.

Exercise

Uncovering your own deeper values and beliefs can be quite hard work. Deciphering other people at this level is even more challenging. Although difficult, any effort in this direction can deliver significant benefits. One of the influencing tactics I share in Chapter 13 is an *inspirational appeal*. This is one of the most effective ways of gaining the wholehearted commitment of other people, and since it focuses on talking directly to their values you can only do this if you know what they value.

The best way to make a start on this is to build your own self-awareness in this area. So, focusing on yourself for a while:

- Make a list of all the key things you think are important at work. My list would begin with things like: results, ambition, energy, profit, efficiency, integrity, doing the right thing and empowerment. Make your list as long as you can.

- Now turn your attention to your personal life and add more things to your list of important things. It should be starting to look like a long list.

- Here's the hard bit – try to pick out eight to 10 items that you think are the most important. Yes, this cuts across the work/ life barrier and aims to discover your core values and beliefs.

- Even harder, now try to order your list. Which is the most important to you? And the next most important?

Tough isn't it? The first time I did this exercise it took me several hours and was of immeasurable benefit because it helped me to understand why I was making the small and large decisions at work and at home. It also helped me to realize that with some of them, I had the priority wrong. There were also some values that conflicted with each other. By raising these values into conscious awareness I was able to reappraise and adjust their relative priorities.

Having applied the process to yourself, now you can start using it to build your understanding of other people. With any person you are considering, ideally you need to be trying to identify as many prominent values as you can. Unless you have the opportunity to take them through the exercise above, it is unlikely you will be able to get as far as prioritization, but that would be the ideal place to get to.

Look at the clues and see if you can make a list of the things they consider to be important, both at work and in their personal life. Look for these clues in:

- topics or ideas that they keep returning to and talking about;
- ideas and suggestions they offer to other people about what they should be focusing on;
- statements that attract their immediate attention;
- things they get excited, passionate and animated about;
- people or events that make them frustrated and/or annoyed.

Once you start to build a list, you can begin to test and refine it through your regular dialogue with them and others who know them. An initial hypothesis makes testing and further research so much easier.

Behavioural style

There is a great deal of variance in the personalities around you, although there are a number of distinct types. This inevitably leads to generalizations and, to an extent, stereotyping. However, this is necessary in order to develop basic principles and approaches before you personalize it to the individual you are analysing.

If you don't have an understanding of their personality there is a danger that you will run into a personality clash or, at least, your relationship will be interrupted by confusion about how both of you are behaving, rather than what you are actually saying to each other. Once you do understand more about their personality you can take steps to remove this risk and maximize your influence.

Back in 2004 Mike Phipps and I developed a tool that seeks to understand personality based on the behaviours typically used to influence others. We have found this tool extremely effective in helping to understand the way people clash and, more importantly, how people can adapt their behaviour in order to exert greater influence. The tool has four distinct areas of behaviour and the way that individuals favour or avoid each:

- *Sociability and networking:* using social skills to build a wide and strong network of valuable contacts versus focusing on the task in hand and avoiding social distraction.
- *Determination:* expressing clear views, opinions and goals while driving them towards realisation versus taking time to consult, accommodate and reach a harmonious solution, direction or view.
- *Tact and diplomacy:* sensing feelings, concerns and agendas of other people and responding in a sensitive way versus being direct and clear with others so they know where they stand, even if this risks upsetting them.
- *Emotional control:* remaining calm and focused on facts and process versus expressing genuine emotions openly as they happen.

The subject of personality will be covered in much more detail later in the book, beginning with Chapter 11 (Understanding influencing styles), but I wanted to introduce it here because it is so fundamental to establishing a good working relationship with people. This is because if someone has a different personality from you they are highly likely to be focusing more of their attention on trying to figure you out rather than listening to what you are actually saying.

Motivation theory

No chapter on understanding people would be complete without touching on this topic. The research over the last hundred years has been extensive and deep. What this research has attempted to identify is the underlying drivers that propel people towards action.

Because the thrust of this book is towards practical action rather than deep theory, I want to highlight a few theories that are particularly interesting and useful when it comes to understanding how to influence people in the workplace. If you need to go deeper into these, I have included additional recommended reading in the online resources that accompany this book.

Herzberg's motivation to work

Based on extensive research, Fredrick Herzberg found that if you want to generate high levels of motivation and job satisfaction, focus on building personal responsibility into the work. If people are involved and given the opportunity to make decisions they are much more likely to be motivated and committed. This research also challenges the notion that people are motivated by monetary rewards. Although money is a good motivator its effect doesn't last very long before dissatisfaction reasserts itself.

This backs up many of the approaches suggested in this book, which encourage building involvement and engagement in the decision-making processes, helping people to take their own decisions and thus becoming committed to the action rather than forcing them to do things that they would rather not do.

McClelland's human motivation theory

This theory developed by David McClelland during the 1950s suggests that people vary in their strength of motivation to satisfy three distinct psychological needs:

- achievement: getting things done;
- affiliation: being accepted and connected with others;
- power: having control over things.

Everyone acquires an element of each of these needs within them, however, according to McClelland, one of them will dominate the others. And the one that dominates in the motivations of the individual you are seeking to understand should be fairly easy to spot. And once you do, you can adapt the way you talk to each of the needs.

For instance, if someone is driven by the need for achievement (always talking about bottom-line results, for instance) then showing how your proposal contributes to their results will be more effective than focusing on how it will unite everyone in the organization and help them work more effectively together (which is what you would do if your target was driven by the need for affiliation). You would also want to be especially careful when suggesting something that erodes an individual's power to make their own decisions, perhaps by changing reporting lines.

Which one is your primary driver?

Deeper understanding

The study of these theories, and others like them, can shed light on what an individual is ultimately trying to gain from their work and life. These are the drivers that sit, often unconsciously, behind the decisions an individual makes and where they focus their agenda (more on that in a moment). One of the key benefits you can gain from this is that you may be able to help them to achieve these things in more effective ways than they have currently thought of.

For instance, if someone is being driven at a deep level by the need for affiliation, they will have decided on a course of action that could be fundamentally flawed. Maybe they are heading in the wrong direction through ignorance or lack of understanding. If you can see this you may be able to help them, and perhaps in the process, also align them more closely to your agenda.

Linking your ideas and proposals to subtly appeal to an individual's deeper drivers is a highly effective influencing approach – providing you are accurate in your assessment of their deeper needs.

Stimulating questions

One problem that is easy to run into when seeking to understand people is getting blinded by your assumptions about the person. These natural short-cuts are useful in order to operate but troublesome when there is a need to take a deeper look at what makes an individual who they are.

To overcome this, here are a collection of interesting, provocative and potentially fun questions to challenge your assumptions about the individual you are analysing. Their intent is to help you to leave to one side your current notions about the person while you have some fun exploring and understanding them from several different angles. This could also be used in the team meeting when you want to enlist the help of others in developing your collective understanding about a particular stakeholder – and have some fun at the same time.

Without any logical thought about their order, here are some questions to play with:

- Who are they scared of?
- What are they always bragging about?
- What do they take courage from?
- If they compiled a list of their achievements, what would be on it?
- What embarrasses them?
- What makes them angry, excited, sad and happy?
- If they were a political candidate seeking election, what would their manifesto contain?
- Who is their favourite business celebrity and why?
- Do they lie about things? Why?
- What makes them envious?
- What are they hiding?
- Do they have any pet hates?
- Why might they have problems sleeping at night?
- What are their career ambitions?
- How do they delude themselves?
- What other questions can you think of like these?

Remember, the point of these is to get you thinking more widely and in different ways. Don't be shy about using your imagination and don't dismiss these questions. Attempt to answer them all. You don't need to rely on the answers you come up with, just have some fun and explore a little further.

Clarifying agendas

Finally, what all of the areas discussed so far contribute to is the individual's agenda – what are they trying to achieve? Everyone has an agenda, in fact they have many agendas. To a greater or lesser extent, everyone will be trying to determine the things they need to focus on and the things they need to do in order to achieve their goals. And if you want to understand people well enough to influence them, you have to know as much as possible about their agendas.

People will have a professional agenda that includes all the formal aims and objectives connected to their role. They will also have personal agendas.

These usually drive the professional agenda because, in most cases, it is the means by which people achieve their personal objectives such as promotion, a comfortable retirement or a much flattered ego.

Professional agendas are not always as clear as you may think, because of the short-term focus of daily life, and sometimes they may be deliberately obscured to protect the personal agenda that is most likely to be hidden from all but the most trusted confidants.

To begin analysing an individual's agendas:

- Study all their official communication. What are they saying publicly about what they are aiming to achieve?

- Consider their unofficial communication. What have they shared more privately with you – off the record?

- Do their actions back up what they are saying, or contradict it? If so, why could this be? What's really going on?

- What is driving this professional agenda? Is it part of a bigger strategic play by the organization, or part of their career plan? If you are not sure, what would your best guess be?

- Talk to them. Encourage them to share at a deeper level what they are trying to achieve and how you may be able to help. Find a positive way to open up the conversation and get them talking.

- Build your relationship with them. The more trust that you can create the more open they will be about what they are really aiming for (see Chapter 10).

- Talk to other people who work with them – perhaps their colleagues or team members. Approach this well and you will learn a great deal about the target of your enquiry. Listen well and match what you hear to what you already know.

- Summarize your ideas and theories. Writing is a great way to distil and clarify your thinking, but don't leave your notes on your desk.

And finally, don't be shy of guessing. Having a working hypothesis about an individual's agenda is a great way of looking for clues, patterns and reality. Scientists start in this way, and it will work for you too. However, be careful of the action you take based on guessing. Determine the probability that you are right and minimize any risks you are taking.

Pull it together

Hopefully as you've been reading you have been using the ideas to develop your self-awareness. Now, to help you to develop your skill of analysis, I'd like you to put it into practice and start analysing people around you. This will give you immediate application and, hopefully, you will gain some practical insights that you can use straight away. It will also be key to helping you to enhance your skill of understanding people.

To help you apply the ideas in this chapter, I'd like to suggest that you decide on two people to analyse, one who you know very well, and another who is less well known by you – ideally someone who you have had dealings with on an infrequent basis.

Once you have settled on the people to focus your analysis on, beginning with the one you know best, reread each section in this chapter and make as many notes as you can about how each topic relates to them. This will collect your thoughts and perhaps highlight gaps in your knowledge too. Take your time, and perhaps do this over a few days by involving other people. Then do the same thing with the one who is less well known to you.

If you do this well, you should be able to give clear answers to three questions:

- What motivates them?

- Who influences them?

- What are their goals?

If you can't answer these completely, what else do you need to do so that you can increase your certainty? The purpose of this exercise is to help you to learn the skill of understanding people. However, you will never be able to completely understand someone, and there will always be surprises. Reducing the element of surprise will make you much more effective as an influential leader.

Getting things done

Important points to remember as you begin to make more progress:

- One of the most important aids to influence is fully stepping into the shoes of other people.

- Analysis of people gets much quicker with practice.

- Decide carefully how much time is appropriate to spend analysing an individual.

- If you cannot work out their personal agenda, you are likely to miss opportunities for greater influence.

- Although imagination can be really useful when seeking deeper understanding, there is no substitute for certainty.

Further reading

When you get a chance, make sure you check the further reading and resources for this chapter online at: **www.learntoinfluence.com/leadership**

As you will find out in Chapter 8 (Increasing your skills as an influential leader), people do not spend enough time seeking to understand others and this creates a big gap in their ability to influence with confidence. Another big gap is their understanding of how individuals fit within groups, and how these groups interact with each other – which is the subject of the next chapter.

Understanding your leadership arena

05

Before deciding strategy, the influential leader needs to consider the dynamics between the people and groups of people in their leadership arena.

Having developed in the last chapter your capability to understand and analyse individuals, you now need to think carefully about the way people interact with each other around the work you are doing or the purpose your are pursuing. This is critical to moving forward safely with your plans and purpose.

In most situations, the influential leader is operating among a large number of groups within their leadership arena. Each of these will have their own agenda, as too will all the ambitious people they contain. Inevitably, there will be times when these conflict with your own purpose. Being proactive in catering for the risks this produces, or the opportunities, will serve you well.

This chapter contributes to the following influential leader capabilities:

Continually develops their understanding of the political aspects of their domain.

Can quickly assess the dynamics operating within any group of individuals.

►

Develops a clear picture of the complete arena or organization where they are active.

Is able to predict future scenarios and how they will affect their purpose.

As you work through this chapter I will be asking you to make it as relevant as possible to your purpose. That will involve identifying all of the main groups of people that can impact your work. Each of these groups needs to be analysed before you can begin to build the bigger picture. Since groups vary in nature, you will need to use your common sense to apply the various analyses below to make them appropriate for the group you are looking at.

The benefits

When people come together in groups it is inevitable that many will have different views, ideas and goals. Often these will conflict and give rise to competition. Learning how individuals are interacting within groups, and also how groups are interacting with each other, raises your potential as an influential leader in three main ways:

- It will allow you to understand where resistance, opposition and challenge will come from as you move forward your purpose. With this knowledge you can take proactive steps to minimize any risks and maximize the opportunities.

- Understanding of the political landscape will enable you to make more efficient use of your time and energy by helping you to link up with the right people and know exactly where you need to apply your influence.

- A true understanding of how groups function will offer you the potential to influence on a group-wide basis. This provides you with economies and this is essential as you rise up through the ranks and progress towards your purpose.

Analysis is always an ongoing activity because of the amount of change and imperfect knowledge that you possess about it. However, once you have done the initial analysis of the groups you are connected with, new information will be able to slot into place quite quickly, provided you make sure that you review your understanding on a regular basis.

In effect, you have already started: in Chapter 1 you spent some time exploring your *leadership arena* and in Chapter 3 you considered how power works in groups. What you now need to do is deepen this initial thinking and extend the exploration into the way that groups interact so that you can develop your own strategy to engage, survive and succeed in the political landscape.

Defining groups

For the purpose of understanding your arena, a group is: 'A collection of individuals who are bound together by a common feature, interest or objective'. The binding comes from the recognition by the group members of their commonality and identification with that group. They may have been brought together by design, such as when an organization is being created. This defines groups such as Marketing, Legal and Operations, which each have a common objective, initially stipulated by the organization. These are usually referred to as formal groups.

Other groups self-organize once a number of people realize they have something in common. As they begin to organize the new group they will recruit additional members and begin to build group identity. Sporting interest clubs (cycling) and professional discipline groups are good examples of these informal groups.

Although informal groups may not be immediately recognized as relevant, they are usually populated by a broad cross-section of people from the formal organization. At this point they become of significant interest because they could provide alternative ways to access and influence senior people outside of the leader's normal circle of connections.

Other examples of groups that may be of interest include:

- religious, race and nationality-defined groups;
- professional bodies such as the Institute of Actuaries;
- academic and qualification-based groups.

The common link between the members can vary dramatically from group to group and the commonality needs to be recognized at least by the members of any group. This is what causes them to come together and begin to function as a group, and is the start of their agenda. With formal groups this is usually orchestrated by senior management, whereas informal groups require the initiative to be taken by those who will become the founder members.

All groups go through a number of phases in their establishment and this is more pronounced in informal groups:

1 Latent: a number of individuals share something significant in common.

2 Recognition: individuals become aware of their common interest or feature.

3 Formation: key individuals take steps to get the new group communicating.

4 Mobilization: the group identifies a purpose/agenda they need to influence in the organization.

As you seek to become more influential, identifying informal groups and assessing their development stage and their potential power can provide exceptional opportunities for developing greater influence within your leadership arena.

Identifying groups

You are already a member of many groups – each of which will exert a degree of influence over your behaviour. As part of understanding your arena and its politics, it is necessary to see what groups could be affecting you, and your purpose. This means looking all around your chosen leadership arena and noticing those groups that have the greatest impact.

To illustrate the complexity and help prepare you for an exercise, here is an example of the groups that a typical chief financial officer (CFO) will be a member of:

- the finance division;
- the executive team;
- their professional body (ICA, ACCA, CIMA, etc);

- the board of directors;
- the Remuneration Committee;
- project steering committees.

Depending on the individual, they may also be a member of:

- the group talent pool;
- the IBM alumni (made up of all who previously worked for IBM now working in the CFO's company);
- the Wharton Club (an annual networking event for those who went to Wharton);
- FLDP (the Finance Leadership Development Programme – as sponsor of this group of highly talented finance professionals from around the group);
- the badminton club (a diverse group from around the organization coming together regularly for sport and fun).

The list could go on. The important thing is to try to notice as many groups as you can and then think about the impact they have, or could have, on what you are trying to achieve.

As you are searching for groups to explore you need to stay focused on groups that are clearly defined and already established, because this will be of most immediate benefit to you where the members have something distinct in common and those that are clearly recognized as being a group by the members. Later I will outline how to create new groups.

Pause now and brainstorm all the groups that:

- you are a member of;
- exist within your leadership arena (or organization);
- are around your arena potentially influencing your leadership purpose.

In Chapter 7 (Creating your leadership strategy and plan) you will be able to target specific groups to influence. This may mean developing your position within existing groups, gaining membership of powerful groups or influencing from the outside. But before that, pick one group that you know fairly well and use this as your focus as you get to grips with group analysis.

Analysing groups

Once you have identified an impactful group, you need to start understanding how it operates. This can be an extremely difficult undertaking, particularly if the group in question is large, complex and/or distant. There are many aspects to consider, and it may involve you researching it over a few weeks and talking to lots of your contacts to gain their insights. Irrespective of the challenge, any attempt to understand it better will yield benefits.

There are several key elements to explore:

1 Structure: not all groups are constructed in the same way, and the politics can vary tremendously due to the way the group has formed and its current state of flux.

2 Maturity: all groups go through fairly predictable development stages once they have formed and will behave differently as the stages progress. This will have a significant effect on the individual members and also the capability of the group to influence collectively.

3 Group agenda: this creates the basis for the way the group works together and competes or collaborates with other groups. Knowing this will help you to forge stronger links and understand why things happen the way they do.

4 Culture: arguably the greatest influence on the behaviour of the individual members. These unwritten rules need to be understood as they exert a huge influence on how members interact with each other and beyond their group.

5 Group politics: all groups of any size will have political wrangling going on between members. Understanding how this is working will equip you with the knowledge necessary to plan your approach and further your interests.

6 Decision making: if the group is likely to rally for or against you, understanding how they collectively reach these decisions will enable you to maximize the probability that it will go your way.

7 Group power: this is the collective clout they are able to deliver as they work together to achieve their objectives and protect their interests. It also impacts the internal pressures and political intensity.

In the sections that follow I will go through each of these in more detail. As you read, make sure that you pause regularly to reflect back on the group you have chosen to analyse. One key reason for this is that you may begin to immediately see things that you can do in order to increase your ability to influence the group and the individuals within it.

Structure

One of the first things to consider is the way that the group is organized and run. This provides insights into what life is like for its members and the parameters within which they need to behave.

Processes

Formal and informal groups can both have well-defined processes to organize the pursuit of their objective, be that to have fun or to produce a product. Formal groups can also have a very low degree of process, especially at the beginning and if they are quite small. The purpose of processes is to help the group to maximize progress. Lack of process in large groups can bring chaos because members will be approaching things in an inconsistent manner.

Typical processes include goal setting, planning, communication, work allocation, roles and responsibilities, governance, recruitment and discipline. The nature of these can all have a bearing on how people within the group interact and, also, how the group interacts with other groups. Once you know their processes, you can start to predict more accurately how its members will behave and also learn the steps you need to take to be able to influence the group more effectively.

Irrespective of the formality of the group's processes, there will always be many informal processes that are accepted ways of communicating and forming opinions. In effect, most formal processes will have a shadow informal process also operating. I'll talk more about that in a moment in the sections on group politics and decision making.

Cohesion

Another aspect that will have a major difference on the way the group operates is the degree of cohesion within the group. This refers to the closeness and interdependence of the individual members.

In tightly coupled groups there will be a high degree of interdependency among the members. Closeness can be both physical (thereby enhancing communication and influence) and/or task dependence (members needing close contact with others to be able to perform). Generally, the smaller the group the more likely it will be closely coupled.

Loosely coupled groups have members who are far more independent of each other. Academic organizations are often categorized in this way, particularly when considering the institution as a group. Individual departments may be more closely connected groups.

Markets are another example of a loosely coupled group (of groups) because of the range of different players involved, from suppliers to consumers, from trade unions to industry magazines. Although each individual group may be tightly coupled as an entity, it resides within a loosely coupled group or environment.

The more cohesive a group, the more effective it will be in relation to other groups in achieving its objectives. They will be able to move quickly and work well together to achieve their objectives and protect their interests. The group's ability to withstand external influence is also likely to be strong. If you are able to tap into their processes correctly you will be able to influence them rapidly.

If you want to influence a loosely coupled group, you need to spread your influence wider and focus on forming opinions and tapping into their common communication methods. A PR-based approach will be more effective here over time, rather than trying to influence the group directly.

Stability

If a group has a high-percentage turnover of members it is likely to lack cohesion and the group's processes will be unstable. With so much change about, it will be difficult to work within. Not only will new members be unfamiliar with the processes that have been established, they will also be unfamiliar with the existing member's roles and responsibilities.

Without doubt, the less stable the group, the more political it will be. Their attention will be inward and the individuals will be more concerned with protecting (or establishing) their position than beating the external competition.

This also applies when a stable group has to absorb a large group of new members. If the incoming members are all coming from the same place, for instance in a merger, then the troubles are likely to be extreme. In effect, what this is doing is forcing the new larger group to begin again. The established group norms (culture) cannot survive the large influx of people with a different way of doing things. Proactively addressing this in groups that are coming together is essential, yet often overlooked.

Maturity

There are various academic models relating to group development, perhaps the most popular being that originally developed by Bruce Tuckman in 1965. He identified four progressive stages of development: forming, storming, norming and performing, as set out below.

Forming

This is where the group comes together. From a political standpoint, during this stage the individuals will be getting to know each other, developing trust (or not) and making initial decisions about who to get close to. It is a stage of considerable uncertainty not only between the members, but also their understanding of the group's objectives, purpose and their role in it.

It pays to get off to a flying start when you are part of a new group coming together, although this requires careful preparation to avoid alienating the rest of the group before you are ready. If you are outside of a group that is forming, building alliances and lending support to those inside could secure valuable loyalty. It is also a time when you might want to be very assertive in helping the new group to settle their purpose and objectives, either directly or indirectly. Once these are clearly established they will be harder to change.

Storming

Once the group members have started to get to know each other they will start working together. In this stage the temperature heats up as the members vie for position, prominence and work hard to influence the group to accept their ideas. It is also a time where cliques and cabals will form as individuals divide up to support mutually beneficial objectives within the group.

Internal considerations will be consuming a high degree of attention and energy and this may lead to the group as a whole being less effective in relation to other groups because they are primarily fighting among themselves. Storming may be short-lived, especially if the leader is knowledgeable about these stages and works hard to drive the group through to the next stage.

Norming

Here things begin to settle down. Individual members accept their relative positions and make the decision to get on with the work. Now the group attention will progressively turn to the task in hand and increase their collective mind to the challenges facing them from other groups. This is where they will begin to unite and influence as a team in the wider organization – drawing on their collective knowledge and power to make things happen.

Performing

Not all groups get to this stage, and much depends on the competence and drive of the key members. In formal groups within organizations, performance is critical and the group will be under growing pressure. Informal groups are more likely to disintegrate if they fail to perform.

From a political point of view this is where the group begins to gain headway in relation to other groups. This may provoke concerted campaigns of action, especially if the group feels that they are being threatened.

Although these stages are well known and fairly obvious, you need to be aware that existing groups can regress to earlier stages, especially when there is a large influx of new members (see 'Stability', above). High turnover of membership can also mean that the group gets stuck in 'Storming' mode.

Group agenda

What is the group's purpose? What agenda is it pursuing? This is a vital element to gain clarity on because it will form the basis on which the group makes decisions and interacts with other groups. It will also equip you with insights about how your purpose or agenda will affect the other groups.

For formal organizational groups, analysis requires delving into their strategies, objectives and plans. It also involves many conversations to add the personal agendas of prominent group members, which may be having an influence on what the group is striving to achieve. These aspects may require some careful detective work, even if you know the group well.

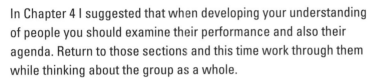

Exercise

In Chapter 4 I suggested that when developing your understanding of people you should examine their performance and also their agenda. Return to those sections and this time work through them while thinking about the group as a whole.

This may be more difficult with informal groups, many of which may have little or no clear agenda if they are formed on the basis of a common interest. Regardless, see if you can figure out what is driving them, because they may represent a significant opportunity for you to develop them as a group and leverage their influence towards your purpose (see 'Developing groups', below).

Culture

Because culture is 'the way we do things round here' it will inevitably have a major impact on the interactions between group members and also the way the group collaborates or conflicts with other groups. In addition to the processes that the group adopts, culture includes the language, humour, stories, rituals and metaphors that members use. All of these combine to produce a common set of values and beliefs about the way things should happen. The benefit this gives to the group is that there is a greater number of things that they don't need to talk about, because they understand each other at a subconscious level. The downside is the reducing level of challenge and stimulation as the individual member's values harmonize.

If you have an unstable group, the culture is likely to be unstable too. This will reduce their effectiveness as an operating unit and distract their attention from what is going on outside of the group. As stability and cultural consistency rise, the members of the group will work together more effectively. One of the drawbacks of a strong culture is that they are likely to find it increasingly difficult to work with other groups who have different cultures.

Some groups have cultural divides within their subgroups. If this is marked, and both are strong in their own right, you should analyse them separately on every aspect but note their common heritage, origin or connections.

Group politics

Who are the most powerful and influential members of the group you are analysing and how do they interact with each other? This will start to reveal who you should be focusing your attention on and who you can ignore. It will also inform you about some of the internal group pressures and how they operate in the wider environment. The relationship between the members can take some time to uncover and there may well be 'history' between them, which has an invisible influence on what happens in the group.

The first thing to consider is the overall political intensity or temperature within the group. To what extent are team members competing or collaborating with each other? There is nothing necessarily wrong with high levels of internal competition. In fact, it can be quite useful in helping the team to innovate to meet the challenges they are facing.

To a large extent, the level of intensity indicates the focus that members place on their individual agendas rather than that of the group as a whole. High intensity is useful for the group when it is assailed by external challenges and doesn't know how best to respond. Key members within the group will compete and innovate to find the best solution. This introduces a risk that they will become too internally focused and neglect the external threats to the group's agenda.

If the group does know how to respond (has decided on the best solution), lower political intensity will bond them together and help them to present a united front to their external challengers. Provided they have a clear and certain strategy, this will make them formidable in the wider political environment.

Noticing this aspect from outside the group may give you clues about how to move forward your own objectives. If the group members are at each other's throats, it may present opportunities for you to collaborate, support and help individuals within the group to win through. The resulting loyalty and goodwill could be extremely useful – but you do need to tread carefully in case those you support lose.

The usual way of building these political insights is through many informal conversations over a period of several months, if not years. I am not talking necessarily about gossip, but rather the sharing of information, knowledge and insights through effective networking. You can speed this up dramatically if you engage in a more deliberate process of enquiry.

The summarized process below involves pulling together a small group of people you know well and who also have a reasonable knowledge of the group you want to analyse. You can do this exercise solo, but it is much more fun and mutually beneficial to get your friends involved.

Exercise

1   Sit around a table with a stack of blank index cards or Post-it notes and marker pens.

2   Instil the culture of exploration, sharing and curiosity – 'let's learn together'.

3   One reasonably well-informed person then spends five–10 minutes using the cards to describe their 'political theory' of the group being analysed.

4   They start by writing the name of the most powerful person in that group (in their view) on a card and placing the card in the middle of the table.

5   Then they write the name of the next most powerful person on another card and place it on the table relative to the power of the first person.

6   They continue in this way, placing names on the table either near or further away from the centre of power. As they do this, they should briefly describe their rationale. The rest of the group should try to keep quiet for at least five minutes – although this is nigh on impossible!

7   Although natural, it is best to try to avoid simply replicating the organizational structure charge. Think of it more in terms of building a mind-map of the politics.

8   When it feels natural, other people can enter the conversation, adding names, moving people, and generally sharing their views. If you can, pass the blank cards to another person, who can then pick up the story and add more names to the map.

As the facilitator, you can add lots of provocative questions along the way to stimulate the debate. For instance:

- What impact does project X have?

- What changes would you predict in the next six months?

- What would happen if you take Ms Z out of the picture?

- Does the recent scandal that hit the press make a difference?

- Where are the greatest tensions?

- How do these people group together – what do people have in common here?

You will be amazed how the time disappears. The conversations are gripping as the picture emerges. I've been using this approach for over 10 years now with a wide variety of different groups, and most people end the exercise with a completely different understanding of the group being analysed. They also end with lots of new ideas about how they can influence the group more effectively. And all of these exercises had to end because we ran out of discussion time.

Decision making

Decisions are central to the way groups work. They range from the formal set-piece processes right down to the most informal and unseen processes by which groups form their collective opinions, values and beliefs. It is the most complicated of areas to analyse, especially if you are external to the group you are interested in. Yet the more often you focus on this aspect of groups and the more you try to influence their decisions, the easier it will become to understand not just their decision-making processes, but those of other groups too.

Without at least a basic understanding of how the group is going to make a decision that you need them to make, you will be reliant to a large degree on luck. Assuming that they follow a logical process, even in the most formal situations, is a mistake. Most decisions are actually made via social connections and include a high degree of emotion.

Apart from your direct involvement with the group, it is also useful to know how they will respond to other groups and changes in their environment. This knowledge can give you a distinct edge when it comes to predicting what will happen next and how to tailor your own strategy for maximum effect. It will also highlight how other people are attempting to influence the group.

The easiest way to begin to uncover these processes is to focus on past decisions that the group members have made, or opinions you know they have formed. If these are similar in nature to the decision you might want them to take, so much the better.

Start by brainstorming a list of decisions and opinions that you are aware of. Consider specific examples in each of these areas:

- strategy, budget and marketing plans;
- crisis responses and reactions;
- internal organization and structure;
- roles and responsibilities;
- communications and reports;
- rewards and recognition;
- opposition or support for external people and groups.

Now you need to select one and begin thinking about the process that the group applied to help them to reach the decision and who was involved. To aid this, think about how the decision you are looking at moved through these phases:

1 Recognition: when those affected become aware that a problem exists and/or a decision needs to be made.

2 Analysis: activity takes place to understand the true nature of the problem, the context and the consequences.

3 Alternatives: various ways of solving the problem are investigated.

4 Decision: after consideration of the options, a decision is made.

5 Implementation: the group does what it needs to do following the decision and resumes their normal work.

The time and effort spent in each phase will vary widely because of the nature of the problem, the competence of those involved and the time available to make the decision. Although the process above looks most applicable to formal decisions, it also applies to very informal decisions and opinion forming. In these cases, the participant's awareness of the process will be minimal and the actual decision point may be fragmented and invisible. This is especially so with opinion forming, because of the combination of many individual decisions to agree with a certain point of view.

In formal decision making, there will also be a point where it will be agreed how to make the final decision. This could be by an individual, a small number of people or consensus of the whole group. Various different mechanisms may also be deployed such as voting. Formal groups may have strict rules about how the decision can be taken. Irrespective of the formality, remember that there will still be a significant social, psychological and emotional influence on the decision.

Speaking of which, a key part of your consideration of the informal process should be how influence is working within the group. In Chapter 3 I asked you to consider how the principles of power were at work in your target group. Make sure you factor this into your deliberations on their decision-making processes. For instance:

- Who is involved in the decision and why?
- Who challenges and why?
- How does the group polarize around the issue under consideration?
- Who isn't involved? Why?
- Does anyone in the group have the power to veto?
- What consequences does the decision have for different factions within the group?
- Who has the greatest interest in the outcome?

Make sure you consider the impact on decisions from external factors such as people, events, legislation and so on. It is not unusual for a senior executive to have the power to veto any decision made by one of the teams in their organization. Legislators are also keen to define minimum standards and specific processes that companies must adhere to.

Group psychology also exerts a tremendous influence on the decisions made by individuals within groups, and groups as a whole. For instance:

- Conformity: many researchers have found that the pressure to conform to the group view can be so extreme (and unconscious) that individuals will agree with the group even though it defies all logic and fact. This seems to happen without regard for their level of intelligence.

- Groupthink: conformity taken to a group-wide level that makes them much more likely to make a decision without due consideration, especially of external evidence.

- Risky shift: groups have been found to make higher-risk decisions than individuals because of the shared responsibility – the risk is divided among the whole team.

- Polarization: any discussions about a potential decision in a group setting is shown to exaggerate the initial views of the individuals.

You can never know enough about how groups make their decisions. It is always work in progress; however, a basic understanding of how key decisions get made will put you in the position where you can begin to consider how different groups interact with each other.

Group power

All groups exist within a population of other groups that are connected together in various ways. They might be connected by industry (which would mean the individual groups are competing businesses, suppliers and other interested parties) or by organizations (whereby they all play a role in the overall mission of their parent (usually split by function and geography).

To begin understanding how these different groups interact with each other, you need to consider the degree of power and influence they are able to exert on different decisions being taken by the parent or higher-level group. Put another way, how powerful is the group you are looking at in comparison with other groups they interact with?

The 'power analysis' exercise in Chapter 2 helped you to identify what makes individuals powerful and influential. Now you can use the same exercise to analyse a group. Group power is simply the combined sources of power available to the individual members plus the effect of that combination (where the whole is greater than the sum of the parts). The exercise below is a simple way to gain greater clarity on this.

Exercise

Return to the 'power analysis' exercise in Chapter 2. Using your power source cards again, prioritize them based on what you believe makes the group influential within their community of groups. Try to focus on examples of when they have been influential with other groups, or when they have failed.

Add extra columns as you analyse more key groups within your leadership arena.

Now I have a couple of questions for you to try to answer:

- Which is the most powerful group in your arena?
- Which group tends to get what it wants?
- When two of the groups being considered are in conflict, which one usually wins and why?
- When are the powerful groups unable to influence? Why?
- Can you order the groups in terms of their power within the community of groups? At least, divide the groups into high, medium and low.

Differences in group power can make organizational life very difficult and can also threaten the survival of the organization. Being ignorant of these power differences can make influential leadership impossible.

Imagine a tug of war between sales and compliance. Which side is the strongest or most powerful? If sales have an extremely strong team, they will easily pull the compliance people all over the field. Exaggerating it a little, they may even just wander where they will, with compliance trailing along behind, picking up the pieces. As soon as compliance tries to put in place a new governance process, sales will just ignore it.

Alternatively, if both sides are equally matched, no one goes anywhere despite the huge amount of energy (meeting time) that is expended. This quickly arrives at a very expensive stalemate: compliance forcing forward on a new procedure, sales pushing back due to lost revenue. The conclusion doesn't suit either side – a classic lose–lose situation.

At the other extreme, if compliance is so powerful that they can put in place procedures to their heart's content, it will stifle the ability of sales to do their job. In addition to risking revenue, it is also likely to cause talented salespeople to seek easier work elsewhere.

Bear in mind that what is really going on here is that each group is seeking to protect and promote its own agenda – it is using power and influence to protect its interests. The extent of selfish endeavour is dependent on the views, attitudes and style of each group's leadership. If the group leader is personally threatened by the activities of other groups, they may use their own group to protect their personal position. This could involve a fair degree of deceit and manipulation, which is unwise – partly because the group members may discover the real personal agenda and react against it (more on this in the next chapter).

Scenario planning

An implicit feature of politics is that of imperfect information – not many know what is really going on. And the actors often relish and encourage that. Mere mortals should keep out of the way, unless they may serve as useful and expendable pawns. I'm going to make the assumption that you don't like to be played and you would like to avoid this situation – or at least feel like you have some control over what may happen to you.

Having considered the various groups in your leadership arena, and thought about how they interact with each other, you now need to bring all the pieces together and consider what the future may hold. If you have been diligent in your research and thinking so far, this step will be much more than crystal-ball gazing – you should by now be able to develop various political theories. Because of the gaps in your knowledge, you are still going to have to take educated guesses, but that is part of the fun.

Scenario planning is a well-established approach that begins with the question: what could unfold here? Then it goes through a series of steps to determine a sound strategy and action plan for each scenario, which has a reasonable probability of coming true. Recognizing and acting on multiple options adds extra work while also reducing the risks if the highest probability scenario doesn't come to pass.

The nature of the options will vary depending on the type of arena you are looking at and the purpose you are aiming towards. In commercial organizations the scenarios might be related to senior-level appointments (or dismissals), restructuring, product launch, geographical expansion or contraction and overall organizational structure. Non-commercial organizations are much more likely to be about values and opinions that gain prominence or dominance in the group as a whole – and usually these are being promoted by powerful individuals who have a purpose. In these situations you'll be considering who the winners might be.

Scenario planning works just as well in the wider sense with loosely coupled groups such as countries, markets and industries. If your arena is like this, you'll need to be considering options around which subgroups will gain prominence. These could be companies, unions, races or any other form of group. Because of the nebulous nature of opinion forming, these are more difficult to predict but not impossible. Industry pundits and analysts trade on their predictions for the future in the same way that commercial strategy directors do.

Although this process is simple, completing it may take quite a bit of time and tenacity. Even if you don't complete it, any effort along this part will dramatically improve your understanding and also put you in a great position to continue building the clarity as the months roll by and you learn more while making progress. In addition, it also provides added clarity to your purpose. This is where visions begin.

Options

Pull together a possible list of two or three scenarios that you think are possible and then consult with a couple of friends – what do they think? This will help to fill in gaps, make sure you haven't missed anything and, in the process, help your friends start to get their heads around the uncertainty too. One important thing to remember as you consider these is not to dismiss options too quickly. Even the outlandish can happen. In fact, I would recommend you keep a full list of all the ideas even if you don't actively work on them right away.

Probabilities

Assign probabilities to each scenario or option you have identified. Again, help from friends will really add value and increase accuracy. You need to keep these under regular review, and this is where the next step comes into play.

Indicators

Think carefully about what you might notice if one of your scenarios is starting to materialize. To help you on this, take each option in turn and imagine that it has come true:

- What would you notice that is different?
- How would people be behaving?
- What announcements would have been made recently?
- What other things would be changing?
- Who would be in favour?
- What changes would they be making?

As you think about these types of questions, start to develop ideas about what things you can observe in the run-up to that scenario coming true. For instance, if one of your options is that the finance director is going to become the new CEO, several weeks before this is announced it is likely that you'll notice him in increasingly good humour. He'll also start to get even busier, delegating more of his work to subordinates; holding meetings with senior people from other parts of the business that he doesn't normally see; having unusual meetings, perhaps several in one week with key shareholders. These could all be indicators of other things too, which is where ongoing vigilance is necessary.

Plan

Develop your own plan of action. You need to consider planning for each option that has a high probability of coming true. You need to be careful that action directed towards one option doesn't damage your preparations for other options. Sometimes this is impossible and you'll have to make a judgement about what to do for the best. At least you are working and thinking about all the possibilities.

I'll talk more about strategies and plans in Chapter 7 (Creating your leadership strategy and plan), especially how this all fits with your own agenda and purpose. If you have succeeded in thinking through several different scenarios – and you may not immediately recognize this – you are actually thinking politically and are well on your way to becoming an influential leader.

Getting things done

Important points to remember as you begin to make more progress:

- Political analysis is an ongoing task that gets easier as your insight grows.

- Involving others in your enquiry has multiple benefits.

- Informal groups represent a significant opportunity to expand your influence irrespective of your position.

- Everyone is influenced by their membership of many different groups, but which takes precedence?

- Group analysis is little more than individual analysis on a more complex scale.

- Culture is perhaps the most difficult element of group analysis to complete, especially from the outside.

- Never forget that no matter how united a group is, they are populated by multiple personal agendas.

Further reading

When you get a chance, make sure you check the further reading and resources for this chapter online at: **www.learntoinfluence.com/leadership**

Having done all of this analysis, you are almost ready to begin finalizing your strategy and plans for achieving your purpose, or at least making a huge step forward. Before you do that, I want to jump into the world of ethics. I have already made various references to it, and by now you should be able to see that the concepts covered in this book can work just as well with unscrupulous intent as with honest endeavour. The next chapter will help you to take a position regarding the ethics of influence and leadership before you finalize your strategy.

The ethics of influence

06

Before deciding on how you are going to move towards your purpose, it is useful to pause and consider your ethical and moral stance.

As you become more influential your ability to get what you want increases. This means that you can satisfy your needs more than ever before. If you are getting what you want, are others getting what they want? To what extent are you creating greater disadvantages for others as you exercise the advantage of your superior skill? Are you creating great harm in the wake of your success as an influential leader?

You have no doubt gathered already that I place a priority on influencing appropriately and ethically. The preceding chapters have largely been exploring the concepts in a neutral way, devoid of judgement about your motives. Now, before you settle on your strategy, I want to give you the opportunity to challenge yourself – and perhaps save you from doing something you may later regret.

This chapter contributes to the following influential leader capabilities:

Operates with high levels of personal integrity.

Understands and makes clear decisions about ethical positioning.

This chapter is a little different in style because of the nature of its topic. Ethics needs a more thoughtful approach before you settle down to getting things done.

The historical perspective

The subject of influence is not new. Aristotle is famed for his rhetorical methods, among many other things. Although he hated the subject of Rhetoric, he felt it important to equip his students with the tools of influence, at least equal to that of the less scrupulous citizens. Or, to put it in today's terms, he noticed ambitious self-serving individuals taking advantage of people of high integrity. He wanted to give these good citizens some skills to defend themselves from the office politicians.

At a more strategic level, Niccolo Machiavelli is infamous for his approach to protecting the state of Florence. He stands today as a role model of all that is bad about influence, having originated the notion of the phrase '*the ends justify the means*'. Yet, to be fair, he (along with Aristotle) recorded his teaching in times that were radically different from today. To judge Machiavelli as good or bad you need to factor in the political setting he was operating in – namely the cunning Medici family, Borgia and several rather aggressive self-serving popes.

Attempting to judge Machiavelli or Aristotle on their ethics is a little like agreeing with a conviction or acquittal in the law courts on the basis of a 60-second news report on television. The simple truth is that it is extremely difficult today to understand the context in which they worked, the challenges they faced, and their personal and professional agendas. Their writing clearly demonstrates that they were masters of their arena, and of influence – at least for a while. They clearly thought that what they were doing was right.

But, are their teachings about influencing right for you in your leadership arena? Are they right for your purpose, passion and followers? The only person who can judge that is you, and the purpose of this chapter is to help you to arrive at some clear decisions on this point.

In the sections below I will introduce you to some of the key ideas that have a direct bearing on taking an ethical approach in leadership. At the end of the chapter, it is important that you arrive at your own decisions about these, and how you will take account of these as you develop your influential leadership practice.

Integrity and influence

I am often asked if it is possible to influence without integrity. The simple answer is yes. To understand why, you need to realize that integrity, in its simplest form, is about living true to your values and beliefs. Influence is about stimulating people to think, act or feel differently. If you don't live true to your values you will still be able to influence.

For example, if someone shouts about the importance of listening skills, but doesn't listen themselves, there is something wrong. Do they really believe that listening is important or are they just saying it? And if they do believe, how is it that they don't live up to their own ideal? Either way, there is a problem. This also applies to many other areas. 'Do what I say, not what I do' seems to be a way of life for people whose behaviour does not match their beliefs and who, as a result, lack integrity.

I expect that at some point in your working life you will have had a boss who fits this description. You probably won't have to think back far in your career to find one. Did their lack of integrity prevent them from influencing you? No, they will have been highly influential in many aspects of your work. You may not have respected them, you may not have liked them, but you will have been influenced by them.

Now think of another boss, one who had loads of integrity. They will also have been influential, probably significantly more influential. These are the type of bosses who inspire and shape, especially the beliefs and values of those around them. Integrity helps people to become more credible, trustable and likeable – which are all beneficial to long-term influence. They help to build relationships and make influencing easier.

Lack of integrity makes people cautious. They wonder what is really going on. Are they being played in some way? Thus the influence that occurs will take longer, be more compliance-orientated and will be far more likely to unravel as soon as that type of boss turns their back. People who lack integrity find it difficult to generate genuine trust and commitment. On the other hand, a leader displaying high levels of integrity grows in power, particularly in the sources of *credibility* and *character* (see Chapter 2).

Another fascinating aspect of integrity within relationships is that it means different things to different people. If integrity is about beliefs and values, it is unlikely that two individuals will agree completely. I have noticed that people tend to judge others based on their own sense of integrity. Maturity and common sense moderates this, although there is still a significant bias. Consequently, you are much more likely to be influenced by someone who shares your values and beliefs.

Questions to ponder:

- What does integrity mean to you?
- How do you feel when someone of high integrity is trying to influence you?
- What are your feelings when someone without integrity is trying to influence you?
- Do they really have low integrity, or are they just different from you?

Tension between influence and ethics

In many ways, the term 'influence' implies win–lose. If I influence you, you will have failed to influence me. If you influence me, I will have failed to influence you. Win–win is the ultimate ethical solution. If both parties can gain from the transaction, it is likely to be an ethical result.

Achieving genuine win–win is extremely difficult because much of the time there is no straight comparison. If you influence me to buy a car I will exchange cash for a mix of wins, tangible (a physical means of transport) and intangible (excitement, pride). An intangible or subjective win can be short-lived if you misled me into believing it was a better car than it actually was. You may not have lied exactly, or contravened any laws. Maybe you just conveniently omitted to tell me about something, or brushed off my concerns about the occasional noise coming from the engine. You may even feel that the flawed motor was fair value. The fact that in six months' time I feel that I have a heap of rubbish sitting on my drive makes no difference.

To gain the ethical tick, what needs to be added to win–win is 'informed and willing'. To be blunt, if you influence people to do something and they are not fully informed about their decision, then in my opinion – and from my culture, with my education, and my experience – you are being unethical. It is also unethical to force people to do things. I am not saying that people must *want* to do it, *willing* to do it is enough for me. Willing implies that they have considered the situation and, although they may not want to do it, they have accepted the rationale and will do what you want. Life is like that, you sometimes have to do things that you don't want to do.

Ethical influence is about gaining people's acceptance and their choosing to do something rather than being forced to do it. Influential leaders aim higher – they aim to get people to *want* to do it. If they really want to do it, have been fully informed, and have been allowed to make their decision without duress or pressure, it is likely to be a win for them. Yes, that's a lot of *ifs* isn't it?

As you may imagine, I read quite a lot of books and articles on the subject of influence. A short time ago I was horrified to see someone offering to show people 'sleight of mouth', to persuade people 'without them even knowing'. Generally, the reason for hiding is so people don't know something important that is relevant to their decision. If they did know it, the influencer would expect them to say no. Sadly, there are many people out there peddling dubious tactics like these.

Some of the most popular authors on the subject of influence fail to address the ethical question in their work. There is a tacit acceptance that, although not stated explicitly, it is okay to influence without full information – a little like leaving the elephant in the corner of the room. Lies of omission are still lies.

I am not suggesting for one minute that the ethical approach to influence is easy. You have lots to do, you are in a hurry and you don't necessarily have the time to spell out every detail. *Caveat emptor* – let the buyer beware – is just one maxim that justifies convenient shortcuts. Yet the long-term benefit from ethical influence is easy to understand – it builds enduring relationships and high levels of credibility.

Tough choices. Your choices. You are the one who will ultimately pay the price and reap the reward from the way you conduct yourself.

Questions to reflect on:

- Is it okay to let the buyer beware?
- What ends justify your means?
- What are your limits?

- What is your balance like between self-interest and the interests of others?
- How does your organization balance 'means' and 'ends'?

Increasing transparency and personal accountability

These days, if you do something wrong it will not take long for word to get around. Social media has its uses. You will not be able to keep a lid on it, and the worse you behave, the bigger and more attractive the share, retweet, or vitriolic comment will become. Your news will travel fast.

And you don't have to have been found guilty of wrongdoing. Trial by social media is hard to control, and extremely difficult and expensive to correct if it is inaccurate or unfair. It is taking a long time for legislators and lawyers to bring a sense of fairness to the online world. Although this is starting to happen more, at present it seems more likely that any attempt to correct these social media injustices could make things very much worse for you.

One of the reasons it is so difficult is that everything that is published online is so easily shared, duplicated, syndicated, stored and indexed. In the online world, things live for a very long time and can easily be found. Your lapse in judgement or misdemeanour may have happened a long time ago, but the internet remembers and reports it in Google searches as if it happened yesterday.

Do you know how easy it is to find you online? Because you have a LinkedIn profile, diligently do your networking, and build your personal image and brand, you are now in the public domain. The PR considerations of the rich, famous or notorious have now entered the lives of all talented and ambitious individuals. You will have an online reputation if you are successful in life, and probably even if you are unsuccessful. Hiding behind the corporate facade and avoiding responsibility when things go wrong is getting harder. Senior bankers, for example, know all about this.

While writing this I tried out a little test on a few people at random, using the names of two people on the first news article on the BBC website, and the Operations Director for the last company whose service I was recently dissatisfied with. I then tried to find these people online. Within an hour I had found out a great deal, including home address (for all of them), family members and also some really embarrassing and potentially slanderous online comments about one of them.

I am starting to think that the online world is beginning to influence good behaviour to a greater extent than the legal system. If you have nothing to hide, then all people can do is to invent things. I would much rather contend with false information than embarrassing mistakes. In the early 1990s a PR specialist offered me this pearl of wisdom about sharing sensitive knowledge: 'Work on the assumption that the whole world will find out.'

Arguably, the best way to avoid trending on Twitter or Google+ is to heed his advice – a man ahead of his time.

Questions to answer:

- What does your online reputation look like? Go on, Google yourself again and see what has changed since you last did it.
- What personal information can you find about yourself?
- How might the public react if they knew what you were doing yesterday?
- What guidelines do you follow when giving online feedback or making comments on blogs?

Cultural diversity

One of the dangers of trial by social media is that the whole world may be watching and forming judgements. A vast array of different cultures and beliefs are watching your online reputation, or at least are capable of seeing it if they want to or if it is brought to their attention.

It is impossible to isolate the influence of one's cultural heritage from judgements of right and wrong. For instance, certain cultures applaud direct and tough communication styles. Telling people what you think and where they stand is the best way to get ahead. If this means being rude or insensitive, so be it. Elsewhere, this would be perceived to be a sign of weakness, immaturity and considered unprofessional.

It was fascinating a few years ago listening to a Chinese friend talking over dinner. His view of the world and what is acceptable and unacceptable differed widely from what I have grown up to believe to be right and wrong. My immediate response was, how can he say that, think that, do that? Yet this was only an internal reaction, as rather than say this to him I instead listened to what he had to say and realized how very different the Chinese culture is from my own. Doubtless, his initial reaction to what I had to say followed a similar path.

The simple reality that is becoming increasingly important is that the decisions you make will be exposed to a wider range of cultures than ever before. You will not satisfy them all – and it doesn't matter how right you are in your own culture if in someone else's culture what you have done is wrong. You cannot please all of the people all of the time.

In addition to the cultural variations, you also have to contend with the way that attitudes change over time within a culture. What a given society believes to be right or wrong now is different from 50 years ago, 10 years ago and even just last year. The changes in general attitudes can be gradual or swift, and this is normal. This is how society develops and evolves. It is very hard to pinpoint the cause of these changes, and it is virtually impossible to predict what will change in the future.

Questions to mull over:

- What examples can you think of where culture impacts decisions and results?
- How tolerant are you of other people's ways of doing things?
- What is normal in other cultures that is wrong in yours?
- How should other cultures adapt to be more accommodating of your beliefs?
- And how should you change?

From complexity to simplicity

The inherent complexity of the ethical question can easily become paralysing or, more likely, will cause many to avoid the question entirely. If a question becomes too difficult to answer, it is likely to float away while people stick their heads in the sand. Resolving the ethics question is not easy, nor can it be done quickly, especially with joint decisions that span diverse cultures. All of the concerns explored above come rushing in to thwart even the most tenacious endeavour to do the right thing.

To be honest, the complexity of the ethical question makes it impossible to satisfy everyone. In my view, probably the only way to resolve this is to look inside yourself: to make it personal. If you consider your own character, morals, values and, in particular, how you treat others, then you can arrive at your own resolution. Developing your own standards, consciously thought through and then rigorously applied, is still going to upset a few people along the way, but at least you will have a defensible position, and one that will help you to sleep peacefully at night.

One of my beliefs is that people who are respectful of those around them are generally going to make ethical, or at least good, decisions. I also believe that those who are disrespectful of those around them are much more likely to make unethical decisions. The distinction between the two animals seems to be that the good are predominately *other-focused* while the not so good, and the downright ugly, are much more *self-focused*.

Questions to challenge:

- Think of an ethical person you know: how do they treat people?
- And someone who isn't so ethical?
- How do you treat those around you?
- Would they agree with you?

So to keep things simple, my advice is to focus your attention on developing great people skills and diligently deploy them for the benefit of those in your immediate circle. Then keep working outwards, which brings me to one of the most troublesome aspects of interpersonal relationships, assertiveness versus bullying – an aspect that ambitious and influential leaders need to pay special attention to.

Assertiveness versus bullying

Bullying is very topical and is an unwelcome feature of many organizations. It is also a key indicator of the way people relate to others. What is the difference between bullying and assertiveness? As a reader of this book I have no doubt that much of the time you are quite assertive. Without wishing to criticize you in any way, merely to provoke your thinking, do you sometimes go too far? On occasion, do you lean too much towards the aggressive end of the scale? When you are under pressure, or managing a crisis, does the *just do it* temptation become irresistible?

Even if you don't tip it too far, I wonder what those around you think of your behaviour? Most people are now working in a very diverse workforce with a vast array of different cultures, attitudes and beliefs. How can you be sure that your definition of assertion ties in with the way your team members or colleagues would define it? This is another subjective area ripe for debate, dispute, conflict and litigation. If they do think you go too far, they will probably regard you as a bully.

It's very easy to push too hard. I recently observed an acquaintance bullying another. To me it was quite clearly bullying. Forcing, cajoling, backing into a corner, and leaving him with no place to go other than do what she wanted. When I challenged her later, quick as a flash she responded, 'But it's okay, I do it with a laugh and a smile and make him think it's just a bit of fun.' I actually think she believed that too. The target of her jokey banter told me later that he wished she would stop bullying him.

Questions to put you on the spot:

- How would you describe the distinction between assertiveness and bullying?
- What would your team say?
- Why do you push too hard sometimes?

Personal pressure and stress

Another very real threat to the ethical approach is the amount of pressure that exists in the workplace. You don't need me to tell you about all the causes of this – I am sure you are very intimately acquainted with them. The pressures that oppose 'doing the right thing' and getting things done land squarely on your shoulders. This creates strain, and if you are unable to handle this strain it becomes stress. The easy way of releasing the pressure is to take the path of least resistance. Because the ethical risk / reward is in the distant future, doing the right thing is already at a big disadvantage to the people screaming to get things done today.

So the temptation to cut a few corners, lie by omission, fail to disclose, or disregard the interests of others, is being dealt with by people every day. An unclear sense of right and wrong makes these shortcuts more appealing, and the trouble with shortcuts is that once taken, it is difficult to backtrack. It also makes taking an even bigger shortcut next time much more likely. So the pattern becomes ingrained, the immediate value reinforces, and the excuses become – 'the end justifies the means'.

In the main, I think that people believe it is an either–or question – shall I be ethical or shall I get the job done? There is a parallel here with the 'working smarter not harder' mantra, which now seems to have succeeded in getting people to step back by habit and look at how they can improve what they are doing rather than responding to pressure by knuckling down and working harder. In a similar way, I believe that a new mantra is needed – 'ethics gets results'.

Questions to become more conscious of:

- How often do you take shortcuts?
- How do you benefit from these shortcuts?
- Is that what you really want to do?
- What will those shortcuts look like to customers, or the public?

Does it pay to be ethical?

This is an important question, and one I am not going to attempt to answer for you. You need to answer it yourself, and only you can answer it. There are plenty of books and speakers out there who can give you all the evidence and cite compelling examples, but you cannot avoid the reality that it is within your own head that you need to answer this question. Indeed, this is a leading question since it presumes that the common belief is that it doesn't pay.

Other questions to get you thinking:

- Does it pay to be unethical?
- What are the short-term benefits of adopting an ethical stance?

- How can you be ethical and profitable?
- Are you paying lip service to ethics?
- Regarding ethics, do your words and actions match?

Your personal position

Now it is time to make all this really personal and pertinent to your work as an influential leader. In this section I will help you to move into the detail of your life at work. I will provide you with a series of questions that will help you to take a hard look at what you are doing as you seek to influence. It is natural to rush around doing things on auto-pilot. Don't you just love to get things done, and quickly? In the process, some things may be missed, the little shortcuts taken. With all the best intentions in the world, the faster you are moving, the more likely it is that you will stray from your own sense of integrity.

So, here is a pause on your journey through life to ask yourself some challenging questions. I do not expect you to get through these questions unscathed. At times I know you will feel like you could have done better. That is good. Being able to reflect honestly on how you have behaved in the past is a sign of maturity, and will help you to be able to take clearer and better decisions about the way you act in the future.

Your influencing strategy

All attempts to influence will have a strategy, irrespective of how conscious this is. This is how you intend to get done what you want to get done. Most of this book is about developing and deploying influencing strategies. The decisions you make will have a large impact on how ethical they are judged to be by others around you.

The questions below will be extremely helpful to you if you can relate them to a recent influencing strategy you have implemented. Remember that proposal you got signed off by the board last month? Or the time you attempted to get the finance team to deliver the numbers for your project steering committee? When answering these questions think of something real, something significant, something personal. Even better, think of an influencing situation you are working on right now.

The challenging questions are phrased towards a current influencing strategy. If you are reviewing a previous strategy, just adapt them to suit:

1 If the target of your influence knew everything you know, would they do it?

2 If you were in their shoes, would you do it?

3 What are you not telling them, and why?

4 Have you told them exactly what you will gain from their agreement?

5 Do you believe that they are willingly doing what you want them to do?

6 To what extent have you exaggerated, omitted or conveniently interpreted the facts?

7 Will they be happy in six months' time with their decision to say yes?

8 What don't you want them to know? What are you holding back?

9 Be honest, have you deluded yourself into thinking it is right?

10 In the cold light of day, will you be pleased with what you have done?

11 Does what you are seeking to influence make the world a better place?

12 How have you manipulated the argument?

13 Is this going to cause them harm?

14 Have you shared your views about how they may be disadvantaged by saying yes?

15 Would it embarrass you if you had to make a full disclosure of everything you know?

16 To what extent are you using confidentiality clauses to your own convenience?

17 What shortcuts are you taking?

18 Can you look them in the eye and say that it is the very best option for them?

19 What is the balance like between your gain and theirs?

20 Does what you are doing breach any of your ethical or moral values?

21 What have you lied about?

I wonder, how far down the list did you get before you started to feel uncomfortable? Perhaps you reached the stage of wishing you had never started this list of questions – maybe this little Pandora's box should have been kept closed?

Perhaps you can forget this list quickly before you go to bed, hoping it will all be forgotten tomorrow. Or perhaps, just maybe, you could take this as an opportunity to adjust your actions. Influential leaders need to be self-aware, and courageous too.

Your influencing behaviour

The list of questions above focused on *what* you are doing, now I'd like to turn your attention to *how* you are doing these things.

In your drive to get results as an influential leader no doubt you can push, and push quite hard. What do those around you think of that? Are you too pushy? Indeed, are you really a bully in the eyes of those around you? Of course you don't think so, in exactly the same way as cold-callers have convinced themselves that they are not selling anything, merely providing a service.

The questions below are designed to challenge your actual behaviour when it comes to influencing. It is based on the typical things that assertive people do in the workplace that can easily be misconstrued or, rather, perceived differently by others.

Assuming you are here with an open mind and wish to explore this sensitive topic in a constructive and very personal way, here are some behaviours that are often associated with bullies:

- interrupting and talking over other people;
- demanding things at short notice;
- forcing people to do things that they don't want to do;
- closing down meetings and conversations before others have had their say;
- dodging questions and giving political answers;
- not listening to others' ideas and suggestions;
- publicly favouring or disfavouring individuals;
- being intolerant of fools;
- telling lies and being dishonest for convenience;
- working on a 'need to know' basis, holding back information until absolutely necessary;
- reacting aggressively when challenged;
- carelessly (or rudely) dismissing ideas;

- taking undue credit for work done by others;
- speaking before thinking and upsetting people;
- asking several people to do the same thing independently;
- allowing others to take unfair responsibility for problems;
- cancelling meetings at short notice;
- demonstrating prejudice when conversing with people;
- telling people what to do and how to do it;
- being tactile on the borders of appropriateness;
- regularly changing your mind, especially without telling people;
- using negative office politics to get things done;
- publicly criticizing poor performance;
- giving helpful feedback about the 'person' rather than the 'performance';
- closely monitoring work – micromanaging;
- using inappropriate humour;
- taking feedback personally and being defensive;
- using emotional blackmail to get things done. In fact, using any sort of blackmail;
- knowing all the answers;
- asking people to do things without giving them a reason why;
- making fun at the expense of juniors.

If you have persevered this far, there may be a little bit of denial going on right now in your mind. Yes, lots of the behaviours above are legitimate (or expedient) ways of getting things done. No, not all of them are bullying behaviours. Isolated occurrences do not mean you are a bully.

However, what you need to take care with is the overall pattern of your behaviour. If you are admitting (at least to yourself) that you are doing quite a few of the above, and doing them quite often, you will need to take some action.

Making some decisions

There is little point reading this chapter unless you actually do something about all this thinking. If you are feeling a little battered and bruised by the relentless questions, please accept my apologies, but it had to be done. If you've got this far and are still feeling pretty good about yourself, congratulations

– but don't be complacent. In the process of writing this I came up with quite a few good ideas for things I could be doing better and I am sure you will be able to do the same.

To drive forward the action, and increase your success in the future, the exercise below will help you to make some clear decisions about how you can develop as an ethical influencer.

Exercise

Making practical changes

Run through the two sets of questions above and make a list of the things you do that you are uneasy about. It may be because you are starting to realize they could damage your relationships, potentially destroy trust or, could get you into trouble. Either copy straight from the list or let it provoke new ideas personal to you. Try to arrive at a list of at least five things you may wish to do something about.

Go through each behaviour on your list and reflect on it by answering these questions:

- What do you gain from the behaviour?
- What could you lose?
- How could you replace the behaviour without loss?
- What could you add to the behaviour to reduce the risk?
- If you do change, how might you benefit?
- Do you want to change the behaviour?

Once you have done each entry on your list, decide on one of these that you can really commit to changing. Then consider:

- What could get in the way of change?
- Do you need help to change?
- Who can support you in changing?
- How will you know you are being successful?
- Specifically, what action are you going to take to change?

Start implementing now and review the exercise again in a month. There are a couple of reasons why I am suggesting that you should focus on just one thing to commit to changing. First, devoting maximum energy to one thing will yield stronger results. During the month you will need to check your progress regularly, review what you have been attempting to do differently and, most likely, adjust your plan. If you try to take on too many different changes you will forget, and you will fail.

The second reason is more important. Providing you do review this again in a month (and that needs some discipline – and a diary entry) it will bring your mind back again to the benefits of taking a more ethical approach. It will avoid the post-course bubble bursting and begin to embed ethical considerations into your normal working life.

Adapting your guiding principles

The above exercise is great in helping you to make changes at a behavioural level in the short term. The regular review helps to adjust your core values and attitudes, which can then have far-reaching effects. If you want to speed this up, you might like to create some ground rules that you can use to guide your general approach to influence. You could call them rules, or perhaps guidelines or ideals. Use whichever term you feel is most appropriate.

To get this started quickly, here are seven guidelines you could consider adopting:

- always help people to make balanced and informed decisions;
- ensure pitches include the drawbacks as well as the benefits;
- whenever influencing, challenge yourself hard on your motives;
- be clear and open with people about your own interests;
- aim for people *wanting* to do what you want them to do;
- never mislead people into doing something that you know will harm them;
- cultivate a genuine interest in those you are influencing.

And yes, I am fully aware that if you live by these rules, at times there will be a personal cost. But I have to believe that in the long term, this is the only way to have a healthy life as an influential leader.

Now, translate these rules into your world:

- Which guidelines don't work for you?
- What is missing from the list?
- Which five rules or guidelines will you use?
- How can you keep your guidelines prominent in your work?
- What can you do to make sure you don't forget them?

Getting things done

Important points to remember as you begin to make more progress:

- Ethics in influence opens up a great deal of complexity.
- An easy way to manage this is to focus on the way you relate and connect with those close to you.
- You are already in the public eye. Behave accordingly.
- Right and wrong means different things to different people and to different cultures. Never assume when influence is important.
- Laying down a set of personal rules or guidelines will help you to move fast and safe as you become a more influential leader.

Further reading

When you get a chance, make sure you check the further reading and resources for this chapter online at: **www.learntoinfluence.com/leadership**

Taking responsibility and making a stand for what you believe in is an important aspect of becoming a leader. You have the opportunity to make these decisions, and as your power and influence grows, so too will your confidence to do what you believe to be the right thing. Now it is time to turn to exactly how you plan to make progress towards your purpose by building your strategy for getting things done.

Creating your leadership strategy and plan

07

> *Building a strategy is central to being an influential leader and to making rapid progress towards your purpose.*

If you have been reading and thinking carefully so far I am sure you will have already identified a great many things you can do that will contribute towards your chosen *leadership purpose*. This chapter is intended to pull all of your various ideas together into a neat strategy and help you to make clear decisions about your plan of action.

This chapter contributes to the following influential leader capabilities:

Develops coherent and robust strategies and plans to achieve their purpose and goals.

Economizes their activities to focus on the most important stakeholders.

Warm-up exercise

Before getting into the guiding principles for developing your strategy, it will help if you pull together your current thinking in one place in your notebook. The questions given in the exercise below should be applied to the primary purpose you have been thinking about so far in order for you to gain the most out of this chapter. They work well for any goal or plan, but since this book is all about influential leadership, focusing you back on your big idea is appropriate.

Exercise

First, recap on the work you did in Chapter 1. Hopefully you will have a clear idea of what it is that you are striving for and also will have developed your compelling vision. The quality of your eventual strategy is wholly dependent on the quality of your vision. If you are still vague, by all means continue with this chapter, but recognize the gap in your clarity and take steps to close that gap quickly.

In Chapters 2–5 you will have been thinking a great deal about the place where you wish to be a leader, the ways that people are influenced there and, also, how this all relates to you as an influential leader. What I'd like you to do now in your notebook is to brainstorm all the ideas that you have about what you need to do in order to move forward on your goal. These questions will help:

- What things could you do to make progress towards your purpose?

- Who do you need to get on side with your ideas?

- What can you do to begin convincing your opposition?

- How can you overcome the significant threats to your plan?

- What don't you know that you need to know?

- Who have you not talked to yet?

- What could you stop doing to allow more time to focus on your plans?

- Whose help do you need?

It is likely that you will now have a long list of unstructured activities. That's fine, but to gain maximum progress, and help you to communicate it effectively, you need to be able to bring these together into the key themes for your strategy. This in turn will help you to identify other actions to take and, vitally, help you to notice the things that are less important. Many things can contribute towards your purpose, but you need to find those that contribute the most value – because you haven't got time to do everything.

To start to bring shape to your ideas, use the following six guiding principles, which all need to be covered in order to evolve a solid strategy.

Principle one: build greater support

Progress becomes easier and quicker if you have the right support in place at the right levels. While it would be tempting to suggest that the more support you have, the more effective you will be, that would be misleading. All you need is just enough of the right support and you can win through. If you are trying to tip the scales in your favour, one heavyweight might be all you need.

Trying to get one powerful individual over to your way of thinking is a high-risk strategy, so instead you should focus your attention on a number of different people who have power to help you in your purpose.

Nor should you be complacent – mere support is not enough, you need to get powerful people shouting from the rooftops on your behalf. Supporters are often taken for granted, and activity intended to build greater levels of support from them brings far greater returns than trying to convert naysayers.

This principle is guiding you to focus your strategy and plans into gaining the maximum *right* kind of support. Some quick questions:

- Who are the powerful people already supporting you?
- Are there other powerful people who might be easy to get on your side?
- Who is critical to your purpose?

Principle two: convert or neutralize opposition

Take opposition seriously and proactively work to convert them to your cause or prevent them from harming your progress. Too often I hear coaching clients telling me that no one is going to lose out when they achieve their goals. Brains work like that, blinkering your mind to alternative perspectives and hiding what others might view as obvious flaws in your ideas. There will always be someone who is upset about losing out – if only because you are changing the way they like to do their job. Overcoming this natural tendency to filter out opposition is almost as hard as becoming proactive in tackling the opposition.

Most people would rather close their mind and ignore opposition until it comes knocking on their door – because it might not. To be proactive is to make the task of handling opposition inevitable. For influential leaders, ignoring opposition is not an option because they are acutely aware of the advantage it gives them to tackle these things head on and, usually, on their territory and at a time of their choosing.

They also know that there is no need to convert everyone. You only have to have the right people on side in order to achieve your goals, provided those who are set against you are unable to counter-influence your friends and cause you problems.

This principle encourages you to take these matters seriously and do something about it. Make sure your strategy and plans cater for these people. Don't stick your head in the sand and hope the opposition doesn't materialize.

Some quick questions:

- Whose world is going to be adversely affected by what you are doing?
- Who doesn't really care for what you are doing and is very powerful?
- Which powerful people ask the most challenging questions?

Principle three: proactively manage risks and opportunities

Project managers take the management of risk very seriously. Without this there is an increased likelihood that something will go wrong. Many things can go wrong within a project and those who are highly competent will also look to risks outside of the project to add an extra measure of certainty to their deliverables. What they don't tend to do is also look for opportunities in the wider environment. Often there are other projects that are going on which could be combined, either by resource or purpose to achieve a more effective solution.

Influential leaders should take into consideration both risks and opportunities when they are developing their strategies. They don't necessarily need to go to the level of detail that project managers do, but they do need to have a clear sense of what might be on the periphery of what they are doing so they can capitalize on it or take immediate action to step out of the way.

Some quick questions:

- What could happen outside of your control that could kill your purpose?
- What might happen that would make your purpose irrelevant/ redundant?
- What other big things are happening around your arena that could help you?

Principle four: accelerate progress

The whole point of influential leadership is to get things done, and quick. Thus a key consideration in your strategizing should be about how you can make things happen quicker. Project managers who are dealing with technical matters need to have a firm grasp on what is realistic. However as a leader, you are more likely to be applying innovative thinking and stretching people's creative talents to make the progress you need.

So a key part of your strategy needs to focus on how you can move it forward much faster. This may be about getting specific people on board, or increasing budgets. Set the delivery date and work hard to keep innovating to make it happen.

Some quick questions:

- What needs to happen for you to halve your delivery time?
- What is holding you back?
- How can you double your resources to make faster progress?

Principle five: protect your progress

Visionary influential leaders seem to be prone to forgetting this principle. Gains and progress need to be protected. Most will be too focused on what has yet to be done rather than how to make prior implementation and progress stick.

This is especially important if you are creating an impact within your *leadership arena*. Aside from the damage you may be causing to other people's dreams and purposes, you may also be exciting envy. While people may not be affected in their work by what you are doing, your brilliance may overshadow their own promotion prospects.

Because of this, influencing people to do things is insufficient – you also need to make sure they stay influenced. It doesn't need to take a great deal of time, but regularly checking back with people is vital, particularly the powerful people.

A good way of doing this is by introducing communication activities into your strategy and perhaps getting people more engaged on an ongoing basis. Make sure to plan these into your strategy rather than rely on your memory.

Some quick questions:

- What have you achieved already that, if lost, would damage future progress?
- What or who are you taking for granted?
- How can you get people more actively involved in your purpose?

Principle six: keep it simple

Project managers are usually meticulous with their planning and implementation. This is great when most of the things are known and technical. Yet leadership as an activity doesn't lend itself easily to these tight disciplines, although I would contend that the closer you can get to specifics in your influential leadership, the better you will fare.

What needs to happen in your strategy is finding the simple principles, guiding thoughts and streams of activity that can serve to organize your communication, action and followers. The easier it is to communicate, the easier it is to follow – and that is certainly something you want people to do.

When building your vision, strategy and plans, keep things simple. Endeavour to break down the big vision into a number of smaller elements. Keep the language simple and the wording unambiguous. Once you have the key themes in your strategy, break these down further into specific goals.

I strive to work on dividing into three, although this is rarely possible. However, I never exceed the guide given by the psychologist George Miller who recommended 7 ± 2. His research on short-term memory revealed that humans can only recall seven pieces of information, or thereabouts. Adding more means losing earlier pieces of information.

Some quick questions:

- What are the key streams of activity in your strategy?
- What three things must you achieve in the next six months?
- Who are your top five targets to build support?

Towards action

Because of the diversity of reader purposes it is impossible for me to be any more prescriptive on how to develop your strategy. In the resources section at the end of the chapter I will recommend some further reading suitable for a range of different purposes. What I want to do now is to move quickly into building your plans to achieve goals within your purpose.

If you have a medium- to long-term focus for your purpose you need to break it down into logical steps. You could do this starting with now and moving forward (what needs to be achieved first?) or by moving backwards in time from the realization of your purpose (to achieve that, what will have to happen before that?). At some stage, doing both will allow you to meet in the middle and then assemble an overall progression of achievements. The further away your time horizon, the more difficult it will be to work backwards.

You can also bring forward your ideas at the beginning of this chapter, cross check with the guiding principles and add new thinking to make sure you have all the angles covered. The main thing to do is to land the key parts of your strategy that you need to begin making progress with – your short- to medium-term goals.

These goals can be hard or soft. Hard goals relate to achievements that are largely incontrovertible. Delivering a report, gaining board sign-off or achieving sales targets are good examples. Soft goals are more difficult to pin down. Gaining support for your purpose or changing cultures are prime examples of soft goals and, to be honest, these types of goal are the primary concern of influential leaders. Usually, soft goals progress towards hard achievements. The most difficult aspect of soft goals is defining them in the first place.

One way of increasing the definition of soft goals is to work backwards from a given hard goal that you want to achieve:

1 Ensure that your hard goal is as specific and unambiguous as possible. 'Generate 12.5 per cent market share in UK' contains ambiguities (definition of market; what product); however, the numbers and geography may be sufficient to avoid later reinterpreting. It is also significantly better than 'Grow market share'.

2 Now answer this question: in order to achieve that hard goal, who do you have to influence and in what way do you need to influence them? Remember that influence is about getting people to do, think or feel differently. Continuing the example above, this might involve influencing the marketing director to get behind your strategy, or for an independent body to rate your product favourably. There are

likely to be many things that you have to influence, so try to record all the key ones.

3 Taking each in turn, write down three to five indicators that will be noticeable when you have achieved the desired influence. You might notice that the marketing director uses your strategy to illustrate to your peers how it should be done, or maybe he or she will put your strategy at the top of every team-meeting agenda. Allocation of funds, public defences of your plans and any direct clues that he or she is wholeheartedly backing your strategy are all contenders for your evidence criteria.

4 Finalize your soft goals with as specific a statement as you can, then follow it with your evidence criteria. There are some examples of well-defined goals in the resources section.

Once you have formulated your strategy and specified some clear goals to influence, you can now start to plan the action.

Stakeholder influence process

The purpose of this process is to help you move quickly from thinking to action towards a given goal. As an influential leader you will use this as a core part of your modus operandi of getting things done. It is this process that will focus you on how to achieve specific goals, and it will stay with you until they are accomplished. As such, you are likely to use this process, or parts of it, every day.

The process should be used separately for each significant goal that you have identified as being important in moving towards your overall purpose. As you work through it, at times you will realize you need to move backwards and that is a normal part of the experience and ensures that everything you are doing is embedded in the real world. The process will keep bringing you back on track (see Figure 7.1).

As you go through the process, apply it to one of the goals that form a part of your overall strategy identified earlier. When you have worked on that one goal, repeat the process for each significant goal you need to take action on.

FIGURE 7.1   The stakeholder influence process

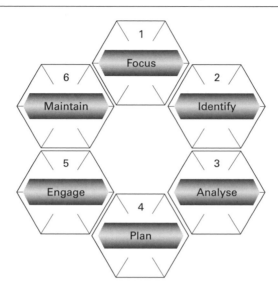

Step 1: focus – assess your priorities and focus your influencing goal

Each iteration of the process should focus on one goal only. By keeping a clear goal in mind, the other steps become much easier and beneficial.

Ideally, goals used for this process should:

- be a top priority for you;
- require many people to think, feel or act differently;
- need to overcome tough opposition;
- be likely to take three or more months to achieve.

Less effective goals for this process would include those that:

- only need one person to say 'yes';
- are likely to be achievable in a single meeting;
- should be driven by someone else;
- have a 'no brainer' logic to them.

These are not hard and fast rules. For instance, if the single person you need to influence is very senior and/or hard to access, you may need to develop a campaign of influence over a period of time using this process. Similarly, your goal may fall into someone else's remit and, if it is allied to your purpose, go for it – just be careful of the political ramifications of doing their job.

Step 2: *identify* – work out which stakeholders can have the biggest impact

The immediate benefit of getting focused is that it is easier to work out who your stakeholders are for the goal you are working on. By 'stakeholder' I mean anyone who has an interest in your success, either positive or negative. Negative stakeholders are those who will possibly lose out if you are successful in achieving your goal.

So this step is really asking: who are the most powerful people who can either help or hinder progress towards the goal you are focusing on? Remember that this must take into account the thinking you have been doing in the chapters on power earlier in this book. There is little point in simply identifying all of the people who can help or hinder – as an ambitious influential leader that will be a very long list. Ideally you might end up with eight–12 people as stakeholders.

Step 3: *analyse* – map the position of each stakeholder

Now you need to consider each stakeholder in turn. Remember to keep your focus clear, and determine where they might be placed on the stakeholder map shown in Figure 7.2. The terms used in the map are intended to be provocative to stretch your thinking.

Where do you think each of your stakeholders should be placed on the map? This is not intended to be a precision tool. Instead you need to keep it simple and estimate the positions. First, consider the nature of your relationship with a stakeholder you are putting on the map:

- Trust: do you trust them and do they trust you?
- Openness: would they volunteer information if they thought it could help you even if you didn't ask for it?
- Frequency: do you interact/engage with them often?

FIGURE 7.2   Stakeholder influence map

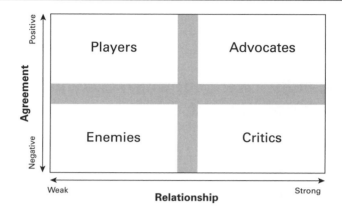

Consider these factors and make an initial decision about where each stake-holder would be on the horizontal axis. If you've got a great relationship with them, they'll be heading towards the right side of the map. However, if you have had some bad experiences, or the evidence is somewhat patchy, maybe they'll fit into the left of the diagram. If you are really unsure, perhaps because you don't know them very well, leave them in the grey zone – that's okay for now.

Then think about the extent to which they agree with your chosen focus. Reflect on their:

● Interest: will they benefit or lose if you are successful?

● Agreement: do they agree with what you are trying to achieve? (It is possible for people to agree even if they themselves are losing out.)

● Activity: to what extent are they actively supporting or blocking you? (This is often an indicator of the way they are thinking in terms of agreement and/or interest.)

What you need to do is arrive at an initial position for them on the vertical axis of agreement. If they are clearly in favour of what you are doing, seem to be a beneficiary and have demonstrated their support, they're heading for the top half of the map.

You may find it helpful to pause a moment in order to understand the different boxes:

- Advocates: these are your fans, those who really believe in what you are doing and are willing to go out of their way to help you succeed.

- Critics: not everyone will agree with you. These people get on well with you but happen to disagree with what you are aiming to achieve.

- Players: people who are a bit of a puzzle as to what they actually think. They say all the right things, but never seem to follow through. In a meeting, they are likely to agree, but their actions speak louder than words!

- Enemies: simply put, these are the people who you don't like, who don't like you and who will go out of their way to hinder your progress.

Where you place people inside the boxes is also important because there is a big difference between someone who is in the bottom left corner of the *advocates* box and someone in the top right. The former is merely an ally who will probably support you if asked to do so. In the opposite corner, these people will be proactively pushing for your success. Similar differences are evident in the other boxes too, so think carefully about the position.

It is not always possible to put people in nice clear boxes. If you are uncertain, perhaps because you don't know them very well, just write their name in the grey area between the boxes.

Step 4: plan – decide your strategy for increasing buy-in

What do you need to change? When you have placed the impactful stakeholders on your map, you need to start thinking about who you need to move.

Quite often, there will be one individual who holds the key to bringing all the others around to your way of thinking – or to your opponent's way of thinking. These people may not be the most obvious. In fact, they are often a few steps removed from the distracting cut and thrust – yet they exert massive influence over the way things are moving.

Questions to stimulate your plan of action:

- What one change would create a massive movement towards your goal?

- Who is the key person blocking you right now?

- What core attitudes need to shift to remove all obstacles?

- If you could wave a magic wand and move one stakeholder over to your side – who would it be?

The principles I covered earlier should be used as a guide to the action you need to be taking for each goal as well as your overall purpose:

1 Build greater support.

2 Convert or neutralize opposition.

3 Proactively manage risks and opportunities.

4 Accelerate progress.

5 Protect progress.

6 Keep it simple.

In addition, consider action that addresses these points:

- *Concentrate on impact:* focus on those who can have the greatest influence on what you want to make happen. There is no point spending time and energy on the minor players unless they are your only route through to the real power brokers.

- *Shift the greys:* stakeholders that ended up in between the main boxes need to be moved fast, especially if they are very powerful.

- *Move up and right:* generally you are aiming to move sufficient power into the top right of the grid by improving relationships and agreement.

- *Movements inside the boxes:* consider opportunities to move people within their box. Moving a powerful critic from the very bottom of their box to the top half may be sufficient to remove their motivation to block you.

- *Advocates are top priority:* this is often overlooked when considering influencing strategies, because they are already on side and thus don't need to be influenced. In addition to finding ways to get them to take more action, you can also work to direct their action towards specific individuals in the other boxes.

- *Critics make great opponents:* because of the good relationship you can have direct negotiations with them. They will tell you what needs to change and this will help toughen up your approach and push you to be your best.

- *Ignore your enemies:* you are potentially wasting time and energy dealing with enemies. Providing you understand them well, one option is to disengage with them and focus more on your advocates (with considerable care, naturally).
- *Remember the indirect routes:* sometimes the most effective influence is created through other people. Look out for other people who can influence those on your map.

An important point to note here is that you don't need to do this in isolation. Both the analysis and planning stages are best done with other people who can contribute to your thinking. Not only will this help you, it will also help them and enhance your relationship.

Step 5: engage – adapt your approach to influence your stakeholders

One thing I consistently notice in people who are not very good at influencing is that they tend to treat everyone the in the same way, and usually in the way that they would like other people to treat them. Because people are different, it is nonsensical to act like this – you need to tailor your approach to best meet the needs, circumstances, preferences and whims of your audience. This may or may not be how you would like to be treated.

To work out how to adapt your approach, you need to start with a clear understanding of your stakeholders as individuals (remember the work you did in Chapter 4 – Deeper understanding of people?) and their position within the political environment (Chapter 5 – Understanding your leadership arena). You need to pay careful attention to their agenda. When attempting to influence, most people automatically focus on their own agenda rather than the agenda of the person they are seeking to influence.

Another key point is to mind your language. If you can adapt your language to suit the other person it will help a great deal. Taking time to understand and then use their favourite words, phrases, terminology, metaphors and clichés will help you to connect more effectively and enter their world – although you need to be careful that this doesn't appear as insincere mimicry.

Another way of adapting is to consider your meeting processes based on the way you have positioned them on the stakeholder map:

- *Advocates:* if you are not doing so already, spend most of your time and energy here. This is the bedrock of your political power and these relationships need careful nurturing and frequent updating if your base is to be solid. Reminding them regularly of your vision and purpose and the progress you are making towards it is key, as is reassuring them of the high value you place on your relationship with them.

  Meeting process:
  - Affirm mutual agreement on your goal.
  - Reaffirm the quality of your relationship with them.
  - Acknowledge doubts and concerns you have with your goal.
  - Ask for their advice and support.

- *Critics:* their purpose is to authentically challenge and test you, in the same way that a good tennis opponent will help you to raise your game. Their questions and challenges will develop your thinking in new and different ways, and while you may not always be comfortable with this, or welcome it, you can be secure in the knowledge that trust between you is high.

  Meeting process:
  - Reaffirm the quality of your relationship with them.
  - State your position regarding your goal.
  - State neutrally what you think their position is on your goal.
  - Engage them in negotiation or problem solving.

- *Players:* you want these people to support you and are encouraged by their apparent agreement with your vision; however, building the relationship dimension to convert them into *advocates* requires a heavy time investment, time that might be better spent elsewhere.

  Meeting process:
  - Reaffirm mutual agreement on your goal.
  - Acknowledge that caution exists.
  - Be clear about what you want from *players* in terms of working together.
  - Ask them to be clear about what they want from you.
  - Try to reach some agreement with *players* as to how you're going to work together.

● *Enemies:* your awareness that their position might change needs to be with you at all times; however, while renegotiation is desirable, conversion will be unlikely. Time and energy is best used working with your *advocates* to protect your goal from any negative action by your *enemies*. And remember, this is a strong label and needs to be used with caution. Most of the time, it is an exaggeration and greater understanding can quickly put them in a different box.

Meeting process:

– State your vision for your goal.

– State neutrally your best understanding of their position.

– Identify your own contribution to the problem.

– End the meeting stating your plans and make no demand of them.

At first sight, this approach with *enemies* may appear to be counter-intuitive. Most people expect that the majority of their work with stakeholders will be about overcoming problems caused by people in the category. By taking care with the approach above you are displaying your confidence, personal power and ability to make things happen. It needs to be done carefully, and with prudent contingency planning. If successful, this sends a powerful signal to the *enemy* that you are confident, capable and not unduly concerned about their dissent. It is also likely that it will encourage them to begin engaging with you and that will substantially change the nature of your relationship with them.

● *Style:* people also have a great deal of variation in their behavioural style and this works independently of the box you have placed them in. All of the processes above can be delivered in many ways, such as with high emotion, or direct and serious behaviour. If you behave in a style different from the stakeholder you are seeking to engage, you will risk distracting them from what you have to say and will make yourself look different from them. Many stakeholders are mature enough to avoid this distraction – many are not. Because this is such a serious factor in your ability to influence, this will be covered in detail beginning in Chapter 11 (Understanding influencing styles).

Step 6: maintain – keep motivated, moving and refreshing

Okay, at this stage this is pretty easy. You're already motivated and moving, so fix a time in your diary to review your progress and refresh your plans. You've got to keep coming back to this process to review how you are doing, what you have learnt and what else you need to do to keep moving towards your goal.

Part of this involves keeping the work you did at the beginning of this book – on your purpose – at the forefront of your mind. The benefits you will gain from achieving (or working towards) your vision should help keep you going. If you have elevated this to the level of passion then all you need to do here is to schedule when you will review each of your goals and your progress towards them. This is especially important if you are involving your team in this process.

The frequency of your review should be at least twice per month. If you only do a monthly review I would seriously question the importance of the goal to you. If you are an influential leader and are getting things done, make these goals your priority.

Getting things done

Important points to remember as you begin to make more progress:

- After all the analysis you have to move swiftly into action.

- If you take no action, you'll make no progress and learn nothing.

- You don't need to get everyone agreeing with you, just enough power on your side to make progress.

- It's okay to ignore your enemies once you've understood the risk they pose and have taken steps to neutralize the damage they can cause.

- Using these simple processes regularly will help to keep you focused and moving forward.

- Always remember that a weak relationship makes influencing extremely difficult.

Further reading

When you get a chance, make sure you check the further reading and resources for this chapter online at: **www.learntoinfluence.com/leadership**

The stakeholder influence process is designed to be simple and straightforward. The complexity comes in its execution. If your purpose is bold, your strategy and goals will be many. Lots of steps will be involved in your route to success and, consequently, you will need to put some time and effort into organizing all of this work.

The disciplines of project and programme management contain many approaches that you can draw from in order to make this easy; just make sure that you only do what is necessary and don't disappear for days trying to get everything organized. While discipline is a necessary element of all notable achievement, action is what really makes it happen.

Having pulled together your strategy and plans, I want to now go into more detail about the various skills you need in the execution of your plans.

Increasing your skills as an influential leader

> *Once the strategy is clear, the influential leader needs to engage with stakeholders skilfully.*

The influential leadership framework shows that there is a great deal more to influence than the skills you are able to deploy. The context in which you use your skills, the manner in which you use them and, of course, the strategy you are engaged on all play their part. However, your skill set remains a fundamental base to rely on as you go about engaging with your teams, followers and stakeholders.

This chapter contributes to the following influential leader capabilities:

Focused on enhancing skills that are critical to more successful influence.

Builds skills through practice, reflection and regular review.

Research background

When I first started to specialize in the area of power and influence I had an intuitive understanding and belief that influencing skills were important to success. In my earlier corporate career I had clearly been influential and achieved significant results, often in very difficult and highly pressured situations. Sometimes I managed to achieve what others considered to be impossible.

How I did this was by staying alert, reflecting and learning at every turn. Flexibility, attitude and intelligence all played a role too. However, I was never quite sure exactly what it was that was creating my success. Somehow I had managed to find a way to be pretty good at influencing.

When I realized that influencing was really hard for so many people I began to get curious and wanted to know what influence was, the role it played in success and, also, how you can develop it. This initial stimulus has now developed into a real passion for helping others to develop these skills.

So, equipped with a lot of practical experience, curiosity and motivation, in 2006 I embarked on a programme of research that uncovered the simple and the obvious. The route began with Gerald Ferris, who at the time was probably the only academic to map out and test political skills. His superb Political Skills Inventory appears to have been the first attempt to codify what it means – at a skill level – to be influential.

From there I toured through the works of Henry Mintzberg, Jeffrey Pfeffer, Cecilia Falbe and many more leading academics. After careful consideration, I constructed a model of influencing skills based on the original work of Ferris, but extended and deepened. One of the great things to come out of this is that there were no magic ingredients, no complicated skills. Nothing, in fact, that in any way struck me as difficult to understand or perform.

Equipped with this model I then began to engage with practising managers and leaders to find out which of these skills they considered to be the most critical to success in the current world of work. It was actually quite difficult to remove any of the skills, as on the face of it they were all important. That's why I focused on the word *critical* – those skills that would put people ahead of the pack and make success almost assured.

Once all the data had been analysed I was able to trim down the original model and transform it into a structure that people could use to develop their ability to influence. In the next section I will take you through a quick tour of the model, which includes seven dimensions or areas of skill and 42 individual skills that were deemed to be critical to success.

Towards the end of the chapter I will share some of the surprising conclusions that came out of the research, which will help you to reflect on some of the natural obstacles you will encounter as you develop your influential leadership.

If you would like to do an online assessment against this model, you can explore the Influencing Skills 360° at: **www.gautreygroup.com/iss**

The seven dimensions of influencing skill

These are:

1 *Self-awareness.* The better you know yourself, the more likely you are to be able to influence other people. This self-awareness helps you to understand what you are capable of, what your limitations are and what you need to do to leverage maximum influence.

2 *Understanding people.* The ability to know what drives people, how they think and how they react is critical. This establishes a firm foundation upon which you can determine the most effective approach to influence.

3 *Understanding groups.* The workplace is a social organization and comprises many different groups, both formal and informal. Understanding them, how they work and how they get results can provide you with many opportunities to gain influence more quickly and thoroughly.

4 *Networking.* This is often seen as the differentiator between the good and the great influencers. To be able to work the room and build a wide array of good personal contacts develops an extremely useful resource that you can call on when you need to for support, information and advice.

5 *Influencing people.* This is the most talked-about area of influence and cannot be avoided. You need to be able to influence people on a one-to-one basis first and foremost. From this base, you can then develop more sophisticated approaches to influence.

6 *Influencing groups.* Influencing groups of people is far more efficient than focusing just on individuals. With your understanding of how the different groups around you function, you can develop strategies to maximize your influence and speed up the results you get.

7 *Building trust.* Research has demonstrated that in the absence of trust, successful influence is unlikely. Therefore, if you are skilled in influencing others you will act in a way that builds trust with the people you are working with.

Self-assessment

As you progress through this chapter, I want to keep you thinking about your skills. To do this I will be asking you to give yourself two scores out of 10 for each of the seven dimensions of influencing skill listed above. The first score should represent the level of skill you believe you possess. If you write down a score of 10 then there is little room for improvement, at least in your estimation.

The second score should represent the extent to which you believe you are currently demonstrating the skill. It is common that people do not always perform at their level of competence, perhaps because of peer pressures, external influences or even stress. If you feel there is a difference between the skills you have and the skills you use, development may become a great deal easier.

To set you up for the scoring, take a page in your notebook now and just write down each of the dimensions with a couple of columns to record your scores.

I explore below each of the seven dimensions in more detail and also share with you the exact item used within the online survey so don't be too concerned about the actual wording – I'll clarify each as needed.

Self-awareness

Many writers have commented on this as being a key aspect of leadership, including Warren Bennis who cited this as one of the four key competencies of leadership, along with creating and giving meaning to a vision of the future. His fourth was building trust.

Naturally there are a great many different aspects to self-awareness, and it was necessary to hone these down to those considered to be most important to influential leadership.

The individual skills within this dimension are:

- Develops their self-awareness.
- Knows what they want to achieve.

- Knows how they are perceived by others.
- Demonstrates awareness of their strengths and weaknesses.
- Understands how their emotions affect other people.
- Remains objective about their own behaviour.

Overall, these skills enable the influential leader to demonstrate clarity of purpose, realistic expectations of themselves and others, and offers the potential of an oft quoted necessary ingredient of leadership – humility. The ability of an influential leader to be able to notice how they are affecting others is vital if they are to stand a chance of being able to flex and moderate their behaviour.

There are many chapters in this book that will help with self-awareness, especially: Chapter 1 (Building your purpose and passion); Chapter 11 (Understanding influencing styles) and Chapter 12 (Understanding and adapting your style).

Exercise

Reflect a little on the six skills listed above and write down a score out of 10 in your notebook to represent the level of skill you think you have in the *self-awareness* dimension. Then write down another score to represent the amount of skill you believe you are actually using in your current role.

Understanding people

This area starts with cultivating a real interest in the lives and welfare of others. Thus the motivation to listen and learn increases – and thorough understanding is just a question of time. The simplicity of these skills hides the time and effort that needs to be placed on them because there is so much to learn, particularly about other people's agendas. As the Native Americans say, 'to understand a man, walk a mile in his moccasins' – and that is a very long mile in the convoluted world of work today.

Individual skills in this dimension are:

- Shows genuine interest in others.
- Listens well to other people.
- Observes the behaviour of other people.
- Senses the feelings of others.
- Understands what motivates others.
- Predicts how people will respond to different situations.

Arguably the most important skill here is the first one. If you can cultivate this and deliver it with real sincerity, it will overcome many other skill deficiencies. And, if you can do this with tenacity and tact too, you'll be well on your way to becoming exceptionally influential. Chapter 4 (Deeper understanding of people) focuses on developing this area of influencing skill.

Exercise

Again, reflect on the six skills listed above and write down a score out of 10 in your notebook to represent the level of skill you think you have in the *understanding people* dimension. Then write down another score to represent the amount of skill you believe you are actually using in your current role.

Understanding groups

This area builds on the previous one to the extent that a group is a collection of individuals. Where it differs is that groups do not always behave as individuals do, and individuals in groups often behave at odds with how they would otherwise behave. Developing a keen sense of what groups are all about and how they function is one of the most neglected areas of learning in the world of influence.

The skills in this dimension are:

- Understands the effect of culture and diversity on groups.
- Knows how formal and informal groups function.
- Observes how different groups interact.
- Understands how powerful individuals affect groups.

- Appreciates various group agendas.
- Identifies how groups make decisions.

As a neglected area of skill, it represents a key opportunity for those aspiring to become influential leaders. Much of this book encourages deeper consideration of the nature of groups, particularly Chapter 5 (Understanding your leadership arena).

Exercise

Reflect on the six skills listed above and write down a score out of 10 in your notebook to represent the level of skill you think you have in the *understanding groups* dimension. Then write down another score to represent the amount of skill you believe you are actually using in your current role.

An interesting footnote to add here is that, based on my experience working with people in this area, this skill is the one most likely to be used without others noticing it. When people are analysing groups they often do it in their own mind, reflecting as they travel and rarely engaging with other members of their teams in their thinking. I'm not sure quite why, because to me it seems like an obvious thing to share and develop together. Pooling insights and sharing perspectives not only achieves greater potential influence, it also builds and bonds the team.

Networking

The case is compelling. The only thing that outweighs the evidence that this is a vital aspect of achieving long-term success is the evidence that people don't do anywhere like enough of it, particularly those who are working inside large organizations.

The notion that networking is a necessary evil to help people find new opportunities, business and jobs is fading fast. Because of the complexity of organizational structures and the popularity of matrix management structures, you are not going to achieve much in an organization like this without an extremely good network, or the help of someone who does have one.

Here are the skills:

- Enjoys meeting new people.
- Quickly finds common ground with new contacts.
- Appears relaxed and comfortable at social events.
- Networks effectively at social events.
- Maintains a wide network of contacts.
- Builds their network strategically.

Two things are striking from the evidence we have collected through the online tool, which calibrates individuals' influencing skill against this model. First, individuals do not generally feel anywhere near as relaxed as they appear to others during networking events. I think that the internal pressure to perform in unstructured social situations may be contributing to this, and gaining the feedback that they appear quite relaxed and comfortable can often help people to relax and just get on with it.

The second difference between self-assessment and observed behaviour is that most people think they are far less effective at networking than they actually appear to others. Everyone else seems to be so good at it and clearly they must have a plan. Again, simple remedies. I'll cover much more about this vital topic in the next chapter, which is devoted to networking.

Exercise

Reflect on the six skills listed above and write down a score out of 10 in your notebook to represent the level of skill you think you have in the *networking* dimension. Then write down another score to represent the amount of skill you believe you are actually using in your current role.

Influencing people

Once you have built a clear understanding of the situation and people you wish to influence, you then have to get on and do something. This is where the skills in this dimension come into play – where theory meets practice.

To a large extent this is about engaging in the political world of work. Influential leaders cannot take a back seat, they have to get involved. This doesn't mean you have to become a Machiavellian schemer. Political activity fuelled by positive intent does a great deal of good in the world (here you might want to refer back to Chapter 6 – The ethics of influence).

The skills that make up this dimension are:

- Builds strong relationships.
- Considers carefully how to influence others.
- Adapts the way they appear to different people.
- Remains calm and controlled when working with others.
- Chooses the right time to influence.
- Persuades using various different approaches.

From the evidence we have compiled since the original research, the main skill gap for most people is being more flexible in their approach. In many ways this is about becoming more strategic in your approach to influence rather than simply doing what you normally do. Assuming you have gained a clear understanding of the individuals you wish to influence, you can then make decisions about what to do, when to do it and how to do it. It is also about adapting your behaviour to suit and this is covered in considerable detail in Chapter 12 (Understanding and adapting your style).

Exercise

Reflect on the six skills listed above and write down a score out of 10 in your notebook to represent the level of skill you think you have in the *influencing people* dimension. Then write down another score to represent the amount of skill you believe you are actually using in your current role.

Influencing groups

This dimension lies at the heart of being an effective influential leader. As you rise through the ranks you do not have the time to influence each and every individual, so you have to develop effective strategies to move the masses. Groups have already featured regularly in this book so this should be no great surprise.

Here are the skills critical to influencing groups of people:

- Identifies key influencers within different groups.
- Plans their approach to influencing groups.
- Builds strong alliances with different groups.
- Builds consensus between groups.
- Senses the mood of an audience.
- Presents to groups persuasively.

Again, drawing from our data and also reflecting on the many coaching clients I have worked with on this topic, most people seem to believe that they are good at influencing groups. That may be the case, but what I also notice is that in the main they are also simply deploying their individual influencing skills. Effective group influence necessitates a strategic approach to the way these skills are focused and used.

Exercise

Reflect on the six skills listed above and write down a score out of 10 in your notebook to represent the level of skill you think you have in the *influencing groups* dimension. Then write down another score to represent the amount of skill you believe you are actually using in your current role.

Building trust

Fundamentally, influence is about relationships and at the centre of all effective relationships is trust. In a good relationship, influence works well both ways and you will trust the other person and they will trust you. Any sizable difference between the relative levels of trust given will lead to problems at some point. Imagine how you feel when you place your trust in someone and after a while you realize that they don't reciprocate that trust.

While most people with a reasonable amount of experience have an instinctive feel for this dimension and how to build trust, few understand what is actually happening beneath the surface and hence miss opportunities to build trust to higher levels with greater speed and reliability.

Here are the final set of six skills:

- Keeps an open mind about the views of others.
- Shows genuine concern for other people.
- Encourages openness and honesty.
- Communicates clear objectives.
- Demonstrates commitment to personal and organizational values.
- Displays confidence and capability.

These speak for themselves. However, they are not necessarily so easy to master consistently. There are many natural obstacles and dilemmas that can get in the way, particularly if you are ambitious and already successful. Chapter 10 (Establishing and building greater trust) will go into much more detail about this topic and help you to see how you can move faster, achieve more and build exceptionally high levels of reciprocal trust.

Exercise

Once again, reflect on the six skills listed above and write down a score out of 10 in your notebook to represent the level of skill you think you have in the *building trust* dimension. Then write down another score to represent the amount of skill you believe you are actually using in your current role.

Now put away your notebook while I share with you some of the interesting conclusions that came out of the original research.

Research findings

Although gratifying, it was not surprising to find that all skills included in the online survey were considered to be important to successful influencing. However, along the way, careful analysis of the quantitative and qualitative data did throw up a few surprises.

Understanding versus influencing

It was surprising to see that those who took part in the survey regarded the development of understanding as less critical than the actual act of influencing.

Based on my experience and the literature review, a great deal of emphasis is placed on developing a keen insight into what is going on, understanding what makes people do the things they do and being able to understand how others interact and respond. The data contradicted this. When I shared this with those I interviewed, they were also surprised, with one quipping, 'how can you influence with any degree of confidence if you don't first understand?'

From the academic world, Gerald Ferris found that social astuteness was the most important determinant of success. He elaborated this point by saying that 'people high in social astuteness have an accurate understanding of social situations as well as the interpersonal interactions that take place in these settings'. Michael Mumford also strongly asserted the need to understand, to diagnose and then to influence.

What emerged during the qualitative stage of my research has shed some light on this area. It would seem that there are barriers to gaining understanding. In some cases, greater value is placed on *doing* rather than *thinking* by senior management. Also, 'we don't have time to develop understanding' was a sentiment expressed by several. In an extreme example, one person stated that 'if you don't get results and fast, you're out'.

Others raised the possibility that the skills of developing understanding are so well developed that they have slipped into unconscious competence and therefore are not as instantly recognized for the value that they bring. This may well be the case. However, I believe that it would be very worthwhile to bring these skills into focus and reassess actual competence.

Men versus women

There was a marked gender difference in the survey; however, this is due to minority position rather than gender itself.

The data clearly demonstrated that women consider these influencing skills to be more critical to success than men do. This was not entirely unexpected given the common notion that women tend to be more socially aware and concerned with relationships. However, the surprise came when probing more deeply into this factor.

It appears from the literature that there has been no successful attempt to find differences between the genders when it comes to perceptions of political skill. Several academics have tried to prove this difference but have failed. What has been found, however, is that major differences appear to be evident among group members who are in minority positions. This feeling of isolation from the rest of the group increases the need to learn influencing skills to overcome their apparently inferior position.

Another potential contributor to this result in my research is the evidence of networking activities by men and women. One researcher discovered that women's networks outside their organization are bigger than those within it, whereas men have larger internal networks. The implication for this in influential leadership is that men seem to have an advantage if the leadership arena is within the bounds of their organization, while women may fare better if the arena is external.

The value of experience

This research has highlighted that different skills within the political domain are recognized as critical by more senior and experienced individuals.

Generally, it was found that senior respondents placed far more emphasis on political skill. This is no surprise, but does provide focus for developing more junior staff, particularly those with talent and potential. In addition to these differences being noticed at a dimension level, several individual skills showed significant differences.

For instance, directors and above considered that developing clear objectives, sensing the feelings of others and being aware of their own emotions are far more critical than their junior colleagues did.

At a more senior level, managing ambiguity is commonplace. Lower organizational levels are much more task specific and there is less need to engage in the social task of influencing. This means that, to achieve success, different skills are required. The need to be able to sense what is going on and notice what emotional response this generates internally and externally becomes far more important at senior levels.

Self-awareness, deemed by seniors as more critical, often only comes at a more experienced level. Training and development interventions change as people rise within the organization and often self-analysis opportunities are encouraged and paid for at senior levels. I believe that everyone can benefit from greater self-awareness but, in reality, this is not easily available at all levels. One interviewee put it well when she said that 'I didn't realize how important self-awareness was until I went on a course'.

For ambitious influential leaders, placing more focus on self-awareness is likely to lead to greater success and progress.

Social niceties

There is clear evidence emerging that less value is placed on social skills in the workplace.

It was established in the literature review that researchers believed that influencing skill needs to be exercised in a social environment. Influence is inherently social in nature.

From my research, it appears that the social aspects of influencing skills are not being recognized by practising managers. This was demonstrated by the fact that half of the ten least important skills all included the word 'social'.

Further insight was gained into this aspect during the qualitative interviews. Many interviewees noted that social skills were not valued by senior management. In the current pressured environment, output is what is important rather than how you get it. Several interviewees reacted with the sentiments that 'business is harsh' and 'time is money'. This corresponds well to the earlier point about the lack of importance placed on understanding. One individual even went so far as to say that we 'don't have time for social niceties here!'

This was expanded by others who responded with 'we don't have time for lunch or golf, cutting the deal is what's important' and 'socializing at work is just work, I keep my personal life separate'. This latter comment seems to suggest an element of doing it just for the job, which is prone to being perceived as insincere.

It was also noted that the appearance of this lack of recognition may in part be due to the UK focus in the research. One interviewee commented that in other European countries higher value was placed on social interactions in the national culture (the problematic nature of cultural differences has already been highlighted in Chapter 6).

The combination of what I found during the literature review, the survey data and the qualitative interviews leads me to the conclusion that, in the current workplace, individuals are under significant pressure to perform and are minded to downplay the importance of sincere social interactions to instead pursue short-term tactical gains. What appears to be missing from their approach is a true appreciation for the benefits to their work of applying sufficient focus to the social aspects of influencing skill.

In fact, this was one of the building blocks of this book and its emphasis on the need to make progress on the short-term imperative, while also building a stronger sense of purpose for the future.

Prioritizing your development focus

All of these skills are really important to the influential leader, but since you are moving fast and don't have much time, you have to make sure that you get a good return on your investment of time and energy in developing skills.

To help you to work out which should get your attention, refresh your mind of the dimension scores you gave yourself earlier. If you wish, you can also complete the self-assessment online and get feedback from your friends and colleagues. This will add a sharper focus to your development: **www.gautreygroup.com/iss**

Here are some questions to help you develop your focus. Which dimension or skill:

- If developed further, would help you to dramatically improve your current performance as an influential leader? You've got to accelerate your progress and also create the time for greater things too.
- Will be most important to your longer-term career prospects? You need to balance short- and long-term focus in your development as well.
- Is in shortest supply in your workplace? This relates directly to the principles covered in Chapter 3 (Why power works in the real world).
- Is holding you back? Lack of skill can be career limiting and may get in the way of gaining the recognition you deserve.

- Have you been told by your manager, mentor, or coach that you need to develop? You don't necessarily have to, but you do need to take their advice into account.

- Would be most helpful in helping you to achieve your longer-term leadership purpose?

These questions are intended to stimulate your thinking and help you begin to identify where you should apply your development effort. The decision you need to make is which skill is most likely to give you a strong return. If you are already fairly well established in your role as an influential leader, stretch your return out to the longer term. Alternatively, if you are just getting going and have a lot of things to straighten out before you can get moving towards your purpose, keep a short-term focus and return again soon.

Before you decide, remember that it is far easier, and more fun, to turn a strength into something truly exceptional than to turn a weakness into a strength. Manage your weaknesses and flaunt your strengths without becoming arrogant.

As a suggestion, settle on one or two to focus your attention on during the next three to six months and pile all your effort into them, then review again later and see where you have got to.

Getting things done

Important points to remember as you begin to make more progress:

- Influencing skills form the base of your capability as an influential leader.

- These skills are not complicated but, they do take consistent practice to hone and perfect.

- Understanding and influencing groups is the most neglected area of skill and presents a valuable opportunity to stand out from the crowd.

- Most chapters in this book contribute in some way to the development of these skills.

- Networking is arguably the most important skill and is a non-negotiable for the influential leader.

- It doesn't matter if you don't have time to socialize at work – it's still vital.

Further reading

When you get a chance, make sure you check the further reading and resources for this chapter online at: **www.learntoinfluence.com/leadership**

On stage I am often heard dismissing influencing skills in favour of having a clear purpose and strategy. Personally I believe that knowing what you want to achieve and having clear ideas is far more important. However, if you get some of these skills wrong, you are unlikely to achieve very much. To address this, the next couple of chapters will focus in on some of these skills to ensure that you are doing what you need to be doing in order to avoid trouble, and also have a clear notion of what you need to be continually doing to make sure these skills are working well for you.

Developing powerful and influential networks

09

> *Influential leaders cannot survive alone; they have to amass a wide network of powerful friends.*

Having a strong and vibrant network brings access to resources, political intelligence and friendly support. It can also be an enjoyable activity that builds mutually rewarding long-term relationships. Success will be short-lived if you have not got the support of a network around you.

The actual activity of networking is about using your social skills to create new connections, contacts and friends. It is about progressing these new relationships from the initial connection (either through work or at an event) into a more rewarding personal relationship. As an influential leader, networking goes far beyond the accumulation of friends – you need to focus on building a strategic web of strong contacts who can, over time, provide maximum support towards the accomplishment of your purpose.

This chapter contributes to the following influential leader capabilities:

Develops strong networks, alliances and collaborations around their domain.

▶

Networking is unlikely to be a new topic for you as an ambitious and fast-moving individual, so what I want to do is to stretch your thinking beyond the obvious working-the-room type of ideas. This chapter will take you into the deeper workings of relationships so that you can see what you need to do in order to create your powerful network.

The networking process

I've found from experience that for many people their networking skill is deficient in just three respects. First, they are not motivated sufficiently to find the time they need to do it properly, hiding behind excuses like 'I'm too busy' or 'I don't see the relevance'. Second, confidence is quite often patchy at best. Social situations are by nature unstructured and there are lots of very successful people who prefer to operate in a well-organized manner. The seemingly chaotic environment of a social gathering can appear quite daunting. The same excuses are used here.

The final deficiency holds the key to overcoming the first two problems with ease. Most people don't apply their networking to their purpose with a strategy and plan. Vaguely wandering from event to event hoping to make useful connections is not appropriate for influential leaders.

To remedy all three problems, the process to adopt is quite straightforward and familiar:

1 Establish a clear networking aim.
2 Analyse your current network and identify gaps.
3 Commit to specific networking objectives.
4 Create a strategy and plan to build and deepen your network.
5 Regularly review progress and adjust your plans.

One common objection to this is that is appears contrived – isn't network-ing supposed to be spontaneous and serendipitous? Yes it is, however, you can retain that while also benefiting from becoming a little more deliberate and targeted about what you are aiming to achieve. Influential leadership is all about getting things done and you haven't got the time to waste. Your networking needs to be quite tightly focused. If you have extra time, feel free to expand your horizons.

Networking aims and objectives

The first step is to consider the question – why are you networking? You'll need to move beyond the reason that you've been told to do it, or it came up on your performance appraisal. Try to get a clear notion of the purpose for all this networking. This way, you can use it as a means of deciding which events to attend, which to avoid and who you need to try to get into your network. It will also help you to set goals and targets for your networking and, ultimately, it will help you to realize your ambitions more quickly.

To maximize your progress as an influential leader, aligning your networking goals with your *leadership purpose* makes sense. If you have already been able to gain clarity on the overall purpose of your leadership, use this as the focus of your networking. Otherwise, take a shorter-term idea of where you are trying to get to and you will still be able to make your networking more effective.

It is usually difficult to arrive at succinct goals for your networking, although that would be ideal. Instead, you may wish to settle for more general aims – you can get more specific once you've started moving.

Example networking aims:

- To become recognized by all members of the board as a valuable contributor to the business.
- To attract challenging new work assignments.
- To become a well-known figure within the profession.
- To advance your career.
- To speak at external conferences.
- To become even more successful in your job.

If you are finding it difficult to define your networking aim, at least settle for the last one in the list above. The only risk with this is that you'll need to be careful to avoid short-term tactical moves, which can create success today but which may move you away from your longer-term leadership purpose, which is where you need to be focused as an influential leader. Don't forget, networking is generally seen as a longer-term investment because it can take a while to develop deep relationships.

Objectives will add more detail to what you are aiming to achieve and how you know you have achieved it. You may have some objectives in mind already, but hold back until you've read the next couple of sections because these will help to form your networking strategy.

Network analysis

There are a number of ways to start analysing your networking. This section will take you through a variety of approaches, which will vary in their suitability to your situation. Appropriateness depends on how well-defined your leadership purpose is and also how experienced you are at networking.

To maximize the usefulness to a wide variety of readers, I'll simply run through each technique and leave you to decide which of them is most appropriate for you to apply. It will then also serve as a useful place to return to as you continue to develop your networking skills.

Territory analysis

If you have a fairly well-defined idea of where you want to go, perhaps with specific career goals or, even better, a clear leadership purpose, then this analysis will be ideal in helping you to identify the direction you need to be taking in expanding your network. It will also help you to deepen your understanding of your leadership arena.

Take a step forward in time and imagine you have arrived at your destination (either your purpose or networking aim). What sort of people would have been helpful in your journey? Figure 9.1 is an illustration of how you could draw this out.

In the examples shown in Figure 9.1, becoming recognized within the industry could be helped by media editors. Editors like writing about movers and shakers in their industry. They also like to receive articles written by people who know what they are talking about. Basically, they provide a potential PR platform. The academics could be useful in helping to raise name awareness among people entering the industry. They may also be very interested in

FIGURE 9.1   Network map

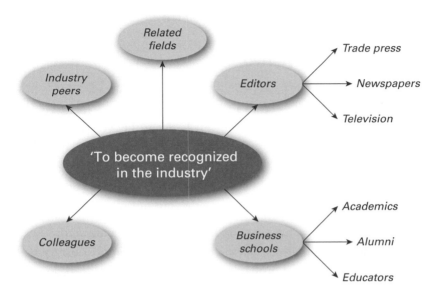

putting practitioners in front of their students in order to share the realities of life in the industry.

The idea here is to move from your purpose to all the different types of people it would be useful to know and who could make a contribution, either directly or in a more supportive capacity. This will help to give your networking more direction. Don't think of individuals at this stage, because it will limit your thinking. Chart out the territory as comprehensively as you can. In Chapter 1 you identified the leadership arena where you wished to be successful. This exercise is intended to take you one step beyond and find the kind of people outside of your immediate arena who could also be helpful.

Depending on your purpose and arena, it may be more appropriate for you to focus your attention within your organization rather than the broader example given in Figure 9.1. The territory within large organizations can be extremely complex and interconnected, so make sure that you include all of the major functions such as Sales, HR and Finance. If you reflect back on Chapter 5 (Understanding your leadership arena), you will want to make sure that you include all of the areas that are powerful. Although it may be tempting to just pull out the organizational structure chart, making your own map will ensure that it stays relevant. You may also feel it is important to add any informal groups you are a member of, such as sports clubs.

Once you've charted the territory in this way, you can then consider how your current network matches. The gaps then become areas on which to focus your networking time.

Quantifying your network

Any attempt to capture the extent and make-up of your network will be a useful exercise if it helps you to identify opportunities to focus your time more effectively. If you can review who you know quickly, you can immediately become a little more deliberate about how you are building relationships.

But, where to start?

Many people have a huge number of contacts on LinkedIn and other social media platforms. They have big address books and many more besides, hidden in the e-mail archives. These days I think it is impossible to analyse your entire network – and probably not worth the attempt.

The quickest way to make some progress here is to remain focused on your priorities – preferably your long-term *leadership purpose*. Assuming you've done the territory-mapping above, an easy way to proceed is to quickly brainstorm a list of people you know in each group on your map.

Exercise

For now, stick with people you have engaged with in some way in the past, perhaps having worked together on a project or attended meetings with. If they are likely to be receptive to an approach of some kind from you then you have a relationship. A later section will look at how to develop these relationships.

Once you have a list of names against the various groups (and I accept that some may be empty at the moment, especially if you are doing this for the first time), run through each list and consider the quality of the relationship you have with each person. Think about the extent to which trust exists between you and them. Are you open with each other and share candidly what is really going on? Do you engage with them on a frequent basis? (This is exactly the same assessment as you did on individual stakeholders in Chapter 7.)

To help make things easier, mark each name in some way to record your view regarding the quality of your relationship, perhaps by grading them high, medium or low.

Now sit back and take a look at what you have got. Which groups are under-represented? Which ones are have contacts that are least well known? What are the most striking gaps in your current network?

The main aim here is to begin to capture the shape, size and location of your network. It is a job that is never finished. Most people don't need to spend much time on this exercise to begin to see where the gaps are and where they need to start focusing more attention on developing their relationships. If you have not yet determined your *leadership purpose* and *territory map* you can still work to quantify the scale and extent of your network, although the gaps to focus on will not become obvious.

If you are in this situation, brainstorm a list of twenty people in your network, then assess the relationship. Then continue adding groups of twenty people until you run out of ideas. Keep adding names on a regular basis and you will soon start to gain a feel for the extent and scope of your network. The benefit of doing this is that you do not need to later rely on your memory when thinking about what and who to build relationships with, you can simply run down your list and realize that you haven't spoken to someone for a while and give them a call.

Which brings me to the final point on this section – find some way of keeping records of all of these. It could be a simple spreadsheet, or even a contact management database. The important thing is to use something simple and not to overengineer it. If you can also add further details about the people as you work your network, so much the better. Memories are fickle and need help, especially if you've got a big and growing network.

Political capital assessment

Developing political capital has to be a priority for an influential leader. Without it, achieving purpose is very hard work. Keeping it simple, political capital is the amount of goodwill and support available to you from within your network. The value of your political capital will be determined by the strength, power and influence of those who offer you their goodwill and support, and also have the potential to assist you in moving forward your goals. There is little point in having lots of goodwill from people who are not in a position to help. You need to be loved by the right people.

To gain political capital, you first need to accumulate social capital. In essence, this is your network and is represented by the quantity and quality of your connections. When you are thinking about developing your network or social capital, don't forget that before you focus on quality, you need to make sure you have quantity. You also need to keep adding new people regularly to develop a pipeline of new potential.

Exercise

To do the political capital assessment, you need to consider two elements for each individual within your network (see Figure 9.2). When all of this is combined, you will then be able to decide on strategies that will be useful in developing higher value in your network.

First consider the amount of goodwill being offered by the contact. This is an extension of the quality of your relationship used in the last section. In addition to trust and openness, goodwill is indicated by evidence of

FIGURE 9.2   Political capital assessment

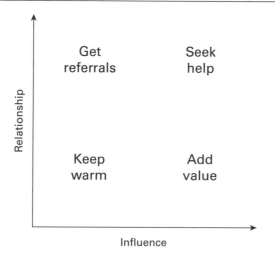

kindness, cheerfulness, generosity, proactive help and friendly support. Goodwill is high if a network contact quickly responds to e-mails and returns calls, and very high if they are frequently going out of their way to be helpful.

It is worth noting that your goodwill does not need to be a two-way feature, although it does help. The reason for mentioning this is that at senior levels it is impossible to have equality of goodwill because of the numbers of people involved. If you are leading a team of several thousand you cannot possibly return the same amount of goodwill as they are potentially offering you. For this assessment, simply think about the amount that they give you. Later you will focus your effort on offering goodwill back to those who offer you the greatest long-term value.

Second, you need to make an assessment of the extent of their influence. You can consider this either in general terms or make it specific to your chosen aim, objective or purpose. If you keep it general you will potentially gain greater long-term potential in your network at the expense of shorter-term gains. Using a tighter focus for your assessment will help you to make progress faster, however there is a danger that your relationship building may be perceived as selfish.

Whichever option you choose, make sure to be consistent when plotting your connections on the grid. Either position people based on their overall power or their power to influence and contribute towards your purpose. If you wish to do both, complete a different grid.

Once you have populated the grid you can then focus your networking effort by considering one of these four strategies:

- Keep warm: don't spend a huge amount of time working with them, but don't risk alienating them either, just in case.
- Get referrals: these are your close friends and associates who will be willing to introduce you to others with more potential to help.
- Add value: find ways to increase their goodwill. Showing how you add value to their work/life will help.
- Seek help: probably all you need to do is ask. But remember to consider reasons why they may not want to help, or be able to help you.

Although it is natural and important to focus your attention on those who you will get the most benefit from networking with, please don't forget that a key principle in networking is about mutual support, not just selfish taking from your contacts. If you come across as too selfish, your contacts will notice this and may be resistant to giving you the help that they could give. Take a long-term view with greater awareness of where the likely payoffs will be.

Contribution assessment

Another way to identify targets for your networking is to consider the people who could potentially make a strong contribution towards your mission or purpose. The aim of this assessment is to ensure that you consider not just the powerful people, but also those who can help in terms of their expertise, people or financial resources, access to others, or even the time, energy and enthusiasm they could bring to your cause. The party faithful are as essential to your success as the rich and famous.

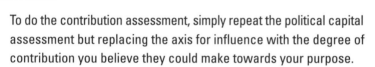

Exercise

To do the contribution assessment, simply repeat the political capital assessment but replacing the axis for influence with the degree of contribution you believe they could make towards your purpose.

In effect, what you are likely to be doing is moving the names around. If you have someone who is very powerful but unlikely to be able to make a major contribution, this may mean you place less emphasis on building your relationship with them. You might also add new names to this assessment because you are thinking about your network from a different angle.

Towards a networking strategy

You must invest a reasonable amount of time doing each of the assessments above in order to stand a good chance of adjusting your activity to maximize your effectiveness. Don't be constrained by what I've included here – if you have used other approaches to improve your networking in the past, do them again if they would be worthwhile. Make sure to keep your notes so that it is easier to review and update your networking in a couple of months' time.

Once you've done these assessments, it is time to begin building your networking strategy. Fundamentally, this strategy should focus on answering four questions:

1 Who in your current network should you focus on building your relationship with?

2 What major gaps need to be filled in your network?

3 Who should you target in order to fill these gaps?

4 How will you move all of this forward?

Try to treat this in exactly the same way as any other aspect of your work that needs to be planned and executed. You may need to do further research to answer question three, or involve others in helping you to identify the optimum targets. Question four involves using your experience and creative thinking to work out the actions you should take. The next section will also be able to stimulate your ideas.

Right now, though, pause for a few moments and make some notes against each of these questions so that you can begin to bring all of your thinking into focus ready to make some decisions shortly about your plan of action.

Developing relationships

There are no shortcuts when it comes to building relationships with people. It takes time and energy and this is why it is so important to be well-focused in your networking.

There are many ways to develop relationships and I am sure that you already know quite a lot about this subject, so here are a few ideas particularly relevant to the influential leader and the ideas covered in this book:

- Become acutely aware of the personal and professional agendas of your key targets (or communities). Make a concerted effort to discover as much as you can about them (refer to Chapter 4 – Deeper understanding of people).

- Make sure you have a clear sense of their values too. You will be able to gain a greater degree of support if you manage to appeal to their values (and emotions) as well as their agenda. Yes, write them down and check them out with your friends too.

- Compare these insights with your own purpose, agenda and values. Where are the common areas? Be honest, where is the conflict? You don't need to act on this immediately, but be aware from the beginning.

- Now, go out of your way to help them. Don't wait to be asked, just do things that make a contribution to their work and life. Be wary of appearing contrived and gaining a reputation for sucking up to people.

- Deepen the relationship by spending more time (particularly informal time) getting to know them and allowing them the opportunity to get to know you. Yes, build more trust and intimacy (see Chapter 10 – Establishing and building greater trust).

- Find ways to encourage them to become more involved in what you are doing. As the relationship builds, it may be possible to motivate (or even inspire!) them to work with you more directly, particularly if what you are doing appeals to their values. Chapter 13 (Tailoring your approach for maximum influence) will help you to find more ways to influence people towards your agenda.

- Ensure you establish a process that will continue to identify new relationships and connections that are worth investing in.

- Stay alert for the potential changes around your goals. Sources of valuable political capital can change and, from a personal perspective, it is important to build a broad base of political capital as well as having it focused on your purpose. Goals and the politics around you can all change very quickly, so remain vigilant. Chapter 5 (Understanding your leadership arena) will help you to do this.

The resources section is the place to go to find more ideas and suggestions about how to improve your relationships and develop your network.

Making networking a team effort

Traditional approaches to developing networks focus on the individual. However, there is an opportunity to adopt a different mindset. As well as considering your own network, also look for ways to help your team to build their networks and, in the process, your collective team network.

Helping your team, company or group to become better connected can yield huge benefits. The World Bank has noted that: 'Increasing evidence shows that social cohesion is critical for societies to prosper economically and for development to be sustainable' (**http://web.worldbank.org/**). If social cohesion can be good for countries, it can also be good for teams and organizations.

Social cohesion is usually explained by using the concept of social capital in economics, which refers to the quantity and quality of the connections that members of a given society or group have between them, and with others outside of the group. More specifically, they look at:

- the number of connections;
- the level of trust within those connections;
- the cultural consistency within the group.

The second and third points in this list are somewhat intertwined. Cultural consistency provides the base of predictable and understandable behaviour between the members. This leads to increasing levels of trust (ie reliability). It is possible to have cohesion without cultural consistency, but that takes a great deal of work to build the level of understanding and tolerance. I'll talk more about trust in the next chapter.

While it may be unrealistic to actually measure comparative social capital between teams, it is easy to imagine that the team with the highest number of high-quality relevant connections will be the most influential. Okay, you have to take into account traditional sources of power too; however, the point is that social capital is something that is easy to increase if you focus on it.

Here are a few ideas for your team:

- put more emphasis on each member, building wider and deeper networks;
- prioritize informal gatherings for your team to get closer – invite other teams along too;
- get your team talking about trust, what it means and how they can develop more of it;
- build a team network map of the organization and look for gaps;
- create a team definition of a high-quality connection;
- set network targets, perhaps even building these into performance reviews;

- ensure each member of your team has a positive attitude to networking;
- bring in external speakers to share their views on building relationships;
- invite other teams to your regular meetings so you can strengthen relationships.

You may find it difficult to quantify the social capital that exists within your team. Instead, look for the anecdotal links to your team's results. The more networked your team, the more politically astute they will become and the results will begin to speak for themselves.

Networking strategy and plan

By now you should be getting a fairly clear idea of your strategy, at least in the short term, and now you need to get moving on it. Unless you plan specific actions to take, and decide when you will take them, you are unlikely to move forward in anything other than a haphazard way.

As you start to finalize your actions, bear these thoughts in mind:

- Favour events that offer the opportunity to meet people in your target groups.
- Find ways of reaching out to these groups and begin to make connections.
- Identify where they *hang out* and get down there to see what's happening.
- Look for others in your network who can introduce you to these missing groups.
- Be clear on what your proposition is for each group; then develop your elevator pitch specific to that group.
- Which networking events can you drop?
- Who should you be spending less time with?

Now, finalize your actions. Make sure you are clear about when you will do things and ensure you are also putting in a formal review action. As you begin to network more effectively you will be learning a great idea, particularly at the start. Adjusting your strategy and plan is the only way to succeed and make sure you also have plenty of time for your other leadership activities.

Getting things done

Important points to remember as you begin to make more progress:

- Focus your networking on your leadership purpose in order to make efficient use of your time.

- Without mutual benefit your network will quickly wither and die.

- Networking quality has to begin with quantity.

- Networking doesn't need to be a solo activity. Get your whole team involved and working together.

- To make this vital task easy, get organized, as you would in any other part of your job.

Further reading

When you get a chance, make sure you check the further reading and resources for this chapter online at: **www.learntoinfluence.com/leadership**

If you have been diligent in applying the ideas in this chapter you should now have a pretty good focus on where you need to build relationships, and also who you need to get closer to. A key part of how you actually build them is the establishment and development of higher levels of trust. How trust works in relationships and how you can engender greater trust is the subject of the next chapter.

Establishing and building greater trust

10

In order to attract a motivated and loyal following, the influential leader has to ensure that trust pervades all aspects of their key relationships.

To do this, you first have to learn exactly what trust is and how it operates within relationships. This chapter will take you beyond the obvious requirements such as telling the truth and doing what you say you are going to do. It will go deeper and take a practical look at what you need to do and what you need to avoid if you are to maximize trust in your relationships.

This chapter contributes to the following influential leader capabilities:

Is able to create and build robust high-trust relationships.

Understands and mitigates the threats to trust.

Although this is a complicated subject, which often disappears into philosophical debates, I will stick to the simple concepts that will make all the difference to your performance. You will also find plenty of ideas here about how you can adjust your behaviours to build and protect trust in your relationships.

Keeping trust simple

Trust is the degree to which you can predict someone or something. When it comes to people, what you are assessing is how well you can predict what they will do, or how they will react, to a given situation. Will they do what they say they will do? Will they keep your secrets? Will they tell you the truth? As your confidence in their reliability grows, you place increasing trust in them.

Integrity is another word usually linked to trust. In this context it means behaving in accordance with a clear set of morals, ethics and values. Although there is a huge cultural overlay to this (as you will have seen in Chapter 6), integrity is essentially internal and personal. Since values drive behavioural decisions, integrity could be said to be how well an individual lives according to their values.

The link between trust and integrity is that the more strictly someone adheres to a clear set of values, the more predictable they become in the eyes of others. From my standpoint, this leads to three important observations:

- Values are rarely expressed clearly, or even understood by an individual. Observation of others' values is difficult, and cultural assumptions (yes, natural stereotyping in action) can be very unreliable when considering an individual. If you cannot determine an individual's values, it is very difficult to judge if they are living true to them.

- Partly in consequence of this, and partly due to human nature, people tend to judge people based on their own values rather than the values the other person holds. When you think someone lacks integrity, what you usually mean is that their behaviour doesn't match with your values. Tyrants usually operate with extremely high integrity, enforcing their values on others.

- People seem to consider trust in a very black-and-white manner – either they trust someone or they don't. The reality, the level of trust you have in someone, will depend on what you are trusting them with. A colleague may reliably keep your confidences, but not if the information you have entrusted with them is threatening to one of their friends. If you can break down the trust and learn what you can, or cannot trust someone with, you can potentially work more effectively with them.

Although I am focusing on individuals, trust works in exactly the same way with organizations and physical things. Do you trust your supermarket, or bank? That will depend on how reliable you have found them to be. Do they stock what you want, when you want it? Can you depend on their accuracy, fairness and customer service? Similarly, does your smartphone do what it is supposed to do?

How trust works in relationships

Be honest, when you meet someone for the first time, a question will be lurking in your mind, probably just outside of conscious awareness – can you trust them? This is natural and healthy. As an influential leader you should not give people your trust too easily or quickly, although you do need to focus hard on building the maximum levels of trust in all of your key relationships. To make this happen quickly, understanding the process that allows trust to develop will help you to speed things up.

Set out below is how trust begins in a new relationship.

Trust orientation

Some people 'trust until proven otherwise', while others 'distrust until they have to'. Each individual will have a starting position between these two extremes based on their personal experiences, bruises and scars.

Relative starting positions can have a big impact on how trust builds. An individual may have a different natural orientation depending on the context of the relationship. For instance, some people are less trusting at work than in their personal lives.

When two people meet for the first time from different ends of this continuum, expect trust to get off to a very difficult start. One person will be open and trusting and will quickly begin to wonder why the other one is not reciprocating their trust. On the other side, the reluctant truster will be wondering why the other person is being so careless with sensitive details – certainly not the sort of person who should be trusted. Once either of these reactions takes hold, mutual trust quickly becomes very difficult to achieve.

Preconceptions

Before you meet someone, you are likely to already know something about them. You will at least have an awareness of their business, job title and objectives. You might even have heard others talking about them – their reputation precedes them.

To an extent, you will also be affected by the stereotypes you have installed in your mind about people in roles such as sales, finance and legal. Stereotypes serve a useful function in helping to economize thinking by relying on assumptions. However, they can also obscure reality. There are always exceptions to any rule and as a mature professional you know you should keep an open mind – but do you? Consequently, by the time you get to meet someone, you have probably already established a starting position for the trust you can place in them.

First impressions

The first impression as you encounter another person will have a long-lasting effect. To a large extent, you are checking to see if the other person conforms to your expectations. Careful appraisal of clothes, body language and mannerisms will all combine to verify your beliefs (or preconceptions). Your ability to filter out evidence that doesn't fit can impede your awareness of the facts before you.

If you have a strong notion of what a person from HR is going to be like, it will be natural to interpret your first impressions to fit that expectation. Unless you are careful, the non-typical HR person will need to really stand out from their crowd in order to avoid falling into your stereotype.

And as you know, first impressions generally stick.

Engagement

Then the dialogue begins. In healthy relationships, each side will be testing and gradually increasing the level of trust bestowed on the other party. Starting with a relatively safe disclosure, and watching what happens. Does the other side respect your confidence, keep your secrets? As the level of confidence grows, so does the willingness to disclose more sensitive information.

At this point, you will also be looking for a reciprocal level of trusting behaviour. As noted earlier, if this is unequal, you may begin to suspect that all is not as it appears. Although the individual seems to be dealing with your secrets appropriately, why don't they share a similar level of sensitivity?

Risk assessment

That said, you also need to take into account that, in any engagement, both sides will be aware of the potential consequences of any disclosure. What might happen if you disclose to a colleague what you really think about your boss? If that colleague happens to be a rival vying for promotion, they may well take advantage of that insight and cause trouble for you. Your risk-weighting will determine the degree to which you are prepared to share, and when. They will be doing the same.

On many occasions, I have heard people in coaching sessions saying things like, 'I don't understand why he's not telling me that, it wouldn't bother me to share that sort of information'. No, it may not bother you, but not everyone sees the world the way you do.

Trust-risk ratings are rarely objective or consciously thought out. If you are feeling pretty confident and secure, sharing your displeasure about a senior colleague may not be a problem. To others who are fearful of their performance rating or even their job, this type of disclosure could be politically foolish.

In order to be reasonable, you have to recognize that the other party might be in a completely different position and either more or less likely to trust. If you think about this sensibly, it will adjust your expectations and potentially avoid hindrances in trust development. If they are scared, you will need to work very hard to get them to trust you.

Challenges and obstacles to trust

Successful leadership and trust go hand in hand. Unless you have the trust of your team and those around you, your leadership is likely to stutter and fail. Probably not a catastrophic failure but you will fall well short of your determination to become an influential leader.

Despite this obvious truth, trust in many places seems to be conspicuous by its absence. And one of the reasons for this is that as a leader, it is so easy to find yourself in a situation that casts a shadow across your trustability.

For instance, have you ever:

- Returned from a senior management meeting that discussed rather sensitive restructure options?

- Disagreed strongly with a decision taken by the senior management committee, yet been told to be a 'good corporate citizen' and toe the party line – especially if you want to get promoted?

- Discussed a pay award with one of your team in order to recognize and motivate them? While you did this with the best of intentions, you then discovered that HR have decided to put a block on all mid-year pay rises.

Innocent and inexperienced leaders can easily fall victim to these dilemmas as they try to figure out what to do for the best. Or, more likely, they don't attempt to figure it out and just stumble around doing their best in the moment. They risk compounding the problem, albeit innocently and with the right intentions towards their team.

Returning to the examples above:

- With a sensitive restructure afoot, the chances are high that your team will have got wind that something is happening and will be very keen to know what it means for them. Saying nothing could allow the rumours to flourish. Be evasive and the rumours will be exaggerated even more. Tell the truth and in the process release news of the decisions not yet made, or not yet ready to be communicated – and your promotion will surely fly out the window (because you will lose the trust of the senior team).

- Toe the company line on decisions you do not agree with and people will wonder why – if they know it is something you are likely to disagree with. So, why aren't you being straight with them? They will think you have been leaned on – a traitor in the camp. Should you argue the decision and isolate yourself from the rest of the senior team? Pretend to the troops that you really do think it's right, but make sure to be convincing and hope your private efforts to reverse the decision don't succeed – because then your team will get even more confused by you.

- And the pay rise – another tough call. You want to reward your supporters and do the right thing. Do you admit that you don't have the influence? Or string them along in the hope that you can force it through eventually? All the while, hoping you can last long enough to prevent them finding a new opportunity elsewhere.

These are the daily dilemmas faced by leaders the world over. It would be easy for me to say you would be best to choose the honest answer, but I also know that life is never that simple. While it would be tempting to offer solutions and answers to these dilemmas, that probably will not help you enough. These are only three of hundreds of different dilemmas that might arrive at your desk and threaten your trustability.

Instead of trying to find solutions to these dilemmas, focus on developing a robust approach to building and protecting trust, which can be used in any situation. What actually needs to happen if you are facing dilemmas of this sort is quite simple. You have to learn from experience. To learn from experience, you need to:

- recognize the issues and the risks they pose to trust;
- reflect objectively on the dynamics of the situation;
- notice your own position within the situation;
- weigh up your options and make a clear decision.

When you are considering your options, what you are looking for is a way that you can respond that will maximize the trust with all parties, and reduce the risk of losing trust. The section below on 'Maintaining confidentiality' will give you more ideas if you need them.

My guess is that you prefer people to be straight with you, yes? And the adult in you would probably prefer that to be the case even if you don't like what they have to say. You probably also don't expect people to reveal everything they know – total disclosure is usually wanted but rarely expected. What you are looking for is an opportunity to treat people as you would like to be treated.

Understanding your trust orientation

Because your own experience of trust is so pivotal to building trusting relationships, at this stage it is important to try to crystallize your thinking with a few exercises. As you do these, make it more than simple reflection; try to summarize your thinking in your notebook in order to make it more concrete and useful.

Exercise

Trusting others

Start off by brainstorming all of the clues that would indicate that there is trust in a relationship. This means thinking about how the other people are treating you (do they trust you?) and also how you treat them. The sort of behaviours you should be looking out for includes:

- revealing things that make the discloser vulnerable;
- telling people things they know might be upsetting or offensive;
- proactively updating people on progress, even if it's not good.

What can you add to this list apart from telling the truth and doing what they say they are going to do?

Exercise

Distrusting others

Similarly, you need to also consider the sorts of behaviour that could be indicative of distrust. Things like:

- repeatedly asking the same question over a number of days or weeks;
- asking lots of follow-up questions and really driving into the detail;
- never giving straight answers to questions – being evasive.

Again, brainstorm your own ideas and add to the list in your notebook. A key benefit of doing this is so that you can audit your own behaviour against this list.

Your relationships

Understanding how you think about relationships is vital to being able to learn how to build greater trust. It may just be that the problem with trust lies at your door rather than the other people around you.

Start by trying to quantify where you are on the 'trust until proven otherwise' versus 'distrust until they have to' continuum. Be objective and be honest with yourself. Both extremes have merit and usefulness and also negative consequences. Knowing where you are will hand you the potential to step outside of your automatic reactions.

Now make this really relevant to your world as an influential leader by writing down your rationale for trusting several people you know quite well. Who do you trust the most and why? Do the opposite too – who don't you trust and why?

On its own this reflection might identify what you need to do to improve your relationships. However, the sections below will give you more ideas on how to establish and build trust.

Establishing trust

In the last exercise you may have realized that a great deal of this subject is common sense. Day in, day out, you are working with trust: assessing how much you can trust someone, taking action to create trust in your relationships and striving to enhance that trust. Hopefully this chapter will convince you that you are already pretty good at doing this. The challenge becomes one of how to do it more frequently, with greater speed and increased depth.

The ideas that follow will help to stimulate your current activities and give you some ideas that you may not have thought about before. From these you should be able to make trust building more conscious and successful.

Becoming more trustable

It is not all about the other person – there is little point in trusting someone else if they don't trust you. You have to get trust working both ways, quickly, and the starting point is making sure you are behaving in the optimum way to encourage them to trust you.

Earlier, I made the point that living with integrity creates a solid foundation on which others can learn to trust you. This is based on having a clear set of values. So, being trustable begins with you making sure you have well-thought-out values and beliefs that you rely on when making decisions about what you are doing. Doing this consistently will help others to see your reliability.

One of the values you need to foster is that of understanding and accepting people with alternative values. Understanding your own values comes first, but you should not allow your increased clarity to push out the reality that others will differ in their values. Once people know that you are prepared to understand their values, they will be far more likely to trust you (we covered this in some detail in Chapter 6).

To maximize your trustability:

1 Establish (and communicate) a clear set of values and beliefs.

2 Work hard to understand and accept contrary values and beliefs.

3 Adhere closely to your values – be entirely consistent.

And remember, you don't have to be an open book sharing everything – that's unrealistic and actually works against being trustable. However, make sure you handle this sensitively.

When starting a relationship

The previous section on how trust works within relationships should have given you plenty of ideas already about making this a more conscious part of your engagement with new colleagues, so the points below will jog your memory and build your practice:

- Notice how you are being affected by stereotypes, gossip and prejudice when thinking of your new colleague.
- What orientation are you taking to the first meeting? To what extent are you prepared to trust?
- What expectations and attitudes might the other person have of you?
- How can you mitigate against any cautions or suspicions they may have about you?

● Can you make trust a more overt topic without being crass?

● How will you know that you can trust them? How will you know if they trust you?

● If total trust is a score of 10, what score would you give them?

● Okay, go on, what score would they give you?

● How can you improve the scores? Yes, both of them!

Thinking proactively about the topic of trust takes a little time, but with practice it gets quicker.

Guarding against the risks

Trust is a delicate dance between two people and you can do all of the above and still run into problems. In particular, you need to watch out for the following risks that are common in the early stages of a relationship, and do all that you can to avoid becoming ensnared by them:

● *Fact, hearsay and distant memories.* In stakeholder mapping exercises, you need to assess the quality of the relationship, particularly regarding trust. Until challenged, this is often based on feelings rather than fact. They could well be right, but they could also be wrong. Having coached countless people on this area, I know that evidence is often in short supply. Reassessing your trust in another, based on evidence, could easily unlock the relationship.

● *Trusting too soon.* If you place a great deal more trust in someone than they would reasonably expect, they are highly likely to close up and trust you less. This is particularly so if they come from the 'distrust until they have to' end of the spectrum. The bigger the gap, the bigger the discord. Would you trust someone who gushes forth their innermost thoughts within five minutes of meeting you? If you have a tendency to do this – don't! Do whatever you can to hold yourself back.

● *Trusting too late.* If the other person is displaying some trust in you, reciprocate. If you leave it too late, they may rethink their approach and it will be very difficult to overcome this change in their trust in you. If you have a tendency to do this, prepare things you can share early in the relationship that will demonstrate trust without introducing excessive risk for you.

● *Unhelpful bias.* Starting with the expectation that the other side is trustworthy or untrustworthy, whether or not you even know them, is potentially a major problem. People can pick up on what you are really thinking through your body language. Attitudes smell. It becomes a vicious circle. Someone who detects that you distrust them will wonder why. They will perhaps think that you are not to be trusted. So, they'll be more cautious rather than less. That will then 'prove' to you that they cannot be trusted. Simple.

● *Forgetting the context.* Building on the last point, don't forget the context in which someone is working. People become more sensitive and less trusting when their job is at risk. If their assessment of the risk is high, it is unreasonable to expect them to continue being open. Respect this. Work with this.

If all of this sounds like a lot of work, yes, it is. Yet if your relationships are important, it will be time well spent – particularly if these ideas help you to increase the level of trust more quickly.

Deepening trust

Once you've got trust off to a good start, you need to keep working hard to protect it and take it to ever deeper levels, especially with your most important relationships. As they say, '*trust takes a lifetime to build and a moment to lose*'.

Maintaining confidentiality

As an influential leader you will be a party to many secrets, and people will be trusting that you handle their secrets with care. Trouble is, when people find out that you know something that they don't, they may put you under pressure to reveal all those juicy secrets.

In your position, you need to think through your processes of accepting and then protecting other people's trust in you. Don't leave it to your automatic reactions, otherwise you may get caught out.

When accepting sensitive information:

● Clarify what level of confidentiality is being asked for.

● Pressure-test the need for confidentiality – is it necessary?

● Discuss the pros and cons of keeping it quiet versus full or partial disclosure.

- Check who else knows what is being disclosed.
- Work to get clear agreements about what can be shared now and what must be withheld.
- Be prepared to negotiate and even deny the request.
- If appropriate, agree the timeline for sharing information with the team/peers.
- Make sure the team/peers can and will also keep the information confidential, and possibly even the fact that you are in the know.

When possessing sensitive information:

- Develop a clear resistance strategy – a repeatable and consistent statement you can make about the current situation and when it might change.
- Take care not to leave the information lying around.
- Consider referring back to the source if you feel the need to disclose it to someone else.

When others know you know something:

- Be sympathetic about other people's desire to know.
- Spend a moment to consider how you would feel in their position.
- If you can't tell them 'what', at least give them a 'why'.
- Call a team meeting to share this with them – so that everyone hears the same message at the same time.
- Reassure people that you will share more as soon as you are able to.
- Remember that people would rather be in the loop than out of it – even if the news is bad.
- Morale might be affected by bad news, but better to let people come to terms with this sooner rather than later.

Much depends on the nature of the secret and the consequences of disclosure, so these ideas may be more or less appropriate to the situation. However, the principle remains that treating people's confidences well and defending them overtly are the very best examples of demonstrating trustability. Even those who don't get you to reveal what you know will respect you for the care you are taking with confidentiality – and know that they can trust you with their own sensitive information.

Building trust beyond the obvious

On workshops, I often ask the question, 'How can you build greater trust in your relationships?' The response is usually fairly predictable and comes down to doing what you say you're going to do, telling the truth, the whole truth and nothing but the truth -- and several related ideas. Yet, I think you can go beyond this. Here are a few ideas:

- *Say thank you.* If you value the current strength of the relationship and want to build it further, openly recognizing it and thanking the others for playing their part in building a great relationship of trust can only help (provided you are sincere). For example, one director did this at the beginning of a meeting with his CEO. The scheduled 20-minute task-focused agenda was immediately ignored and they had a rich 90-minute debate about how to move forward the key projects he was working on.

- *Demonstrate your trust.* If you signal your trust in others, they are far more likely to reciprocate. And, vocalizing clear criteria for your trust helps people to know what they need to do to gain more trust from you. For instance, 'to be convinced about your commitment, I need to see you doing x' is one way to do this without saying, 'I will only trust you if you do this', which is a little crass. As well as clarity, it also sets the example for appropriate behaviour – they are more likely to reward you with the same high-integrity behaviour.

- *Trust and verify.* Blind faith lacks credibility and begs the question, why are you so trusting? It's okay to trust first, but it is prudent and respected practice to seek verification. This approach sets up open dialogue and does not mean saying you trust someone then sneaking around their back to verify!

- *Manage expectations.* Trust is about reliability or, at best, dependability. Therefore, if you say you're going to do something, and then find you cannot deliver – talk to them, don't leave them guessing.

- *Be frank with sensitivity.* Don't fudge the feedback. If you think something negative about another and it is in all of your interests that they improve, say it as it is, but with care. You don't have to be rude or insensitive, but being direct will be valued, even if in the short term it makes people uncomfortable.

- *Make serious commitments.* Rather than make promises on the fly, demonstrate that you are thinking seriously about making a commitment to someone. Show your workings and let them see how serious you are about keeping your promises. If something goes wrong later, managing expectations will also be easier if they know the challenges you are facing.

- *Tackle breaches.* If someone lets you down, don't just pass it off, tackle it head-on with sensitivity. Leaving it to fester will hurt in the long run. Explain what you expected, what you seemed to get, and hear their side too. Then agree future conduct for a great relationship.

- *Demonstrate understanding.* If you can show how well you understand the other person, they are far more likely to think you care and, also, far more likely to place their trust in you. Acknowledge the inherent downsides for the other party from your proposals: ignoring it and hoping it goes away is not a high-trust approach. Unless they are convinced you understand, they will proceed with caution.

- *Respect reservations.* There is a time and a place for every disclosure and, unless the other person is personally ready, it is unwise to force it. Doing so will make the other party feel uncomfortable because it demonstrates (potentially) lack of care and interest in their welfare. Be realistic about what others can and should trust you with. Everyone has different levels of tolerance, and just because you would feel comfortable sharing doesn't mean someone else will.

- *Be prudently open.* Be as open as you can be. It is often wise to withhold, but this needs to be kept to a minimum. When you do withhold, taking the opportunity to explain why also helps. Avoid waiting for the other person to ask the right question and, in so doing, avoid the later accusation, 'You could have told me that!' And this includes being open about your own vulnerabilities and worries. Everyone has them, and if you don't share yours (carefully), people may wonder what else you're holding back.

- *Segment trust.* You can trust someone with *this* but not *that* – and that's okay. Being clear in your own mind helps unlock relationships and allows them to work more effectively. The statement, 'I don't trust Peter' is not only unhelpful, but it is also a sweeping generalization. Distrusting someone in one area shouldn't mean you distrust them completely.

- *Be realistic.* Everyone has their limits and boundaries. Someone may be entirely predictable in most circumstances; but, at the extreme, they will probably look after number one. Under threat of dismissal, people talk.

Some of these ideas are more difficult than others, and most of them require practice and careful execution. Yet, if you invest in these behaviours, over the long term you will accumulate an enviable reputation and maximize the value of your relationships.

Getting things done

Important points to remember as you begin to make more progress:

- Building trust should never be left to chance, it is far too important for that.

- Trust begins before you meet, and builds or declines before you even speak.

- Diagnosing the basis of trust in a relationship helps to identify ways to enhance trust.

- Demonstrating trust in others is a critical step in gaining their trust.

- You cannot tell everyone everything and no one expects you to, even if they want you to.

- There are plenty of opportunities for the influential leader to inadvertently damage trust.

Further reading

When you get a chance, make sure you check the further reading and resources for this chapter online at: **www.learntoinfluence.com/leadership**

Yes, there is lots to do when building trust, which makes it all the more important that you are paying heed to the lessons in the last chapter, on networking. With the basics of building trust firmly established, I'd like to now turn to how your personality and behaviour may be distracting people.

Understanding influencing styles

11

> '*It ain't what you do, it's the way that you do it, and that's what gets results.*'
>
> **BANANARAMA**

My memory for popular music is somewhat limited, yet whenever I get to the subject of influencing styles, this song reverberates around my head. Relationships are extremely important to influential leaders and they can be dramatically improved, or spectacularly destroyed, by the 'way' the leader deploys their skills. At times I am sure that the manner in which you use your skills will create more influence than the content alone. As an influential leader, you need to be capable of adapting your behaviour to remove the distraction that may interfere with your communication.

This chapter contributes to the following influential leader capability:

Has learnt how personality affects engagement and is tolerant of diversity.

The primary purpose of this chapter is to introduce the framework of influencing styles, get you intimately involved with understanding them and provide a foundation for the next chapter, which will help you to learn how to maximize your flexibility.

Why behavioural style matters

The behaviour you use when you deploy your skills matters a great deal, especially to the person who you are focusing on. The underlying skill can remain the same, yet the effect can be dramatically different. Imagine for a moment that Raj and Susan have both developed the skill of problem solving. When Raj is asking questions as part of his process of enquiry, he comes across as an interrogator – often brutal in his pursuit of the facts. Susan achieves the same outcome in a gentle and encouraging manner. She helps people to open up and share everything they know.

How would you react to each of these people when they come to ask their questions? Well, that will depend on how you prefer to behave, your own behavioural style. You may react badly to Susan, thinking her to be too soft and timid: 'Why doesn't she just get straight to the point?' Alternatively, you may be the sort of character who detests disrespectful behaviour and find Raj to be arrogant and rude: 'It doesn't cost anything to show some manners and courtesy.'

This illustrates the complexity of human behaviour, the distraction that behaviour can create and, also, the importance of this topic within influential leadership. If your style differs from the style of the individual you are attempting to influence, it is likely that their internal dialogue will be distracting them from what you are actually saying. It will also shape their response to your request and set up their motivational bias. Go about it the wrong way and they may be thinking, 'Over my dead body!'

The ideas within this chapter are likely to be especially important if you have ever been told by a mentor, manager or friend that you:

- 'are too nice';
- 'need to be less flippant';
- 'should develop more gravitas';
- 'wear your heart on your sleeve';
- 'need to open up a bit more';
- 'are too rude';
- 'should be doing more networking';
- 'need to go easy on people';
- 'get far too emotional about things'.

It will also be really useful if any of the following apply to you:

- you struggle to make a personal connection with an important stakeholder;
- in some of your important relationships there are big personality clashes;
- there is no identifiable reason why your stakeholder should be resisting;
- people don't seem to understand 'you';
- you find it difficult to get to know others;
- you wish to be a phenomenally successful influential leader.

As a skilled and successful leader you have to know how people are responding to your behaviour. You need to be able to predict likely reactions and, also, you need to be able to adapt your behaviour to suit your purpose. This is why I have included *style* as a key element of the influential leader framework.

Introduction to influencing styles

Back in 2004 when Mike Phipps and I were first getting immersed in the subject of influence and how to help people to become more influential, we wanted to focus people on the behaviours people use when influencing. To do this, we searched for a psychometric that would do this in a simple and practical way – adding a little science to their development without going over the top on theory. We needed something that was accurate and accessible to busy people without a degree in psychology. After drawing a blank in our search, we created our first psychometric instrument, with a little help from a chartered psychologist and lots of willing guinea pigs.

Since then it has evolved while being used live in the training room and during coaching sessions. It has demonstrated time and again that it sheds light on relationship challenges and provides people with simple things they can do to become more influential. It doesn't take a great deal of effort to gain successes with this model.

The tool we developed is publicly available and you can find out more about it at: **www.gautreygroup.com/ipp**

CASE STUDY

Here is just one example of how understanding influencing styles made a difference:

> Javier, a financial manager loves his sport. Whenever he starts a meeting he enjoys sharing his reaction to the latest match. He thinks it helps to warm things up and relax people before the business starts. To be honest, he also really enjoys talking to people. He knew that one of his stakeholders liked sport, but whenever a meeting started, he was unwilling to talk about it. When Javier mentioned the previous week's game he simply scowled at him and looked at his Blackberry. What Javier learned through coaching on influencing styles was that with this particular individual he needed to get straight down to business and talk about the match afterwards. He did this and the effect was instant.

Understanding influencing styles is not complicated, it is actually very straightforward. To make it easy to use you have to learn the model of behaviour that sits behind it. Once you have learned that and practised it you will be able to quickly assess a stakeholder, decide what style and approach will be most likely to work, and then just do it. While I cannot guarantee that you will achieve the influence you want, it will at the very least make sure that the relationship is optimized and any failure will be down to it being a rubbish idea that you wanted them to support.

Our original research has evolved over the last 10 years and the framework now divides influencing behaviours into four broad categories or dimensions: *determination*; *tact and diplomacy*; *sociability and networking*; and *emotional control*. During your lifetime you have developed a mix of these behaviours based on what works best for you. For each of these dimensions you will have arrived at a comfortable level that you will tend to use in most situations automatically. Everyone does this quite naturally and unconsciously, yet there are often substantial differences in style. What works for you may not work for someone else.

Here is what you can expect of those who favour each of these dimensions of influential behaviour:

- Favouring *sociability and networking*: using social skills to build a wide and strong network of valuable contacts.
- Favouring *determination*: expressing clear views, opinions and goals while driving them towards realization.
- Favouring *tact and diplomacy*: sensing feelings, concerns and agendas of other people and responding in a sensitive way.
- Favouring *emotional control*: remaining calm and focused on the facts and the process.

It also needs to be recognized that to some extent people may have learned to avoid each of these dimensions:

- Avoiding *sociability and networking*: focusing on the task in hand and avoiding social distraction.
- Avoiding *determination*: taking time to consult, accommodate and reach a harmonious solution, direction or view.
- Avoiding *tact and diplomacy*: being direct and clear with others so they know where they stand, even if this risks upsetting them.
- Avoiding *emotional control*: expressing genuine emotions openly as they happen.

The fascinating part comes when you start to pull all of these together in real life. Each day as you go about your work you are *behaving* all the time. In any situation you will draw unconsciously from these dimensions of behaviour. The actions that get triggered depend on many factors and it is only through awareness that you can begin to take conscious control of your behaviour selection. Before going into the more detailed behaviours that these dimensions cover, I'd like to take you through the key concepts that lie behind this model.

Influencing styles: key concepts

1 *You have a preferred way of influencing others based on your personality and life's experiences.*
As you live your life, you are learning and adapting all of the time. If something works for you, you will tend to repeat it. Providing it keeps working, the behaviour becomes easier to perform and more

likely to be called upon automatically when you need it most. Other behaviours will tend to get pushed out as your favoured approach continues to bring the results you want.

For instance, what was your childhood tactic to get more sweets? There are many choices, including stamping your feet and demanding 'More, now!', smiling sweetly and saying 'Pleeeeeeeasssse, pretty please Mummy', and snatching them out of the hands of your little brother. The one that worked best for you will have been repeated, strengthened and rendered automatic.

These preferences becomes very strong – it is your way of engaging with the world. It becomes automatic and requires little or no thought to perform. And, when it stops working, you will keep using it even harder until you finally realize it is time to change.

Try this little exercise. Read the instructions then carry out the simple steps as quickly as you can:

- Put down your book, pen etc.
- Quickly fold your arms.
- Now just as quickly, fold them the other way round.
- Relax and pick up the book again!

Most people who do this exercise struggle the second time around. The first arm folding was your default or automatic way: the second demonstrates your level of flexibility or skill. You probably found the second arm folding more difficult, or even impossible. Over time your muscles have become accustomed to working in a certain way, and because there is little need to fold your arms the other way, you haven't had much practice. Some people on my workshops confidently fold their arms the other way without realizing that all they have done is to cycle their arms right round to the original position again.

Although this is a simple physical example, it demonstrates exactly what I mean about how embedded and automatic behaviour can become. Your brain becomes conditioned just like your muscles do. Unless you consciously focus on adapting your behaviour, you are likely to do it your preferred way. When the pressure comes on, people revert to type – and there is no shortage of pressure at work today.

As you will discover later, the different behaviours are not necessarily difficult to adopt once you have presence of mind to do so.

2 *People prefer to be influenced in the way they prefer to influence others.*
Most humans are programmed to think that the world should be just like them. Despite sound evidence-based logic of the benefits of diversity, and the accompanying political correctness, most people feel more comfortable associating with people who are similar to them.

Part of the reason why you may do this is that you can take much more for granted. Having attitudes and dispositions in common with others means you don't have to do so much processing; you can get straight to the heart of the problem in hand. Spending time trying to work out where someone else is coming from will slow you down, confuse you and casts a shadow of doubt about your course of action.

This applies to many aspects of your life, and the implication for influence is that you are more likely to be able to influence an individual if you adopt their way of doing things. In the sales world this is often referred to as building rapport; however, this oversimplifies what is needed to become truly effective.

3 *Any difference in behaviour between two people is likely to create a distraction from the content of their communication.*
As I described above, if someone comes to influence you with an approach contrary to your preferred way of doing things, you are likely to be distracted. This is natural as you try to figure out how to read them, what their motives might be. Unfortunately, this all needs to be processed at the same time as listening and thinking about what the person is actually saying.

4 *Adapting your behaviour to match the person you wish to influence is likely to reduce distraction and increase success.*

5 *In certain situations, it is easy to transform your behaviour.*
Fight-or-flight responses free your physical capabilities from their usual constraints in an instant. In a similar way, your thought processes and behaviours can also change instantly when triggered by unusual or extreme events.

For instance, a normally placid individual can be pushed too far and become angry and aggressive. Very confident people can quickly become timid and retiring when exposed to an unfamiliar senior-level audience. This type of change is easy, although may be a little unpredictable. It takes little effort or thought to behave in a radically different way.

6 *In most situations, it takes conscious effort to adapt behaviour.* Generally your behaviour is automatic and corresponds to your preferred way of doing things. Auto-pilot mode switches on as you concentrate on the deadlines, meetings and tasks you have to accomplish. In fact, the more pressure you are under, the more likely you are to behave automatically.

7 *No style is inherently good or bad. It is more a question of which will create the optimum effect in a given situation with a certain person.* I cannot stress just how important this point is. All of these dimensions can bring great benefits and also significant drawbacks, as you will see later. This is true whether you are favouring or avoiding the behaviours in a given dimension.

CASE STUDY

Here is a quick example of behaviour style and its effect:

Belinda prefers to avoid the *sociability* and *networking* behaviours. This really helps her in her rather technical work because she has to concentrate for hours on end evaluating data and producing reports that she has to present at board meetings. However, her avoidance of sociability and networking behaviours means that she finds it very difficult to acquire anecdotal or qualitative information from different parts of the business. These critical insights cannot be gained by a questionnaire but only through talking to the salespeople. Her reluctance to get out there and meet people also means she is not really known around the business and has meant she has recently been rejected for a new role.

'The only right style is the one that worked best.'

In order to maximize the potential of influencing styles as part of your approach to leadership, the simple process that drops out of the concepts above is:

● develop a clear understanding of the behaviours that contribute to each dimension;

- assess yourself between favouring and avoiding on each dimension so that you are clear where your preferences lie;
- determine where a stakeholder you wish to influence would be on each dimension;
- analyse the gaps between you and your stakeholder;
- make clear decisions about how you will adapt to remove or lessen the potential distraction your behaviour causes.

This chapter, and the next one, will help you to move through this process.

The dimension behaviours

It is important to understand the detailed behaviours that make up these dimensions because it will help you to understand yourself and others more clearly. Additionally, it will enable you to select behaviours that you can use to adapt your style.

As I take you through each of the dimensions I will concentrate on the extremes for the sake of illustration, although it is actually quite rare for someone to score at the extreme end of any of these dimensions. Each section will follow broadly the same outline:

- consideration of the behaviours and attributes of people who favour and avoid the dimension;
- understanding of the benefits and drawback of each extreme position;
- consideration of the impact these create in the minds of others (the distraction).

Sociability and networking

The two extreme positions on this dimension are: 1) *favouring* sociability and networking: using social skills to build a wide and strong network of valuable contacts, and 2) *avoiding* sociability and networking: focusing on the task in hand and avoiding social distraction.

TABLE 11.1   Preference indicators for *sociability and networking*

Favouring sociability and networking	Avoiding sociability and networking
• Comfortable at informal meetings and gatherings.	• Develops deep relationships over a long period of time.
• Knows exactly what is going on in the organization.	• Careful observer of people.
• Always looking to meet new people.	• Great at listening.
• Likes being the centre of attention.	• Able to concentrate for long periods without getting distracted.
• Has many superficial and short-term relationships.	• Detail-conscious and meticulous.
• Has lots of interesting things to say.	• Finds it hard to share personal information.
• Finds it difficult to stop talking.	• Displays closed body language, folded arms, buttoned jackets.
• Not so good at listening.	• Does very little talking.
• Is never at their desk.	• Gives short answers to open questions.
• Shares lots of smiles, laughter and hugs.	• Avoids eye contact.

This dimension is all about the extent to which people like to be with people. Those who like to use these behaviours love being around others and learning all about them. Table 11.1 shows some indicators commonly associated with people at the extremes of this dimension.

Pause for a moment and try to add to the lists shown in Table 11.1. When doing this, it helps if you can think of someone who you believe epitomizes favouring or avoiding sociability and networking.

So, if this is how people are behaving, what are the implications of these behaviours? During workshops I ask people to indicate where they think they are on the dimension. Then, working the extremes, I want to know from them the answers to a few questions that help to build their understanding of the implications.

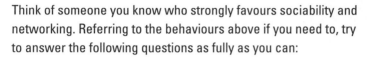

Exercise

Think of someone you know who strongly favours sociability and networking. Referring to the behaviours above if you need to, try to answer the following questions as fully as you can:

1 What benefits do they gain using these behaviours?

2 What drawbacks might they experience?

3 In what situations does it really help their work?

4 When does it really hinder their work?

Take your time thinking the answers through. If you are not someone who favours sociability and networking and you are finding it difficult to answer these questions, I strongly recommend that you share this exercise with someone who does strongly favour this dimension.

Next I'd like you to think about someone at the opposite extreme – avoiding sociability and networking. Pause and answer the same four questions for this alternative perspective.

Here are a couple of examples, collected during workshops, of when people find the two extremes of sociability and networking useful:

Favouring sociability and networking is really useful when:

- informal team building is needed to help foster stronger relationships;

- it is difficult getting all the information you need to make a decision;

- people need to be fully bought in to what you are doing.

Avoiding sociability and networking is really useful:

- when there is complicated work or analysis to be done;

- where enough facts are known and a strategy is needed;

- in crisis situations where decisions need to be made;

- when you need others to feel the gravity of the situation.

Having spent some time doing this carefully, I now want to challenge you in a different way. One of the elements that is essential to fully utilize influencing styles is building understanding and tolerance for people with different styles from your own. It also helps if you understand what others may be thinking about you too.

In workshops I like to ask people to share their real feelings and thoughts about people at opposite ends of the dimension. Below is a list of typical responses. My challenge to you is, if you were strongly *favouring* or *avoiding* sociability and networking, what comments would you add to the lists shown in Table 11.2?

The serious point to notice is that these are all genuine responses – typical internal dialogue working to distract people from the content of the communication they are receiving from other people who are different from them.

TABLE 11.2   Reactions to *sociability and networking* preferences

People who *favour* sociability and networking express these thoughts about people who are *avoiding*:	<ul><li>Very difficult to get to know.</li><li>Hard work – sometimes it's like pulling teeth.</li><li>They need to lighten up and have a bit of fun!</li><li>Boring and miserable.</li><li>They're the sort of people we give the work to because we know they will get it done.</li><li>I wish I could concentrate like them. I'd get a lot more done.</li><li>It doesn't cost anything to be friendly, does it?</li><li>Why don't they pick up the phone or come see me rather that send e-mails or whatever?</li><li>Rather disconnected with what is really going on – good job they like being in the dark!</li></ul>

TABLE 11.2 *continued*

People who *avoid* sociability and networking express these thoughts about people who are *favouring*:	<ul><li>Self-obsessed and talking all the time, usually about themselves!</li><li>I never get a chance to speak.</li><li>They seem to get all the attention – whatever happened to doing a good job?</li><li>When do they actually do any work?</li><li>To be honest, I wish I was more like them, I'm sure I'm missing opportunities.</li><li>Why do they need to have meetings all the time? Especially meetings before meetings!</li><li>They seem to know everyone.</li><li>Luckily for them, they have us backing them up and doing all the work.</li><li>Can I get back to work now please?</li></ul>

CASE STUDY

Chuck had asked me to run a workshop on influence for his team of operations managers. He wanted them to become more influential through their respective parts of their global organization. As usual when exploring the impact of influencing styles, we started off with *sociability and networking*. After presenting the relevant behaviours to the team (about 10 people as I recall) I asked them to position themselves along a wall that represented the dimension. Chuck went right down to the far left in the extreme *avoiding* position, while one of his team members, Dan, went to the opposite corner signifying how strongly he favoured *sociability and networking*.

It was quite a moment as they looked at each other across the wide expanse of floor tiles between their respective positions. Without saying a word, they both smiled and quietly nodded to each other. I later found out that in that moment they had both realized exactly what they were struggling with in their relationship. Chuck had been preparing to fire Dan because of their 'personality clash'. What this exercise did in an instant was demonstrate what was wrong and why they didn't really have a problem, they just preferred different styles. They were able to quickly build their relationship; Chuck avoided an expensive exit and rehire and Dan didn't have to look for a new opportunity.

As you work through the remaining dimensions, please make sure you spend plenty of time thinking of your own answers to the questions. You will notice that the questions are broadly the same for each dimension because these are the things that I have found to be most useful in helping people to make practical use of the concept of influencing styles.

Determination

The two extreme positions on this dimension are: 1) *favouring* determination: expressing clear views, opinions and goals while driving them towards realization, and 2) *avoiding* determination: taking time to consult, accommodate and reach a harmonious solution, direction or view.

At its heart, this is all about the amount of drive and energy an individual likes to put into the pursuit of their own agendas. It doesn't mean that those who are avoiding these behaviours do not have an agenda – they are simply more likely to let others have their say first (see Table 11.3).

Exercise

Consider the benefits and drawbacks of both favouring and avoiding determination. Make sure you answer the questions for people at both ends of the dimension:

1　What benefits do they gain using these behaviours?
2　What drawbacks might they experience?
3　In what situations does it really help their work?
4　When does it really hinder their work?

Take your time, there is no rush. The longer you spend reflecting on these questions the more you will gain.

TABLE 11.3 Preference indicators for *determination*

Favouring determination	*Avoiding* determination
• Drives their views/agenda as a priority.	• Relaxed and easy-going.
• Intense, direct eye contact.	• Responsive and flexible towards others.
• Always stretching others' performance.	• Seeks to compromise rather than compete.
• Focused on results, ratios, KPIs and plans.	• Easily influenced by those of greater status.
• 'Here's what I need you to do, now.'	• Good at 'fitting in' and working within the hierarchy.
• Walking fast, walking with purpose.	• Easily sees other's points of view.
• Unwilling to listen to dissenting voices.	• Quiet, hesitant voice.
• Very articulate and clear about their goals.	• Uses words like 'maybe', 'perhaps'.
• Demanding, asking for more and more.	• Uses phrases like 'would you have any objection if...?'
• Turning assertively demanding to know what is wrong and why.	• Not saying anything.

Here are a few examples of situations where favouring and avoiding are especially useful:

Favouring determination is useful when:

- the pressure is on and time is short;
- breaking through a deadlock;
- the answer is pretty clear and implementation is critical.

Avoiding determination is useful when:

- it is unclear what the right answer is;
- consultation is essential to a quality outcome;
- helping others to figure out their own answers.

Can you add to these lists?

Now for the interesting part: Table 11.4 shows what people who *favour* often think of those who *avoid* determination and vice versa.

TABLE 11.4   Reactions to *determination* preferences

People who *favour* determination express these thoughts about people who are *avoiding*:	<ul><li>Waste of space, irrelevant.</li><li>Lacking in substance and weak.</li><li>Certainly very relaxed and calm.</li><li>Indecisive and overly cautious.</li><li>I wish they would speak their minds.</li><li>They probably have something useful to contribute but I've yet to hear it.</li><li>Behind every great leader...</li><li>When they do speak you need to listen.</li></ul>*Can you think of any more?*
People who *avoid* determination express these thoughts about people who are *favouring*:	<ul><li>Arrogant – overly confident in their own abilities.</li><li>Intimidating and don't like to be challenged.</li><li>Not very good at engaging us.</li><li>They think they have the right answer and are just driving for the goal.</li><li>Make decisions too quickly without considering all the risks.</li><li>I generally try to keep out of their way.</li><li>They certainly seem to achieve a lot.</li><li>Bit of a bully – their way or the highway.</li><li>Okay, they achieve a lot but is it the right thing to achieve?</li></ul>*What would you add to this list?*

You will notice that the responses listed in Table 11.4 are mainly critical. That's just how it seems to happen in the training room. I think it is probably symptomatic of the preferred behaviours of those who are highly driven and determined. If they are talking about you, listen to what they are saying, they may have a point you need to take serious notice of.

Before I leave *determination*, you may well be thinking that you have to be highly determined in order to get to a senior position in any organization. You may recall that my focus here is how people 'prefer' to behave rather than how they 'actually' behave. I agree that senior people need to behave with determination, but that does not necessarily mean that they prefer to be that way – often they have just learned to be like that when it is needed. My research indicates that preferred *determination* levels do not correlate with seniority, whereas behaviour does. This principle is at work in each dimension. I'll talk more about this in the next chapter.

Tact and diplomacy

The two extreme positions on this dimension are: 1) *favouring* tact and diplomacy: sensing feelings, concerns and agendas of other people and responding in a sensitive way, and 2) *avoiding* tact and diplomacy: being direct and clear with others so they know where they stand, even if this risks upsetting them (see Table 11.5).

TABLE 11.5   Preference indicators for *tact and diplomacy*

Favouring tact and diplomacy	*Avoiding* tact and diplomacy
• Prefers indirect communication.	• Quickly cuts through the sensitivities.
• Slow at making decisions.	• Direct and blunt in style.
• Always checking their understanding.	• Often speaks without thinking.
• Promoting harmony and defusing conflict.	• Outwardly tough characters.
• Respectful of the views of others.	• Not easily swayed by emotional appeals.
• Reputation for being a good listener.	• Likely to 'call it as they see it'.
• Asking lots of probing questions.	• Talks over people – finishes their sentences for them.
• Dancing around the issues.	• Very straightforward approach.
• Concerned about how people may react.	• Being surprised when others get upset.
• Afraid to speak their mind.	• Disregarding others' concerns.

The essence of this dimension is the degree to which people are able to naturally tune in to the thoughts and feelings of others. It does not necessarily mean that they care about people, but they are sensitive to what is going on in the hearts and minds of people.

Exercise

As with the other dimensions, consider how someone at each extreme would see the benefits and drawbacks of their behaviour:

1   What benefits do they gain using these behaviours?
2   What drawbacks might they experience?
3   In what situations does it really help their work?
4   When does it really hinder their work?

Remember to answer each question for someone who is *favouring* and also someone who is *avoiding*. Again, it really helps if you have got someone in mind as you are doing this.

Here are some examples.

Favouring tact and diplomacy is cited as useful:

● when there are sensitive people issues in hand;
● when there are no right answers and consensus is important;
● in situations where the individual needs to arrive at their own answer.

Avoiding tact and diplomacy is cited as useful:

● when time is of the essence and buy-in is less important;
● when emotions are getting in the way of clear decisions;
● in a crisis when the task has to be delivered.

Having said the above, in my view there are no excuses for being rude and discourteous to others who you are working with. Sometimes straight and direct dealing is necessary and, if you are careful, that can be done without damaging the relationship. The important thing is that if you prefer lower levels of tact and diplomacy you need to be able to modify your behaviour suitably and, also, be able to minimize the damage or risks when you elect to drive through regardless.

And at the other end, you need to recognize that you cannot always take your time trying to find out everything that everyone is thinking and feeling. Apart from taking a long time, it also alienates others around you who would prefer to crack on and get the job done.

Differences on this dimension can be especially distracting to people, causing frustration on both sides. Table 11.6 shows some common sentiments expressed in workshops.

TABLE 11.6   Reactions to *tact and diplomacy* preferences

People who *favour* tact and diplomacy express these thoughts about people who are *avoiding*:	• Why do they have to be so rude? • They really need to think before they speak. • I try to avoid people like that. • That's no way to treat people. • At least I know where I stand with them, but it hurts. • Bit of a bully. • They can be quite intimidating. *What else can you add?*
People who *avoid* tact and diplomacy express these thoughts about people who are *favouring*:	• I wish they'd hurry up. • Stop dancing around the issues and speak plainly. • Excessively worried about what people think of them. • They need to toughen up. • It's really hard working out where they are coming from. • They need to learn how to use tough love. *Feel free to extend this list.*

CASE STUDY

When running a seminar on influencing styles some years ago, one of the coaches approached me afterwards to thank me for the help it had given her. She explained that when we were working on the *tact and diplomacy* dimension it suddenly dawned on her that one of her clients was avoiding those behaviours – being very direct, brisk and businesslike. It is not unusual for coaches to be pretty high on the *favouring* side of this one – and she was. What she now realized was that her coaching client needed a little more directness from her, and that it was okay to do that, because that's how he was. She still faced the difficulty of overcoming her own dislike of behaving like that, but she had now realized the key to unlocking the current strained relationship – she was going to be quite a bit more assertive in her views at their next session.

Emotional control

The two extreme positions on this dimension are: 1) *favouring* emotional control: remaining calm and focused on facts and process, and 2) *avoiding* emotional control: expressing genuine emotions openly as they happen (see Table 11.7).

It is important to realize that this dimension is focusing on the degree to which people prefer to share what they are feeling. Everyone has feelings but intensity varies as does their willingness to share their innermost emotions.

So, how do people at either end gain and lose from their preferred behaviour?

TABLE 11.7   Preference indicators for *emotional control*

Favouring emotional control	*Avoiding* emotional control
• Appears calm and in control of their emotions.	• Easily provoked into emotional reactions.
• Difficult to read or second-guess.	• Factors emotions into their decisions.
• Not easily provoked into emotional reactions.	• Lively and exciting characters.
• Uses logical influence.	• Connects with people at an emotional level.
• Expressionless, dead-pan.	• Overreacting to what people are saying.
• Possessing gravitas and maturity.	• Voice rising and falling quite quickly.
• Limited movements of the body – stiff and robotic.	• Very enthusiastic and passionate.
• Even or monotonous voice.	• Appears about to burst into tears.
• Manages complex situations.	• Talking too fast.
• Lack of emotive words.	• Using emotive words like passionate, enjoy, fun or depressing.

Exercise

Here are the questions again to help you think it through:

1 What benefits do they gain using these behaviours?

2 What drawbacks might they experience?

3 In what situations does it really help their work?

4 When does it really hinder their work?

Again, make sure you pause for a moment to consider when strong *favouring* emotional control is most useful and, also, when it can really hinder a relationship or situation. Similarly, those live wires who are very spontaneous and emotional (preferring to avoid emotional control): how does this really help and hinder different types of work?

Here are some examples.

Favouring emotional control is useful when:

- there is a crisis that needs to be handled carefully;
- negotiating important agreements;
- investigating something without revealing what you are thinking.

Avoiding emotional control (displaying lots of emotion) is really useful when:

- projects need to pick up energy and enthusiasm;
- it is important that others know how you feel;
- gaining emotional buy-in and commitment.

Table 11.8 shows some common sentiments expressed in workshops.

TABLE 11.8   Reactions to *emotional control* preferences

People who *favour* emotional control express these thoughts about people who are *avoiding*:	• They need to calm down. • It's okay when they are in a good mood, well, some of the time. • They are very easy to bait. • It's great being able to see their agenda all the time. • They are very volatile and unpredictable. *What would you add?*
People who *avoid* emotional control express these thoughts about people who are *favouring*:	• Are they alive in there? • Not sure what they are thinking – can I trust them? • They don't seem to care. • I wish I could be more like them. • They don't seem very interested in what we are doing – do they even care? *Can you think of anything else?*

CASE STUDY

Michael is a naturally bouncy kind of guy. He likes to roll in in the morning and let everyone know what's been happening in his life since yesterday. All the little dramas play out and secretly everyone is hoping that on balance he is in a good mood. Secretly they joke about him being like the girl with the curl in the nursery rhyme: 'when she was good she was very very good, but when she was not, she was horrid'. Unfortunately his boss is completely the opposite and they simply don't get on. In fact, Michael had been told that unless he learns to control his outbursts he will never make it to a higher grade. In fact, his boss has even side-lined him on certain jobs, especially negotiations with suppliers, because there was no way Michael can hide what he is really thinking.

There are some quite severe distractions that can creep in on this dimension because these two extremes simply do not understand each other. A natural influencing strategy for someone who prefers to be fairly low on emotional control will be to pack in as much emotional communication as possible so they can appeal to the other person's heart. Mr Cool will wonder what on earth they are waving their arms about for: can't they just calm down? Their typical reaction will be to close down even more. Trouble is, those who trade on their emotions are searching for a reaction, good or bad: they need to feel and see what their approach is doing to the emotional world of the other. But non-verbal communication is reducing so they are likely to jump even higher. And so the two naturally and quickly move further apart and, unless someone intervenes, they are likely to completely fail to communicate.

Another aspect of note is what is happening on the trust side of the relationship here. Humans are programmed to seek information on many different channels: words, gestures, eyes, etc. Psychologists concur that for someone to believe another, they need to see congruency between their words and all the body language cues available. Mr Cool at the extreme may be utilizing only 7 per cent of his communication potential as he closes down the body language even more, so it is difficult if not impossible to gain assurance that what he says is true.

To balance that, because he is so predictable, that can be a source of trust, which is the last thing that can be said of the person waving their arms at the other end. They are demonstrating lack of predictability because they are so volatile, but at least you can see and hear what is actually going on.

Getting things done

Important points to remember as you begin to make more progress:

- Styles evolve naturally as people experience the results of their behaviours: what works for them will get repeated and become automatic.

- Removing the distraction that different styles creates will clear the way for influential communication.

- Clear understanding of the different styles is important preparation for making adaptation easy.

- Distraction does not occur if the other person understands and accepts the difference.

- The only correct style to use is the one that works.

Further reading

When you get a chance, make sure you check the further reading and resources for this chapter online at: **www.learntoinfluence.com/leadership**

Hopefully you've been diligent in thinking around the ideas and points made in this chapter. It is vitally important to translate these into the world around you. In the next chapter I will take you deeper into the application and help you learn how to develop your style flexibility and apply it appropriately with the people you need to influence.

Understanding and adapting your style

12

> *Influential leaders need to be able to tune in to styles and adapt quickly when the need arises.*

As a human being with personality you are a unique mix of the four dimensions of influencing style described in the last chapter. To make practical use of this, you need to gain a clear understanding of your own preferences and those of the people you wish to influence. Thus, as an influential leader, you can begin to flex your behaviour to suit the influencing situation far more effectively.

This chapter contributes to the following influential leader capabilities:

Can instantly adapt their behaviour to suit the individual they are seeking to influence.

Analysing your style

During the last chapter I am sure that you would have begun to get a sense of where you prefer to be on each of the dimensions. Now it is time to clarify this ahead of deciding what implications your style has for you and the way you interact with others.

To keep this as simple as possible, I will tell you how our online tool works. You are welcome to complete this online assessment and find out exactly how others may be perceiving you. However, it is not critical to being able to make use of influencing styles in order to become more successful in your communication.

When doing the questionnaire, you will be presented with pairs of statements that are drawn from different dimensions. You are asked to select the one that you prefer in each pair. When you make a selection it will add to your score for the dimension from which the statement came. Because of the way the statements are worded, each selection you make indicates that you are favouring that dimension when compared to the other statement.

At some point during the questionnaire, most people find some of the comparisons difficult. Sometimes they want to select both statements and, at other times, neither. This is because we are seeking to establish preference and mimic the subconscious trade-offs that are made in real life when selecting the behaviour to use in any situation. The main point is that we are hoping people will follow the instructions and go with their gut feel.

Some people resolve the tension between the statements by indicating the behaviour they would normally use rather than the one they prefer. Others are more aspirational and answer based on what they would like to be able to do. This is okay providing it is taken into account when looking at the results: learning is still possible. Unfortunately, some also try to select the one they think we are looking for, which denies them the opportunity to develop their self-awareness and influence.

There are 30 pairs of statements and at the end you will have a score for each of the four dimensions. This score can be anywhere between 0 and 15 for each dimension, contributing to a total or maximum score of 30. The combination of these four scores gives an indication of how you may come across to others if you behave according to your preference. For instance, someone might score:

- sociability and networking: 12
- determination: 5
- tact and diplomacy: 9
- emotional control: 4

In this case, it would suggest someone who is pretty lively, who loves meeting new people and quite often wears their heart on their sleeve. They are not too pushy and have a good level of understanding about how other people are responding to what is going on around them. The online report goes into more detail, but this is the gist.

Exercise

Consider how you might score if you did the questionnaire. Refer back to the previous chapter and the behaviours related to each dimension. Try to gauge your position between the two extremes of *avoiding* and *favouring*. If you find yourself recognizing all of the behaviours related to favouring the dimension and none of the avoiding, you are likely to be heading towards a score of 15. If you like, you are welcome to complete the online assessment, which will give you a highly accurate assessment and also a short report. You can find out more about it at: **www.gautreygroup.com/ipp**

Normally people feel good about getting a high score but, as I stressed in the last chapter, strongly favouring a dimension can also have some drawbacks. Similarly, a very low score is not necessarily a bad thing; just that you prefer to avoid that type of behaviour. It is not so much where you score that counts, but what style will be most effective and how easy it is for you to adapt to that style.

The more extreme you are, the more ingrained your behaviour is likely to be. Or, the less likely you are to be able to adapt your behaviour. It is very rare that I meet anyone who is right on the extremes, but anyone close to them is going to have a hard time adapting their behaviour. People who score low on emotional control (*avoiding*) seem to have lived many career years with the development need to be less emotional, more controlled. They just cannot help but show what they are thinking on their face – you can read them like a book.

The consequence of this ingrained behaviour is that when they meet someone at the other end of the dimension, the distraction risk is high and they are unlikely to be able to do much about it. People who score in the middle territory are far more flexible in being able to move up and down the behaviour spectrum and are thus more able to adapt to a wider range of different styles.

Ultimately, with sufficient experience and time, I'm convinced that individual preferences gravitate towards the middle ground. The more self-development you do, the more experience you have with people who are different, the more comfortable you will be using a wide range of different behaviours. Sure, this isn't always the case and some people are destined to remain grumpy and cantankerous.

Role suitability

As with other psychometric profiles, there tends to be a few clear occupational biases. Certain styles are particularly well-suited to different jobs. To do a little check on how you are absorbing these ideas about styles, given below is an exercise to do.

Exercise

For each of the jobs listed below, indicate if you think it would help them to be successful if they *favoured* or *avoided* different dimensions. Indicate your thoughts with SF (strongly favour), F (favour), A (avoid) or SA (strongly avoid) and record your responses in Table 12.1. As you do this, remember that you cannot strongly favour all of the dimensions – there has to be some trade-offs between them, as explained above.

Naturally there are a lot of variations within each category, so here are just some broad ideas to help reinforce your learning:

- *Salesperson:* they have to be totally out there meeting new people without hesitation, so I would place a priority on *sociability and networking*. One of the troubles with avoiding this dimension is that people get really creative at finding excuses not to go and meet new people. Generally they also need to be favouring *determination* because of the usual target-driven nature of their work. Sure, you might also think of favouring *emotional control* for high-level negotiators, or you may favour *tact and diplomacy* so that they can really tune in to their

TABLE 12.1 Mapping potential reactions to behaviours

	Sociability and networking	Determination	Tact and diplomacy	Emotional control
Salesperson				
Auditor				
Lawyer				
Executive				
Coach				

customers' wants, needs and concerns. But overall, I'd look for someone favouring *sociability and networking* and *determination* for my term.

- *Auditor:* avoiding *sociability and networking* and favouring *emotional control* is what I'd go for. I'd want auditors who can concentrate on their evidence for hours on end while not getting distracted or perhaps feeling they want to be liked by those they are auditing. The *emotional control* will help them to keep drawing more information out of people without giving them any clues as to what they are really thinking. They share this with police, fraud investigators and the people who like to search you at airports.

- *Lawyer:* avoid *tact and diplomacy* and favour *determination.* I once met a lawyer who proudly stated that he was absolutely committed to his brief and didn't care who he trampled over to get there (he actually scored 0 on *tact and diplomacy* and 15 on *determination*!). If you want a lawyer who will get the result you want, this is exactly the person you should be selecting.

- *Executive:* I included this for a bit of fun and to challenge your thinking, because there is probably no general theme to this one, so much depends on the role and also the company. However, many companies would cite avoiding *tact and diplomacy* and favouring *determination* as being important. I can see why that works, yet cannot quite agree that it is optimum – maybe I just don't want to think of my lawyer running the corporation. Here I think you really need to look at the remit of the executive and, based on the people who need to be influenced, what is most likely to enable them to be successful.

- *Coach:* favouring *tact and diplomacy* (so they can see what is really happening for their client) and avoiding *determination* (so that they do not try to push through their own ideas and instead encourage their client to find the answers that are right for them).

Be wary of these generalizations because there are always exceptions. The important thing to recognize here is that certain jobs require different styles in order to succeed. Regularly behaving contrary to your preference is likely to put a strain on your performance. If your preferred style is not suited to your job you may find it very difficult to succeed or even enjoy your work.

Analysing others

As an influential leader it is vital that you understand those around you and gain an appreciation for the problems that different styles of behaviour can create in the relationships you wish to influence. Already you should have a good idea of the preferred styles of those around you who you know well. But, what about people you are only meeting for the first time, or those you can initially only glimpse? Sometimes it is important to be able to style-spot in e-mails too. As people interact with others, they are giving off clues about their preferences all the time. These clues, if you are observant, can help you to build up a picture of the individual and make a shrewd guess as to their preferred style.

It is not my intention to turn you into an expert at this in just a few pages, but what follows will point the way and get you started. It will also start to prepare you for working out the simple things you can do to start to adapt your behaviour or style when the need arises.

Different types of clue

There are four main types of clue that you can look out for:

- voice: often the pitch, pace and tone of voice will give you a clue about which type of style is in play;

- expression: faces are mobile features of the human body and often tell a story all of their own;
- body language: in a more general way, how an individual makes use of their body can provide valuable clues about what is really going on;
- words and phrases: selection of different words gives an insight into what is driving behaviour at a deeper level.

Clues are just clues. To build an accurate assessment you need to build the full picture. When you are people watching you may realize that some clues could be suggesting more than one style. For instance, a smile could indicate that the individual is favouring *sociability and networking* and/or avoiding *emotional control*. Similarly, a pointing finger may indicate avoiding *tact and diplomacy* and/or favouring *determination*. Curiously, the difference on this one lies in the direction of the finger. A finger pointing down suggests *determination* (the emphasis on assertion); however, if the finger is pointing towards someone, it is more likely to be accusing someone and demonstrating lower levels of tact.

If you have been paying careful attention to the rest of this chapter, the clues will start to become rather obvious, so let me stretch your learning further with a little challenge, set out in the exercise below.

Exercise

Think of an individual you know well but do not necessarily have a particularly good relationship with. Take a piece of paper and use lines to divide it up into two columns (portrait orientation) and then further divide it into four rows. Title each row with the four dimensions. At the top of the first column write the title 'avoiding' and put 'favouring' as the title for the second column.

What I'd like to challenge you to do is to fill each box with the clues you notice in the individual you are thinking about, which could indicate a preference. If your top row is *sociability and networking*, you need to fill the left-hand box with all the clues that you have observed that could indicate they are avoiding these behaviours, such as rarely going for a beer after work or not engaging in small talk. See if you can fill all of the boxes. Some will be easier than others for the person you are considering. This could be a good indication of their preferences.

Finally, try giving them a score for each dimension. Don't forget that the scores need to total 30 and some adjustment to your initial figures may be necessary. I will talk shortly about the implications for you and how to adapt your behaviour to remove or lessen the potential distraction between the two of you.

There is, of course, a very slight flaw in this process – you are calibrating their behaviours rather than their preferences. Experienced people can be quite good at delivering the required behaviour and the more they practice, the easier it becomes for them to operate differently. However, most people are prone to revert to type, especially when the pressure is on, so the gap between actual behaviour and preferred behaviour may be very small. The only way of being sure about their preferred behaviour is getting them to do the questionnaire, so I'm afraid that this exercise has to remain in the behaviour side of things – which in reality is probably a pretty good estimate, so don't worry too much about it. With time and practice you will become more skilled and begin to notice the real preference peeping through the deliberate behaviours.

But this is just the beginning: to really make the most of this and set yourself up for becoming more influential, you need to make this process almost automatic. So before you move on, do some more analysis. To keep it relevant and useful I would recommend drawing up a list of significant stakeholders that have an impact on your work. Start by analysing those who are the most different from you. To an extent, if you think they are the same as you there is not much point in analysing them because there will be little distraction or need to adapt your behaviour. Good practice, nevertheless.

Focus on those who are the most different from you and keep going until you are able to give them a score for each dimension. Then you will be ready to start to make decisions about how best to adapt your behaviour so that you can become more effective in your communication with them.

Developing your style

The secret to becoming more influential is removing as much of the distraction as you can to make your communication more effective. This can be done by minimizing the difference between your behaviour, and the preferred behaviour of the person you are trying to influence. To make this as simple as possible, you need to develop your style in order to feel increasingly comfortable moving up and down the dimensions.

The trouble comes in that adapting your behaviour, like folding your arms a different way, is not always easy. Sometimes it takes extra skill, increased motivation and gritty determination. Other times, just a simple idea can unlock the behaviour naturally. Your job now is to take this opportunity to move forward and unlock greater potential for influence. Quite likely, over time, this effort will result in you moving towards the middle ground by preference, and for some this can take many years of effort.

The first step is to identify where to focus your development effort. There is no simple answer to this because it depends on your situation, your job and the people you need to influence. These questions will help you to get a little focus:

- If you had to move from your current position on each dimension, to the extremes, which would make you feel most uncomfortable?
- Which dimension scores are most different from the colleagues you work with?
- In your role, how might your scores differ from the perfect score for your job?
- To be more successful at your job, which dimension do you need to become more flexible in?
- What have you always been told to work on?

The following coaching questions will help you to develop options and ideas for improving your versatility. If you can, hand them over to a friend who can do the asking while you concentrate on figuring out the answers:

- In which dimension do you want to develop more flexibility?
- Which end is most difficult for you, favouring or avoiding the behaviours?
- Who can be a role-model for this style?
- What do they do that indicates they prefer this style?
- What makes them really good at it?
- What are the simple things they do that illustrate this dimension?
- What do they do that may detract from that position?
- What could you do differently?
- Why do you find it difficult or uncomfortable to adopt this behaviour?
- What is stopping you from using this behaviour?

- What examples can you give of times when you have found it easy to do this?

- How will you benefit if you can behave in this way?

- Can you think of a situation in the next couple of days where you could try some new behaviours?

- What will you do?

Don't forget to refer back to the previous chapters where the behaviours were listed for each dimension – all the clues are there. The most important thing is that you find things that you can do with a reasonable degree of comfort. You don't have to wince and do things that are totally alien to you. In fact, that is likely to be a bad idea because you will increase your stress and probably communicate that you are pretending, or are not confident in what you are saying, thereby creating other problems. So focus on things that will not stress you out too much – and the more you practise, the easier they will become. Sometimes the simplest adaptations are the best, like smiling more – or less. Asking different questions, or perhaps simply reordering the discussion.

The questions above can be used for any new behaviour you wish to develop, and you should return often to these as you progress. The greater flexibility (and comfort) you can develop on all of the styles the better. What comes next is making decisions about what style to adopt to remove or lessen the distraction.

Adapting your style to suit

And now for the final piece of the jigsaw, making decisions about how to adapt your style.

In the last section I pointed out that it can take many years of practice to enable you to move up and down the dimensions with ease. However, that does not mean you have to wait until then before you start deliberately adapting your behaviour. The more real-life experience you get at doing this the better.

Earlier I asked you to analyse the preferences (or at least the behaviours) of a number of stakeholders who are quite different from you. Deciding how to adapt your behaviour to remove the potential distractions is now a simple process. For each stakeholder you want to improve your influence with:

1 Write your scores next to theirs for each dimension.

2 Notice the big differences. Which dimension has the biggest gap?

3 How can you reduce the gap in your next interaction with them?

4 What benefit might you gain from clearer communication with them?

5 Make a strong decision to give it a go.

Step three is the hardest to begin with. If you have been studying this chapter and doing the exercises, you should be full of ideas. As with any new skill, you will be stepping out of your comfort zone. Be wary of your self-talk; don't talk yourself out of the attempt before you have even got going. Self-talk is immensely powerful and needs to be kept positive. Some of the thoughts to watch out for include:

- 'I can't do that – it's not me';
- 'it may work for others but I could never pull that off';
- 'they will be suspicious';
- 'this is manipulative and I am not interested in pretending';
- 'I will look stupid trying that'.

Be honest, there may be an element of truth in all of these, and you may be persuaded out of the attempt – but I hope not, because you can do it if you try, and if you want to enough. Most of the time it is far easier than your imagination would have you believe.

Advanced thoughts on style

We've run out of space for this topic. What you have here are the basics of the framework of style that will serve you well providing you apply it. Before I summarize what you can do as a leader to get more done using a different style, there are a few things I want to stimulate you with and, in so doing, demonstrate how much more there is to this if your interest has been piqued. If you're just getting started, feel free to skip over these and come back later once you've got to grips with beginning to adapt your style.

Maintaining integrity

Sometimes, people in the training room question the impact that adapting behaviour could have on their integrity. Acting in a way contrary to their usual way lacks integrity – pretending to be something that they are not.

To test out this concept, in 2010 I ran a discussion with colleagues in the American Society for Training and Development group on LinkedIn. When the initial, almost ferocious volley of 'absolutely, you lack integrity if you pretend to be something you are not' subsided, a more thoughtful debate developed. Professionals gave many examples of how in different roles you need to behave in different ways. A policeman doesn't lack integrity because he behaves differently with criminals than with his family. The consensus of nearly 200 contributors to the debate seemed to be that within certain boundaries it is appropriate to flex your behaviour. The key boundary seemed to be the intent rather than the act that determined the potential damage to integrity.

One friend neatly summed it up, that when travelling abroad it makes sense to learn a little of the language to help you to communicate more effectively – that doesn't mean you lack integrity, you are just being sensible. As we help people to learn on our workshops, each individual needs to make their own decisions about what integrity means to them, because each group you are associated with is doing so (albeit subconsciously).

Portfolio of preferred styles

While I maintain that in general people have one preferred style or way of behaving, the style they use and prefer to use may be subject to other influences in their surroundings. Indeed, certain triggers may launch them immediately and easily into a completely different style. For instance:

- People who generally favour *tact and diplomacy* will have a tolerance limit. Breach that and you will quickly notice them very comfortably (for them) telling you exactly what they think of you – they will appear to snap and leap for the jugular.

- Those who tend to avoid *sociability and networking* at work may feel completely different when they are out with their friends. The different surroundings and greater familiarity of their friends will unlock their natural enjoyment of being with others. Consequences can act as a brake on these behaviours. At work, the consequence of an inappropriate joke may be extreme. With friends, they will probably retort with another inappropriate joke. The risk of losing your job will make you behave differently, as will the less familiar people you are dealing with.

- At work you may be highly determined and driving through the results. The level of comfort doing those things may evaporate as soon as you step through your front door. Consequences again. Asserting yourself at work gets a wholly different result than asserting yourself at home and in your personal relationships.

One of the most interesting implications of this is that if you are comfortable using different styles in different situations, it can make it very much easier to unlock the behaviour you need. You already have it, but somehow you have chosen not to use it in a particular environment. As you enter the office you have changed your style, as you did your clothes. This gives you the opportunity to challenge yourself – why did you choose to do that? Making the unconscious conscious can enhance your flexibility quickly, and dramatically change the way you are perceived in the workplace.

That said, be careful that you determine what needs to change for you to open up the other behaviour options, and what differences will remain. No, you still cannot use those inappropriate jokes at work, but you could translate that fun into other ways to socially engage with your peers, perhaps by turning on (appropriate) banter.

Balance and flexibility

Earlier I made the point that scoring high or low on the dimensions is not necessarily bad or good, and that preferring the middle territory is the optimum. This is because it makes it easier to flex up and down the behaviours. Moving from the extremes is much harder.

But this introduces a risk – blandness. If you always behave in the middle ground, there is the danger that others will not notice you perhaps as much as you would like. You are neither one thing nor the other. People who are avoiding *tact and diplomacy* certainly don't suffer from not being noticed – they may have other problems, but standing out will not be one of them. Behaving in the middle ground is like sitting on the fence. It is still the optimum place for your preference, but not your actual behaviour.

If this applies to you, what I would suggest is that you increase the deviation in your actual performance, dancing up and down (within reason) the scales as you adapt to match or mismatch other stakeholders around the organization. I say within reason because you don't want to inadvertently appear unpredictable and, dare I say it, unstable. That said, if you can practise greater versatility you will begin to stand out as a more vivid and colourful character to engage with.

A closely related consideration that really stretches the thinking is how to flex your behaviour in front of an audience. If you assume (and it is not a given) that the audience has a wide range of different styles, it would be impossible to please all of the people all of the time. Dumbing down your presentation to the middle ground will probably leave it unremarkable to all of them. Instead, what if you could dance up and down each dimension, appealing to different styles within the audience at different times. Providing you don't step to the extremes and alienate whole swathes of them, all of them are likely to go away with something to remark upon. Careful preparation is warranted on this one.

Rapid flexing

Imagine you have to handle a performance issue with someone who is strongly favouring *tact and diplomacy*. The theory goes that if you adapt your style to match their preference you will remove the distraction and therefore be able to communicate more effectively. That is true, but there may be an even better strategy.

To make sure you get their attention, you may wish to dive down to the avoiding end momentarily. This could alert them to the seriousness of the situation and prepare them to listen even more closely. Once you've got their attention, shift straight back up to the favouring end and engage with them on solving the problem. Some call this 'tough love'. Provided you do it quickly and instantly, it can prove very effective and dramatically reduce the time it takes to get them to take responsibility and make decisions about how they are going to change – while at the same time protecting the relationship.

This can work in lots of other situations and on different dimensions too. Remember, learn to dance up and down to maximize your results. No one said you have to match people all the time, and deliberately creating wider gaps can prove highly effective.

Cultural conditioning

As individuals have different preferred styles, so do cultures. American, British, Chinese will have slightly different expected norms of behaviour that can be described using this framework. For instance, it is fairly apparent that (sweeping generalization, of course) the American culture is far more direct than the British, who seem to have a finely developed art of subtlety that charms and also befuddles Americans. From the British position, the American approach can appear to be rude and discourteous, even though they think it is absolutely the prudent way of doing it because it is straight and honest dealing. I am, of course, talking about the *tact and diplomacy* dimension.

So, do all Americans prefer to avoid *tact and diplomacy*? No, my research is crystal clear in this respect. Americans are no more likely to prefer to be rude than the British. What is different is the way they have been conditioned to behave by their culture. In order to be successful in America it really helps if you can be very direct. Those who find it easier to move from their natural preference to the behaviour expected in a given culture will likely be the most successful, or at least those who distract others the least – they will fit in well.

My personal belief is that if you want to understand the differences between cultures, and need to be more successful working on the global stage, developing your cultural understanding around these dimensions will significantly enhance your ability to fit in and be successful. It will also help you to learn where it is easier to fit in and, also, where in the world not to go.

This aspect does not just relate to countries or races; it is evident in any distinguishable group of people of sufficient size to have its own unique culture – including companies, clubs and departments. And this is something you should be particularly careful of when moving from one job to another. Before you leap, recognize the behaviour that will be expected of you and decide if you will be able to deliver. Do this before you leap rather than find out in the first performance review.

Gender differences

I often get asked about this and my response is very similar to the cultural conditioning points. The differences that you would expect to see show up in the observable behaviour rather than the underlying personal preference. Again, my data shows quite clearly that the styles you would reasonably expect men and women to prefer are non-existent. You might think that women would favour *tact and diplomacy* and *sociability and networking* more than men. In preference, they don't. In behaviour, yes, they generally do. Again, it is a result of being conditioned to meet expectations within the culture and be successful that elicits the behaviour, rather than the underlying preference.

Acceptance of diversity

This final point lies very close to my heart – or my values. There is nothing wrong with being different from others except to the degree that the difference is not understood and accepted. It is the lack of understanding that is probably at the root of most intercultural (or intergroup) discord. The lack of understanding leads easily to lack of tolerance – and who knows where else. The world is full of discord.

The strange thing is that to get along well with others you don't have to be exactly like them. In fact that would be a pretty boring world, wouldn't it? But, you do have to understand and at least tolerate the differences. If you (and they) can do that, you will not be distracting each other by your behaviour and you can both spend more time being yourselves. Much healthier for all concerned.

To prove this, just look at the relationships that you know have lasted a long time. Are the people in these relationships the same? Unlikely. Why have they lasted? Because they have developed over time a deep understanding of their differences and have decided that they can live with those differences. They recognize their differences and often delight in them.

Consequently, the sooner you can get everyone around you understanding and accepting your preferred way of doing things, and you theirs, the better off you will all be.

> ### Getting things done
>
> Important points to remember as you begin to make more progress:
>
> - Become acutely aware of your preferred way of behaving and how this can affect others.
>
> - Hone your ability to observe and analyse differences between you and those you lead and wish to influence.
>
> - Find simple ways to adapt your behaviour so you present a different style. Sometimes it's as simple as frowning or smiling a little more.
>
> - Make clear decisions about when and how to flex your behaviour with different people in different situations.
>
> - Don't be afraid to deliberately increase the gap when the need arises.
>
> - Share these insights with your team and learn and grow together.

Further reading

When you get a chance, make sure you check the further reading and resources for this chapter online at: **www.learntoinfluence.com/leadership**

Since Chapter 7 you have covered a great number of other topics related to engaging more effectively with people and becoming more influential. There is always more to learn about influence; however, the final topic I would like to turn to before closing this book is the range of different approaches and techniques you can deliver with skill and style depending on the situations and the person you are facing. It is also important to consider how others may be trying to influence you and what your response will be.

Tailoring your approach for maximum influence

13

"You cannot escape the fact that most influence is the result of engaging with individuals. Influential leaders need to be exceptionally good at this.

It is impossible to avoid the need to influence at an individual level. While at a senior level a great deal of your work will be with groups of individuals, getting that moving still requires that you gain the buy-in from senior colleagues and stakeholders. As you approach the close of this book – a book all about influencing people – it is important to pull together the threads of individual influence touched on earlier and fill in the gaps.

This chapter contributes to the following influential leader capabilities:

Thinks carefully about the influence they want to create in any situation and responds appropriately to meet the needs of any individual.

As you go through this chapter it will help to think of a specific influencing attempt that you soon need to make. There is a great deal offered here that you can use to prepare for influence and you need to make sure that you adapt what follows in order to suit the situation and the time available to you. Overpreparation can lead to delays and paralysis and underpreparation can lead to failure. Your decision.

Individual influencing process

The process that follows brings together a great deal of what you have been reading about during this book. As you begin to use the process you will probably find you need to refer back to the content of the chapters indicated. As you become more accomplished, it will begin to become automatic, and quick. Now is the time to apply what you have learned to an individual influencing situation.

Step 1: clarity

Exactly what do you want the stakeholder you are about to engage with to do, think or feel? Influence is about creating change, so how do you want them to change as a result of your conversation? Any uncertainty on your part will delay your influence – you may or may not choose to disclose exactly what you want, but not being clear in your own mind should be avoided. No, you cannot always be precise and sometimes that comes from the actual act of engaging with them, but you do need to do your best to be un-ambiguous in your own mind about the change you want to effect in them.

In Chapter 7 (Creating your leadership strategy and plan) the section titled 'Towards action' provided an approach to gaining clarity on your overall influencing goals: now you can use this for smaller, specific influence attempts. When you sit down with the stakeholder, what outcomes do you want to achieve?

Step 2: reflection

Collect your thoughts on what you know about them. You will need to decide on how much time you are able to devote to this, or how much time you need to invest in this activity. This can range from a momentary investment of time as you are going to meet them or a full-blown team review for the most important influencing attempts.

In particular, reflect on their:

- *Agenda:* how does it connect or disconnect with your agenda? Make sure to factor in their personal agenda too. See Chapter 4.
- *Context:* their performance, outside influences and commercial pressures all act to help or hinder their agenda. Look at Chapters 4 and 5.

- *Power:* what power do they have, respond to and have access to? How does this compare with what you have at your disposal? Revisit Chapters 2 and 3.

- *Personality:* what type of person are they and how does this compare with you? In addition to their style, are they data/detail focused or big-picture thinkers? See Chapters 11 and 12.

- *Risks/rewards:* be frank with yourself, how are they going to win or lose if they agree to what you want? Review Chapters 1 and 4.

- *Category:* where do they sit on your stakeholder map? If they are over to the left you will need to focus hard on building your relationship with them. Over to the right and candour and openness comes to the fore. Review Chapter 7.

- *Perceptions:* what do they think of you? Do they see you as powerful, insightful, irrelevant or an idiot? These expectations make a huge difference when you come to attempt to influence them. See Chapter 3.

- *Trust:* how much do you trust them? It may not be prudent to fully disclose everything about your request and if you are going to hold something back, think about the consequences. Review Chapter 10.

- *Competition:* what does your idea compete with? It is unlikely that they will be able to agree to all requests and agreeing with your proposal may push out someone else. If you are competing, expect the competition to be influencing against you. Review Chapters 1 and 4. (I'll cover this aspect in more detail shortly.)

- *Responses:* how do you think they may respond to your request? If the probability of yes is high, then you can economize on much of the preparation but don't become complacent: cover the options and have a plan in place in case it goes wrong. See Chapter 4.

Lots to think about, and the more you think about them, the more successful you will be as an influential leader, provided you quickly move into action.

Step 3: decision

Decide on your influencing approach. Don't delay too long, you have to move it fast. With sensible preparation you ought to find this step much easier. Here are some of the things to decide on:

- *Direct or indirect?* As mentioned in Chapter 7, you don't necessarily need to use a direct approach. Influencing the influencers brings great economy of effort.

- *Face to face or remote?* It is not always possible or desirable to physically sit down with the stakeholder. Often the drive to do this creates substantial delays. Remote mediums vary greatly in effectiveness and also in their receptivity. If you know they don't like e-mail, don't e-mail them for an important decision.

- *Alone or with a friend?* Bringing along support might be appropriate. It might also be wise to ensure the stakeholder has someone else there too. If you think that they will delay a decision in order to give them an opportunity to consult with someone else, get them there too. Embarrassing them in front of their colleagues is rarely a good idea.

- *Simple or planned?* Aiming to achieve your influence in a single meeting or conversation can move things along quickly. However, it may not be feasible or have a high probability of success. In some situations you may find it more useful to warm them up in writing, and then have a preliminary meeting before going for a decision. If you find yourself planning, beware of appearing manipulative or scheming. You might also elevate it to the full *Stakeholder Influence Process* in its own right (see Chapter 7).

- *Influencing style.* From the exercise comparing their style to yours, what do you need to do differently when you meet them in order to remove the personality distraction that may creep in?

- *Influencing tactic.* There are many different ways of engaging when it comes to influence. Sometimes you may choose to add a little force, at others take a more consultative approach. Below I'll share with you the *Nine Influencing Tactics* that can be used in isolation or used in combination. Don't work on auto-pilot or just with your favourite approach – adapt.

- *Timing.* When are you going to do it? If you have a choice, use it. In addition to times of the day, you also need to make sure to optimize around other things that may affect their state of mind. For example, immediately after an announcement of poor company results might be the perfect moment, or a recipe for disaster.

- *Pitch structure.* Do you start with the problems and the conclusion or pump up the benefits right up front? Designing your delivery should be included in every influence attempt, no matter how small.

Overall, influence works best if your approach demonstrates that you have a clear understanding of the stakeholder's position, care about their interests and present a rational and balanced review (including the drawbacks for them). Success is most likely if you are appealing to their agenda, demonstrating power they respect and showing how they will become more powerful as a result of saying yes. If they also feel in control of their decision – even better.

Step 4: action

All of the above considerations are great, but nothing substitutes for taking action. Don't overengineer and fail to act because there were too many things to think about. Try to make your reflections and decisions fit for purpose and avoid the trap of lack of preparation – it could save you your job.

As I've been making clear throughout this book, the influential leader is swift to action, so go to it.

Step 5: review

The final stage is to spend a few moments learning from what happened. It is unlikely to go exactly as you planned and there will be surprises along the way. You have to be learning with every step.

After you have made your influence attempt:

- What happened? What worked and what didn't work?
- Why was it different from what you planned/expected?
- What do you wish you had done differently?
- How might this change your approach with others?
- What did you learn?
- What will you do differently going forward?
- What are you going to do now?

Be cautious about drawing radical conclusions from each individual experience. If you are influencing a wide variety of people, they will be responding in different ways and just because your influence didn't work with one it does not mean it will also fail with everyone else. Notice the trends and then make big changes. Knee-jerk reactions are seldom prudent.

Nine influencing tactics

There has been a great deal of research done over the last few decades on influence, which has yielded some fascinating insights into how to engage with your stakeholders. Cecilia Falbe and her colleagues compiled and researched a range of distinct tactics that are commonly used in the workplace. They then set about considering the likelihood of the tactic being successful. The great thing about their work is that it provides a quick checklist of different approaches you could use, so that you can decide which one fits your purpose best. Provided you are aware of the likely consequences, you can potentially engage much more effectively with the right selection.

Inspirational appeals

Here you seek commitment to your goals by appealing to your stakeholder's values, ideals and aspirations. This is directly related to the earlier sections of this chapter, as it is the behaviour built on your vision and benefits work. Unless you did that preparation, you are likely to be unconvincing if you try an inspiration appeal.

Consultation

The essence of this tactic is engaging your stakeholder in developing your detailed proposals or plans – before you've made up your own mind. Care is needed in order to avoid the accusation that you are just going through the motions. A sincere inclusion in your decision-making process is a great tactic to get people onside before you've even started. Or, if you have already got moving, this tactic could involve you engaging them in problem solving.

Rational persuasion

The use of logic and rationality is an extremely popular tactic when dealing with stakeholders, but there are limitations and research has shown that, in actual fact, it is not the tactic most likely to succeed. That does not mean that you do not need to cover the rational side of your proposals; just that it is rarely the most important tactic to use.

Ingratiation

In a nutshell, this tactic is about getting a stakeholder to like you so that they are more likely to agree with you. Of course, everyone wants to be liked or at least respected, but this specific tactic focuses the main influence attempt on being liked, rather than rationality or inspiration.

Personal appeals

Help! Often referred to as emotional appeals, this is where you might try to call in a favour from a stakeholder, or simply beg them to do it. It plays heavily on the personal relationship, friendship and sense of loyalty.

Exchange

Typified by the phrase 'you scratch my back and I'll scratch yours', this is often an open negotiation of terms. In an organizational setting, it could be a bargain struck with a stakeholder that if they support you on your goal, you'll withdraw your objections to their projects. Sometimes these exchanges are implied, with a nod and a wink.

Pressure

Assertion and aggression are effective influencing tactics, but are often criticized as being unfair or wrong. This applies less to assertion, but aggression is to be avoided for most people. The type of pressure applied can also vary; and as it changes, so does the common view of its acceptability. Culture informs the relative acceptability of different types of force. Pressure can include threats, bullying, nagging and public humiliation (either verbal or through e-mail).

Legitimating

This tactic differs from rationality because it attempts to gain agreement due to its fit with other policies, procedures or regulations, rather than relying on its own merits. There may be good logical reasons for retaining a poor performer, but this tactic uses the legislation as the reason to keep the individual. In many ways, this tactic is borrowing power from other sources.

Coalition

In the research, this tactic is referring to the use of others to do your influencing for you. It is important to have other people on your side; however, excessive reliance on their influence is of limited benefit and risky in the long term. Unless you can win unaided, you will always be reliant to some extent on other people's power.

In their results, Falbe and her colleagues reported that the most successful tactics were *inspirational appeals* and *consultation*. Somewhat surprisingly, *rational persuasion* languished in the middle in terms of success. Least likely to be successful were *pressure*, *legitimating* and *coalition*. At first sight, the surprise here is that *coalitions* were in the bottom group. When you go deeper into the research, what becomes clear is that it is the specific use of a confederate to do your influencing for you that is less likely to be successful. It does not mean that you should not build coalitions – these are extremely useful in getting more and more people on the right page and is really what the influential leadership is intended to achieve.

Remember, there are no hard and fast rules here. What you need to do is adopt a tactic or a range of tactics that have been selected for a particular situation after careful thought. Blundering around with your favourite tactic will not be anywhere near as effective as selecting the right tools for the job in hand.

Responding to political rivalry

Throughout this book I have avoiding giving credence to the office politicians and schemers who inhabit organizational life. Instead I have focused almost entirely on giving you the various ideas in a neutral manner so that you can apply them to whatever purpose you have chosen and in a way best suited to you. The processes of analysis, particularly of agendas, will have given you plenty of opportunity to think through the forces arrayed against you and, I hope, will have begun to help you to feel competent to deal with opposition, whatever form it takes.

However, the fact remains that in all organizations conflicting personal agendas will give rise to unhelpful and unwelcomed political rivalry and you need to become skilled at dealing with it – not playing it, but cutting it down and making sure it does not spread and interrupt your progress towards your goals.

In order to do this, you first have to understand the motives and drivers before you can make a judgement on the means they are deploying. Some seemingly negative practices may in fact be for the longer-term good of the organization and those who remain. Organizations are not generally paternal and forgiving places to work and, as mentioned in Chapter 6 (The ethics of influence), different actions will be perceived differently. Once you have gained a reasonable understanding of what is going and why, then you can make clearer decisions about its impact on you and your purpose, and then how best to respond to the risk it poses.

In the main, this type of activity arises when individuals, for whatever reason, decide to pursue a self-advancing agenda. To an extent everyone does this, but it is the strong leaning towards self-interest that is the hallmark of the office politician. They have chosen to pursue matters for their own purposes at the expense of, or at least with disregard for, those around them. The consequences of their political machinations on the lives of those around them matter little. They are also quite adept at making use of others' generosity, energy and hard work while giving little loyalty or goodwill in return. Once they have expended their value, they get jettisoned.

One of the main techniques used by these people to advance their cause is deception, either by blatantly lying about the facts, obscuring the critical details or simply saying nothing. They do this because they fear that full disclosure would make it harder for them to achieve their goals. That it damages the long-term relationship matters little to them.

Yet it is still important to realize that, irrespective of their motives and means, they are still doing it for a purpose, however selfish it may seem to others. They are human, however, and while you may disagree with their approach, understanding the human drivers may enable you to make a more balanced response. This offers the opportunity of harnessing their energy and channelling their skills in more productive ways.

This may not be possible or desirable and there are people out there who are playing these games for fun. Some even have sociopathic or psychopathic tendencies and, in my view, are too risky to have anywhere near your leadership purpose. Taking pleasure in other people's misfortune and being prepared to exacerbate their misery is not something that you, as an influential leader, want to tolerate in anyone.

A great deal has been written on this subject and I don't intend to repeat it here. The resources section later will give you plenty of references to learn more about this area. What I will do is share with you a few general guidelines that you can adopt when people like this start to trouble your purpose:

- Do as much as you can to understand their real motives and the way they operate. The ideas and processes in Chapters 4 and 5 will be helpful, with the addition of being more cautious in believing what you are hearing. Don't take things at face value and verify everything if you think people are playing games with you.

- Try to gauge the lengths they are personally prepared to go to in order to get what they want. Consideration of their ethics and integrity will help you to do this; however, diligent observation is essential. It may even be important for you to test them out in safe areas.

- Stay alert for people who seem to be playing games but actually have the best of intentions. Some people just enjoy the cut and thrust of organizational life a little too much and are not necessarily bad. Working on your relationship with these people and just making sure they don't go too far is usually all that is needed to contain any risks.

- Don't try to play them at their own game. They are likely to be much more competent in their methods than you are, especially if you are honest and straightforward.

- Play to your own strengths and rise above their approach by managing your stakeholders. By resisting the temptation to join in you are demonstrating strength and empowerment. In any case, most of your senior stakeholders will probably recognize what is really going on and will respect your handling of the situation.

- Make sure you stay grounded in your own sense of integrity and ethics. This is where the personal rules you developed in Chapter 6 really come in handy.

Responding to dirty tricks

Particularly at junior to middle levels, there can be a lot of office politics going on around you. These are the small techniques that people learn in the playground and perfect in the workplace. My first book, *21 Dirty Tricks at Work*, written with Mike Phipps, identified games such as:

- *development opportunity:* the tactic of motivating someone to take on a task, project or assignment they might reasonably refuse, by pretending it is a development opportunity;

- *rock and a hard place:* manipulating people by offering limited or fixed choices, expecting the victim to choose the lesser of two evils;

- *creative magpie:* exaggerating involvement in the ideas and good work of others, or blatantly stealing them whilst hiding the originator's worthy contributions;

- *tell me more:* the tactic of delaying decisions or honest disclosure by requesting more work, research or data, which often includes the efforts of others;

- *my hands are tied:* pretending to be helpless due to the influence of a higher authority or process, when under the same circumstances, but with a different person, there would be a different outcome.

The full catalogue ran to over 70 discrete games of varying intensity and damage. Core to all of them is a deceit of some kind. There is an unwillingness to be open and honest on the part of the game player. Whatever the reason, they are playing the situation, and you. Whatever you call it, the important thing is that you need to recognize what might be going on and how you are potentially being deceived. This is the first step in handling the situation; then you can decide what to do for the best outcome.

In general you should:

- keep your emotions under control, manage your fear, and look for the facts;
- consider the bigger picture;
- offer ways forward / ways out;
- put out fires and build bridges;
- walk in their shoes;
- take some time to think;
- look for positive intent;
- ask them what they want;
- not fight every battle.

But whatever you do, don't ignore or avoid the reality; otherwise it will catch you out – and probably at your most vulnerable moment!

Responding to other influence attempts

This is a topic that receives little coverage yet is increasingly important as you rise up the ladder becoming more influential – others will be breaking down your door trying to influence you. The more successful you are, the longer the queue will become.

Rather than putting up barriers, developing an effective response and providing people with an easy way of getting air time is sensible. In fact, welcome with open arms the people who are trying to influence you. One of the problems with denying them this opportunity is that their influence may go under-ground, which could cause you more problems later. This problem can be largely removed by investing the time dealing with it in an open and con-structive way at the outset.

Many think that the last thing they want is to be influenced by others – this book is all about exerting greater influence, not being influenced. There are several reasons why the influential leader should be amenable to this:

- It can help to grow an increasingly loyal network if you give people attention.
- Opportunities for expanding your sphere of influence will grow without you needing to proactively build it.
- If someone wants to influence you, there could well be an advantage for you too.
- When you have someone looking to gain something from you, they are acknowledging your power and in the process building it further.
- Even if you still say no, the approach can give you deep insight into other areas of the organization, which may help you in other areas.
- A constructive and open dialogue may limit downstream problems, politicking and vendettas. It will give you a good moment to make forthright and final decisions.

All of this is naturally dependent on the manner in which you do it. Here is an outline approach that you can use when you notice someone attempting to influence you:

1 Do a quick importance assessment – based on your short-term goals and longer-term purpose. This will help you to decide how best to handle the situation and reduce attention in the remainder of the process.

2 Try to get to the bottom of what they really want. Go beyond the obvious and dig into the personal agenda that is driving their request.

3 Be open and encourage honest assessment of the request. Engage them in debating the detail of the request, the consequences and the fit with your own agenda(s).

4 Agree a decision-making process that will serve their needs as well as respecting your own. Show them what they need to do in order to move it through to a final decision.

5 Take your time to verify the information they are providing, especially if you have been unable to understand their personal agenda.

6 Manage their expectations. There is no need to be vague and try to discourage them. If it is a definite no, be definite. Any lack of clarity can easily begin to fuel the dirty tricks and game playing explored earlier.

7 Consider doing a deal. If they have something that would aid you in your purpose, which is not currently on the table, and it is appropriate for you to make a request in return, now is the optimum time to influence them. This is collaboration in action, although some call it bargaining.

8 Above all, respect their attempt and desire to do the right thing. Potentially they are putting innovation and opportunity on your desk.

The bottom line on this event is that by welcoming the approach you will build trust and stay more in control of what is happening around you. Taking this authentic approach will maximize loyalty and ensure that there is a continual supply of new ideas coming across your desk. The moment you deflect, resist, or simply ignore these, it will send out the message loud and clear that you are not interested – a sure sign of falling power. Strong, confident and powerful people are more than happy to entertain the influence of others.

Further study

Before closing this chapter, I want to suggest that you extend your learning into three other topics that have a direct bearing on individual influence and, I have to say, stand out as exceptionally fruitful areas to apply: rhetoric, consultative selling and negotiation.

Rhetoric

Yes, rhetoric has a shady reputation. However, the fact is that it was originally developed by Aristotle to empower honest citizens with a means of defending themselves against their more self-serving peers with inferior ideas. Rhetoric gives power to weaker arguments, and learning their ways is a prudent approach to levelling the playing field and exposing their flaws. Eloquence and communication skills are rightly applauded among leaders, and the rules of rhetoric lie behind every famous speech – so why not study how they do it?

When you do you will quickly realize that it enables you to structure your communication in efficient and compelling ways. You don't need to be a master wordsmith to benefit from even a cursory study of the subject. And it is not just for those who give speeches and make grand presentations. The same rules apply to all communication, right down to performance appraisals, one-to-ones and even e-mails.

Consultative selling

At the end of the day, influence is all about selling to people – or rather, getting people to buy your ideas. This seems to have been missed by a great many people who do not have sales careers. Head office and management training is more likely to elicit rational argumentation than effective sales pitches. As someone with a sales background I can certainly vouch for its effectiveness. People with an experience and training in sales are at a distinct advantage in teams who do not have that capability.

Over the last few decades there have been a great many sales processes developed. Paramount in my eyes is the work on *consultative selling*. The essence of this approach is that as a sales person (influencer) you accept that the client (stakeholder) is going through a buying process (making a decision). Added to this is the wisdom that if people feel that they are in control of this process – and that it is their decision – they are much more likely to be receptive to the influence of the sales person. In this method, the sales person is merely facilitating the decision – well, almost.

By following this approach with your individual influence you will get much more robust decisions made and avoid the risks of decisions being reversed.

Negotiation

This takes it up a level from selling, and the study of negotiation will yield immediate benefits, especially if you have big plans and ambitious purposes. You don't need to apply it to a set-piece deal between two big players. Everything that they talk about in books on negotiation can be applied to, for example, getting a stakeholder to agree to your restructure, or getting a steering committee to sign off your budget.

The techniques may be a bit more hard-nosed and orchestrated than the influence that is normally exercised by an influential leader, but the lessons are there and should be applied appropriately to the situation. One of the big lessons coming out of all books on negotiation is that of preparation. Throughout this book I have been labouring the need for preparation – and studying this topic will add more questions for you to answer.

A return to ethics

By way of closing this chapter, which has focused on how to get your way with others, it is appropriate to return to the subject of ethics and integrity, which are central to the work of influential leaders. The most likely threat to your personal ground rules comes in the individual attempts to influence rather than the sweeping big-purpose and strategy areas. If you have a clear idea of what you want, will you let one individual stand in your way? A little lie here, or a bit of deceit there will be easily justified by the bigger picture. Well it may, but equally, it may not.

Here's a quick reminder of the ethical rules (suggested in Chapter 6) to use as a base for your own approach to influence:

1 Always help people to make balanced and informed decisions.
2 Ensure pitches include the drawbacks as well as the benefits.
3 Whenever influencing, challenge yourself hard on your motives.
4 Be clear and open with people about your own interests.
5 Aim for people *wanting* to do what you want them to do.
6 Never mislead people into doing something that you know will harm them.
7 Cultivate a genuine interest in those you are influencing.

If you can stand by these you will not go too far wrong and will be able to build excellent long-term relationships. Sure, at times all of these will be threatened, but making decisions about your actions from this base will at the very least enable you to minimize and counter any negative consequences from doing what you have to do.

Getting things done

Important points to remember as you begin to make more progress:

- Before you attempt to influence an important individual, make clear decisions about your approach based on careful analysis.

- Your automatic approach to influence is rarely the most effective option.

- Influential leaders are swift to action once their analysis is sufficient. And that is quick too.

- Welcome the influence of others as an opportunity to learn and grow.

- Diligent application of processes and careful learning will dramatically increase influence and progress.

- Rational persuasion is pretty much useless on its own for the purposes of an influential leader.

- There is always more to learn about influence.

Further reading

When you get a chance, make sure you check the further reading and resources for this chapter online at: **www.learntoinfluence.com/leadership**

Yes, there is much more to learn about the detail of influence – it is an ongoing task. The ideas, tools and concepts I have covered in this book will be sufficient to help you to make substantial progress towards becoming an influential leader, providing you develop persistence. And that is the subject of the final chapter.

Influential leadership and persistence of purpose

14

Great achievements happen because of the relentless focus and persistence of influential leaders.

There is little doubt that when you start to make great things happen, many obstacles will surface. They come in many forms, both external and internal to your organization. Perhaps the most damaging to real progress are the internal ones, and the way external obstacles threaten internal resolve. This is where the skill of persistence becomes vital to you as an influential leader.

This chapter contributes to the following influential leader capabilities:

Injects passion into their purpose and is able to maintain momentum.

Is meticulous in preparation, swift to action and tenacious in the pursuit of their purpose.

There is no substitute for persistence! It cannot be supplanted by any other quality! Remember this, and it will hearten you, in the beginning, when the going may seem difficult and slow.

Napoleon Hill, *Think and Grow Rich* (1937)

The value of persistence

Here, at the end of this book on *Influential Leadership*, there remains but one task – to help you to build persistence. To be an influential leader you need to be persistent in the pursuit of your purpose and in the application of the tools and techniques you have learned about in this book.

Being persistent means that when things get in the way, as they will, you will find a way of overcoming them. If people knock you down, as they will, you are able to pick yourself up, dust yourself off and return to your path. It also means that when doubts creep into your mind, as they will, you are able to listen to their message without being distracted from your purpose.

At its best, persistence allows you to remain open to new ideas because you want to keep learning. If you are persistent, you will seek opportunities to bring people towards your purpose, even if that means modifying your route or some of the detail along the way. You hold true to your purpose.

The persistence displayed by influential leaders should not be confused with being bloody-minded, stubborn or pig-headed – none of these will help your relationships at work. Another word that helps to explain what you need to avoid is intransigence – unwilling or refusing to change one's views or to agree about something. These attitudes create discord within relationships. In effect, they scream, 'I'm right, you're wrong, and to hell with what you think'.

The ultimate value of persistence is that it gets things done, it makes progress and it achieves the defined purpose. And persistence uses passion as its fuel.

Definiteness of purpose

In Chapter 1 I encouraged you to spend plenty of time reflecting on what you wish to achieve, and where you want to achieve it. There is little point in persisting in ambiguity – so the bedrock of persistence is being clear about your end goal, vision or purpose.

At the beginning you may not be too clear, especially if you are in a position where you are beset with difficulties and challenges. If you have not had the time to think about your long-term future, all you can do is concentrate on what is right in front on you.

Make sure that you aim to make enough progress to free up time to think about the longer term, rather than create the capacity to do more short-term work. The only way to become an influential leader is to develop a long-term vision of a future that people want.

Inevitably, in the early days as an influential leader, when you start to apply the tools and techniques in this book, you will be focusing on short-term goals and purposes. However, as you begin to make progress, your ideas will expand and you will realize that you can be bolder. The same principles and processes work regardless of the purpose you apply them to.

You need to keep thinking and keep working on your ideas. As they evolve in your mind, the clarity of your purpose will grow as will your desire to achieve it – your passion. And with clarity and passion, your persistence will grow quickly.

Flexible route

Once you have determined your end goal, or your purpose, and you begin to be persistent in its realization, don't become fixated on the route you have decided to take. It is actually quite rare for someone to achieve something noteworthy by following their initial plan.

As you will have seen in the various chapters in this book, there are a great many related agendas that are being pursued by other talented individuals within your leadership arena. This creates a huge amount of uncertainty. Add to this the way the world is rapidly changing and it makes it almost impossible to believe that any long-term plan will be executed unchanged.

So, as you begin to make progress, stay very alert for the need to change your route. It doesn't mean you should jettison well-founded plans when you meet the least resistance, it means you have to accept the possibility that there will always be a better way of achieving what you want to achieve – you've just got to spot it when it appears.

Make sure you focus your persistence on your purpose, not your plan.

Listen, learn and reaffirm

What needs to be happening when you are making progress is the regular review of what you are doing, where you have got to and what you are going to do next. This encapsulates the previous point and makes it more systematic.

When a serious challenge arises, don't ignore it and hope it goes away. Get curious and find out as much as you can about it. What are the pros and cons of the challenge? Make sure that you listen well and analyse not only what is on the surface, but also the personal agendas that are hidden beneath.

From the analysis, draw some firm conclusions and lessons. Learning through the challenge may help you to find an easier or quicker way to make progress. By welcoming the challenge you will be more likely to keep your mind open and learning rather than descending into defence. You are also likely to enhance the relationship with your challengers and may be able to win them over more easily.

Irrespective of your conclusion, make a clear decision about how you are going to let it affect your plans and then move on, keeping your persistence focused on your purpose.

Resilient defence

If your purpose is clear and you are passionate about its achievement, don't allow yourself to become distracted by other things. There will be plenty of people trying to dissuade you from your goal, or tell you that it is not possible. At times you will also be distracting yourself. If you yield to these distractions too easily you will find yourself aiming for a different goal or purpose.

Pursuing a purpose with persistence for a few months is easy. Persistence to a single purpose for years takes real dedication and focus. Yet the reward is that progress speeds up the longer you remain focused on a single purpose.

It is also true that many people find that their biggest breakthroughs come right after their bleakest moment. What happens at these times is that a new route comes into view as a result of the challenge, obstacles and learning that is provoked.

Build emotional support

Few leaders are able to survive on their own. They may be resolute in their purpose, fixed on their plan and making progress, but there will come a time when they are assailed by doubt. It's at times like these when friendly encouragement and support is vital in helping them to keep the faith and remain on their path.

As an influential leader, you need to develop your own support network. In Chapter 9 (Developing powerful and influential networks) there were a lot of ideas shared about how to build a wider group of connections. These same principles can be used to build your own personal inner-circle. Make it a priority to build up these special relationships where you can reciprocate emotional support. With these people, and these people alone, you can share you innermost thoughts, reservations and fears. If you've selected them well and nurtured these relationships, they will be the ones who will see you through to the achievement of your purpose.

Prominent benefits

There will come a time when you don't need to keep reminding yourself of the benefits that will arrive when your vision and purpose have been realized. They will be so well embedded as to not be questioned or needed to propel you forwards. Until that time, you need to do something to keep reminding yourself of the benefits.

In Chapter 1 you learned ways to build and maintain your motivation. Make sure to implement these and keep reinforcing them regularly. If you remain focused on your purpose, and mindful of the benefits, there will quickly come a time when persistence becomes automatic and progress assured.

Influential leadership: a leader's guide to getting things done

The world is in desperate need of influential leaders of all kinds, in all sorts of different organizations. These leaders need to be able to balance the needs of today with those of tomorrow, and take into account a bewildering array of vested interests. They need to make rapid progress, incrementally develop their purpose and fuel this with a passion that makes success an inevitability.

This book has been 10 years in the making and nearly a year in the writing – and now it is done. There was more I could have included, but space denied me that opportunity. Hence, please make sure to refer regularly to the online resources dedicated to supporting *Influential Leadership* at: **www.learntoinfluence.com/leadership**

My most fervent wish now is that you take what you can from it, do something with it, and become a more *Influential Leader* tomorrow.

INDEX

NB: page numbers in *italics* indicate figures or tables.